CEMETERY INSCRIPTIONS
of DYER COUNTY, TENNESSEE

Compiled by:
Mrs. Quintard Glass
Newbern, Tennessee

The Key Corner DAR Chapter of Dyer County Bicentennial Project

Book Publishers

Published by:
SOUTHERN HISTORICAL PRESS

Please direct all correspondence and orders to:

www.southernhistoricalpress.com
or
SOUTHERN HISTORICAL PRESS, Inc.
PO BOX 1267
375 West Broad Street
Greenville, SC   29601
southernhistoricalpress@gmail.com

ISBN #0-89308-085-3

Printed in the United States of America

CONTENTS

Atkins Cemetery

Atkins Cemetery consists of approximately one acre of ground. The land was originally owned by the late James Atkins. It was first used as a family plot but was later used as a community cemetery. According to tombstone inscriptions the earliest grave was in 1784 though many graves are unmarked and the date may be indefinite. James Atkins was the great grandfather of Mrs. Betty Jane Atkins Caldwell and Franklin Milan.

To reach Atkins Cemetery cross the Illinois Central Railroad tracks in Newbery at the intersection of Jefferson and Parks St. Travel due East to the city limits. There Parks St. runs into Ditmore Road. Travel 1½ miles on Ditmore Road and turn south on Atkins Lane for approximately ½ mile before turning right on little lane for 400 fee is the cemetery.

Atkins, James M.
Dec. 8, 1817
Oct. 17, 1895
Atkins, Mary E.
  Wife of J. M. Atkins
June 12, 1821
Feb. 25, 1894

Atkins, Mary J.
  Wife of J. A. Atkins
Nov. 19, 1847
Aug. 26, 1869

Baker, Jewell S.
1906-1921

Chapman, J. C.
1852-1932
Chapman, Arebella
1865-1898

Chapman, Robert
Aug. 9, 1888

Chapman, Lora Vernie
Sept. 2, 1887
May 18, 1927

Chapman, Sallie Loraine
July 11, 1920
Mar. 15, 1962

Chapman, Viola Bell
June 6, 1918
Jan. 4, 1930

Chapman, Virgie "Bud"
May 9, 1902

Chapman, W. T. (Brother)
1851-1920

Chapman, W. W.
May 12, 1823
Dec. 18, 1901

Clanton, Felix
1858-19
Clanton, Hattie Ann
1862-1932

Clanton, Fred Edward
May 4, 1889
Jan. 11, 1970

Clanton, Lela Caroline
April 27, 1893
Jan. 1, 1969

Clanton, John A. Sr.
Aug 22, 1918
April 23, 1962

Clanton, Murrell E.
Dec. 15, 1911
Feb. 14, 1912

Clanton, Rena
1889-19
Clanton, Charlie
1888-1942

Clanton, Russell Lee
June 1, 1906
Aug. 20, 1916

Cole, J. M.
Dec. 27, 1821
Sept. 25, 1884

Cook, Elizabeth
  Wife of John Cook
Died Oct. 9, 1861
46 years

Doak, Thomas
Nov. 29, 1784
March 1852

Dozier, Beatrice
Feb. 8, 1916
Jan. 18, 1919

Harrison, Charley "Tay"
April 9, 1863
Jan. 31, 1903

Harrison, John L.
1852-1911
Harrison, Martha J.
1866-1910

Heath, Elizabeth
  Wife of Richard Heath
Aug. 8, 1813
Sept. 21, 1889

Heath, Dr. J. M.
Sept. 30, 1950
Oct. 11, 1897

Heath, Richard
Jan. 8, 1811
Feb. 11, 1877

Jones, Jas. M.
July 13, 1850
Nov. 4, 1910
Jones, Martie (Hiw Wife)
July 27, 1864
Oct. 21, 1907

Mallard, Guy
Florida
PVT
U. S. Army
World War I
Dec. 18, 1886
July 6, 1970

Payne, William H.
Feb. 12, 1848
Mar. 6, 1916

Payne, Louisa J.
April 8, 1958
May 8, 1913

CENTER CEMETERY

Center Cemetery is located approximately eight miles from
Newbern. From Newbern, cross the Illinois Central Railroad at
the Jefferson St. intersection and travel to the city limits.
Then, continue on the Tatumville Highway for 2½ miles before
turning east on the Edgewood road. Travel 5½ miles on the Edgewood Road, and Center Church and cemetery are located on the
left hand side of the road.

Center received its named because it was in the center of
four communities, namely Churchton, Nebo, Tatumville, and Edgewood.

In 1851 six acres of land was purchased from J. A. Temple-
ton for the purpose of building a church with an adjoining cemetery on the grounds. A large two story building of logs was
erected. The upper story was used for the Order of the Sons of
Temperance and the lower story was used for a community school
house. The seats were made of split logs with pegs to hold them
together.

In 1875 a new frame building was erected 50 years east of
the old log structure. In 1949 a new church building of brick
was erected because the old building was inadequate.

Adams, Docie E.
1869-1913

Akin, B. J.
Died Nov. 29, 1875
22 yrs., 3 mos., 25 days.

Akin, Emma
Mar. 19, 1891
Mar. 9, 1920

Akin, James G.
1856-1930
Father
Akin, Sudie C.
185701930
Mother

Akin, M. A.
July 31, 1860
May 21, 1917

Akin, M. B.
 wife of F. R. Akin
Mar. 6, 1884
July 28, 1909

Akin, M. J.
 wife of T. B. Akin
Apr. 24, 1851
July 22, 1876

Akin, Mollie
Nov. 18, 1844
Jan. 4, 1922

Akin, Stephen B.
Aug. 2, 1816
June 25, 1861

Akin, Thomas H.
Master of
Lucinda Akins
Dec. 23, 1822
Sept 28, 1787
55 yrs, 9 mos., 5 days

Akin, W. H.
1872-1952
Akin, Dora B.
1875-1951

Akins, Lucinda
wife of
Charlie Akins
Died 1890

Akins, T. R.
April 19, 1887
Jan. 21, 1919

Arnold, Baxter
1874-1929

Arnold, Dora
1878-1960

Arnold, Sarah E.
June 10, 1860
Jan. 24, 1920

Austin, Almous
April 14, 1889
Feb. 20, 1918

Austin, Arthley O.
son of
J. F. & M. E. Austin
Aug. 2, 1885
Oct. 4, 1888

Austin, Claude D.
Jan. 19, 1888
July 16, 1921

Austin, Gorgan
Jan. 31, 1862
Oct. 10, 1932
Mother

Austin, Ora Bell
dau. of
J. F. & M. E. Austin
Jan. 30, 1895
July 10, 1898
3 yrs, 5 mos., 10 days

Austin, W. L.
Sept. 7, 1853
Jan. 31, 1923

Balthrop, Bobby
Born & Died
Sept. 1, 1940

Balthrop, Dr. J. G.
1858-1923
Father
Balthrop, Kittie
Born 1870
Mother

Balthrop, Mary
1893-1894

Banks, Biram
July 27, 1809
July 1, 1977
57 yrs, 5 mos., 4 days

Berryman, Jennie
wife of J. C. Berryman
1883-1917

Boon, Edward
son of
A. D. V. and Mary Boon
Born April 5, 1855
Feb. 21, 1873

Brewer, Caroline
1845-1929
Mother

Brewer, James
Dec. 6, 1888
June 12, 1911

Brewer, Robert L.
Aug. 31, 1872
July 1, 1909
(Woodman of the World Memorial)

Brewer, W. Q.
Dec. 4, 1845
Oct. 3, 1891

Brown, A. W.
son of R. M. & M. V. Brown
Oct. 22, 1877
Dec. 17, 1877

Brown, G. O. L.
dau. of R. M. & M. V. Brown
Aug. 28, 1892
Oct. 16, 1893

Brown, Laura Augusta
dau. of W. H. & S. A. Brown
Dec.10, 1871
Sept. 16, 1873

Brown, R. M.
1852-
Father
Brown, M. V.
1855-
His wife

Brown, Silas
Aug. 27, 1858
April 4, 1882

Bryant, John A.
Nov. 23, 1828
Sept. 25, 1885

Bryant, Nancy
April 7, 1835
Sept. 25, 1889

Carroll, Charley
1875-1955
Carroll, Ethel
1881-1934

Carroll, Eli D.
1875-1964
Carroll, Ella F.
1883-1935

Carroll, J. M.
Feb. 25, 1864
Sept. 30, 1908

Carroll, Susie F.
Daughter
1912-1928

Churchman, M. M.
Wife of
J. R. Churchman
July 30, 1840
Dec. 23, 1887
47 yrs., 4 mos., 23 da.

Churchman, Ruth
Wife of
T. C. Churchman
Feb. 20, 1815
Dec. 5, 1882

Clanton, Leonard
Aug. 14, 1910
Feb. 25, 1957

Clark, Jake
1870-1934
Clark, Lula
1884-1933

Clark, Infant son of
J. H. & S. F. Clark
Born & Died
Nov. 27, 1878

Clark, Infant son of
J. H. & S. F. Clark
Born & Died
Nov. 28, 1876

Clark, Infant dau. of
J. H. & S. F. Clark
Born & Died
July 9, 1880

Clark, Sarah F.
Wife of J. H. Clark
Sept. 9, 1853
Feb. 1, 1882

Cole, Charley
Son of
B. G. & M. C. Cole
Jan. 21, 1876
Aug. 25, 1876

Cole, Dr. E. A.
Jan. 21, 1824
Mar. 12, 1897
73 yrs., 3 mos., 16 days

Cole, Issabella G.
Wife of
E. A. Cole
Died Oct. 12, 1874
45 yrs., 8 mos., 23 days

Cole, Dr. J. D.
Aug. 30, 1861
Aug. 29, 1917
56 yrs.

Cole, James M.
Son of S. A. & N. C. Cole
Sept. 12, 1859
Feb. 12, 1861
4 yrs. 5 mos.

Cole, Jas. W.
Son of B. G. M. & M. C. Cole
June 29, 1872
Sept. 24, 1877

Cole, Joseph E.
Son of B. G. M. & S. M. Cole
Aug. 15, 1861
Aug. 23, 1862
1 yr., 8 days

Cole, Martha C.
Wife of B. G. M. Cole
July 1, 1839
May 10, 1876

Cole, Richard Lee
Son of B. G. M. & Susan Cole
Dec. 30, 1868
July 31, 1869
1 yr., 7 months

Cole, Robert L.
1866-1929
Cole, Robert L.
1866-1911

Cole, Sally E.
Dau. of E. A. & M. C. Cole
Aug. 3, 1863
Aug. 6, 1863

Cole, Susan
Wife of B. G. M. Cole
Oct. 19, 1828
July 10, 1870
41 yrs., 8 mos., 21 days

Cook, Edgar Clay
Father
Mar. 10, 1887
Oct. 16, 1969

Cook, Gladys Louise
Dau. of Ed Cook
June 23, 1916
May 11, 1917

Cook, William
Jan. 12, 1848
Mar. 17, 1912
Cook, Mary E.
Nov. 7, 1853
June 6, 1912

Cook, William Edward
Son of C. A. & Velma Cook
Sept. 13, 1916
May 29, 1917

Corley, Willie Nona
Oct. 13, 1903
Aug. 20, 1904
Dau. of L.C. & S. C. Corley

Cowan, Elizabeth C.
Wife of John Cowan
Aug. 12, 1809
July 31, 1856

Cowan, J. A.
Mar. 30, 1838
Dec. 24, 1861

Cowan, John F.
May 30, 1803
Aug. 7, 1856
53 yrs., 2 mos.

Cowart, Mary L.
1935-1954

Cowsert, A. P.
Wife of
W. S. Cowsert
Aug. 25, 1824
Aug. 21, 1894

Cresap, Alice
Aug. 17, 1896
July 13, 1907
Cresap, Infant Son of
J. A. & A. V. Cresap
Cresap, Gracie
Feb. 27, 1903
Jan. 14, 1904
Cresap, Finis N.
Mar. 19, 1905
Nov. 27, 1905

Cresap, Paul
Sept. 17, 1906
Nov. 11, 1908

Cummings, Birdie P.
1905-1956

Cummings, Herman
1901-1959

Cummings, Rita Carroll
1964

Dennison, Joel David
Mar. 16, 1955
Apr. 25, 1955

Dickey, John F.
1839-1931
Dickey, Margaret K.
1839-1925

Doak, Babe
Son of
W. & G. J. Doak
Aug. 10, 1871
July 18, 1877

Doak, Eller
Dau. of W. E. & Martha A.
Sept. 9, 1866
Sept. 10, 1968

Doaks, J. W.
Born and Died 1865

Doak, Robert L.
Dec. 10, 1836
Arp. 11, 1869

Doak, Sammie R.
Mar. 8, 1865
May 16, 1872

Doaks, Mrs. Sue
Died April 24, 1975
92 yrs.

Dozier, John Henry
Dec. 6, 1917
Jan. 8, 1922

Dozier, Leacy C.
Wife of H. C. Dozier
March 4, 1846
May 26, 1873

Dozier, Savannah
Wife of G. S. Dozier
Jan. 26, 1871
Oct. 26, 1903

Dozier, Tollie V.
Oct. 2, 1896
July 15, 1914

Dozier, Woodrow
Son of O. H. & T. V. Dozier
Oct. 3, 1913
Jan. 18, 1919

Dunn, Miss F. D.
No Dates

Dunn, Mrs. J. L.
No Dates

Dunnagan, Emma
wife of W. H. Dunnagan
Jan. 10, 1871
Oct. 10, 1898

Faris, Flora Hall
Nov. 11, 1887
Nov. 16, 1923

Featherston, A.C.
Aug. 25, 1830
July 29, 1878

Featherston, A. T.
(Broken Stone)

Featherston, Azza Lee
May 17, 1874
Feb. 25, 1947

Featherston, Daniel Eugene
son of W.V. & S.A.
O'Neal Featherston
May 2, 1870
Feb. 13, 1948

Featherston, Freda
dau. of O.E. & B.B.
Featherston
Feb. 5, 1905
Jan. 9, 1908

Featherston, H. B.
July 17, 1826
Oct. 26, 1903
77 yrs., 3 mos., 8 days

Featherston, Joe
Nov. 9, 1895
April 7, 1926

Featherston, John V.
son of A. T. &
A.C. Featherston
Mar. 8, 1862
June 10, 1880

Featherston, Laverne
son of O. E. &
A. Featherston
Mar. 26, 1899
July 29, 1899
4 mos., 3 days

Featherston, Maggie J.
dau. of A. T. &
A. C. Featherston
Aug. 18, 1870
July 26, 1875

Featherston, Napoleon E.
son of W. V. & S. E.
Featherston
Dec. 11, 1866
Sept. 18, 1886

Featherston, Netta
dau. of W. V. & S.A.
Featherston
Aug. 9, 1872
Sept. 20, 1873
1 yr., 1 mo. 11 days

Featherston, Sally V.
Died Sept. 27, 1975
95 years

Featherston, Samantha A.
wife of
A. L. Featherston
Mar. 6, 1880
July 25, 1913

Featherston, Sarah Ann
dau. of
Henry D. Featherston
May 6, 1832
May 9, 1858

Featherston, Shadrack Ezra
son of W. V. & S. A.
Featherston
July 17, 1875
Sept. 8, 1891

Featherston, Sudie A.
wife of
O. E. Featherston
Feb. 8, 1881
June 16, 1899
18 yrs., 4 mo., 10 days

Featherston, Thomas
1865-1926
Father
Featherston, Fannie
1865-
Mother

Featherston, W. V.
Sept. 19, 1839
June 19, 1908
Featherston, S. A.
March 15, 1844
Sept. 21, 1923

Fisher, Mary E.
1832-1901

Fisher, T. E.
Nov. 3, 1841
Dec. 13, 1878

Flovad, E. L.
wife of
W. S. Flovad
June 9, 1829
Nov. 24, 1868

Forsythe, Nuten E.
son of T. D. &
A. E. Forsythe
June 28, 1880
Jan. 20, 1898

Gannon, Infant son of
W. C. & Amanda Gannon
Born & Died
Sept. 5, 1864

Gibbons, A. B.
July 28, 1867
Dec. 15, 1923

Gibbons, Edward D.
1861-1935
Gibbons, Emma J.
1867-1954

Gibbons, Infant of
E. D & E. J.
Gibbons
May 10, 1892
Oct. 25, 1900

Gibbons, Guy Porter
May 22, 1918
Jan. 18, 1919

Gibbons, James Rice
Nov. 3, 1889
Nov. 20, 1912

Gibbons, J. T.
Father
1864-1933
Gibbons, Dora
Mother
1873-1954

Gibbons, Lamigra V.
Died Dec. 3, 1800
51 yrs., 1 mo., 3 da.

Gilmer, N. G.
May 6, 1861
May 29, 1920
Gilmer, Martha
His wife
Aug. 4, 1865
Nov. 26, 1928

Grigg, Mrs. L. R.
No Date

Grograns, John C.
Aug. 7, 1860
Feb. 23, 1893

Gwaltney, Thomas A.
May 26, 1787
Mar. 30, 1867

Hall, Alfred
Nov. 27, 1876
57 yrs., 2 mos., 27 days

Hall, C. M.
wife of T. H. Hall
Nov. 13, 1861
Aug. 13, 1886

Hall, Mrs. G. A.
wife of J. H. Hall
Feb. 15, 1847
Mar. 10, 1904

Hall, J. H.
July 22, 1844
Jan. 23, 1918

Hall, J. J.
Husband of M. C. Hall
Mar. 17, 1837
1879 (Broken Stone)

Hall, Joel J.
Died Aug. 14, 1879
42 yrs., 11 mos., 2 days

Hall, Joseph W.
May 18, 1863
20 yrs., 8 mos., 20 days

Hall, J. W.
Jan. 10, 1858
Aug. 6, 1891

Hall, Loucenia A.
dau. of
W. A. & E. F. Hall
Sept. 26, 1881
Aug. 20, 1885
3 yrs. 10 mos. 24 days

Hall, Luther Ray
1941-1945

Hall, Margaret E.
wife of T. W. Hall
July 9, 1840
Oct. 29, 1883

Hall, Mary J.
wife of W. M. Hall
Died Mar. 22, 1869
34 yrs., 11 mos., 3 days

Hall, Mary Jane
dau. of A. & Eliza Jane
Dec. 23, 1847
May 23, 1864

Hall, Sallie
wife of S. S. Hall
1825-1868

Hall, Sarah
wife of Wilson Hall
Dec. 25, 1802
Oct. 23, 1886
83 yrs., 9 mos.
28 days

Hall, Sarah E.
Mar. 3, 1847
No Date 1857

Hall, S. S.
1821-1877

Hall, T. A.
Nov. 23, 1872
July 18, 1922

Hall, Thomas E.
May 10, 1870
July 15, 1871
1 yr., 4 mos., 5 days

Hall, T. W.
Nov. 18, 184
Aug. 21, 1891

Hall, Warn
Husband of Rebecca Hall
Feb. 23, 1851
Nov. 25, 1895

Hall, William A.
Aug. 22, 1846
Oct. 10, 1927
Hall, Eatha F.
Feb. 22, 1851
Jan. 14, 1917
His wife

Hall, William Lee
son of
W. A. & R. E. F. Hall
Oct. 18, 1875
Feb. 28, 1888
12 yrs., 4 mos., 10 days

Hall, Wilson
1798-1868

Hampton, William
Mar. 10 (No Date)
July 13 (No Date)

Harrington, E. S.
wife of R. P. Harrington
April 4, 1870
Oct. 6, 1903

Harrington, Katie
wife of R. P. Harrington
Nov. 12, 1883
Sept. 12, 1914

Harris, Thomas Blunt
Jan. 18, 1865
July 1, 1940
Harris, Rebecca Elizabeth
Jan. 28, 1870

Harris, William B.
Arkansas
Pvt. 15 Inf. 87 Div.
Died Jan. 24, 1927

Hendrix, Manerva Jane
wife of W. H. Hendrix
No Dates

Hendrix, Martha
wife of James Hendrix
June 12, 1812
Sept. 15, 1873
71 yrs. 3 mos., 3 days

Hendrix, Samuel
son of W. H. & M. J. Hendrix
Oct. 20, 1861
June 10, 1865

Hendrix, William L
son of W. H. & M. J. Hendrix
Died Aug. 22, 1882

Hollister, James F.
1853-1935
Hollister, Martha J.
1861-1937

Hollomon, Christopher R.
Dec. 15, 1887
Feb. 22, 1939
(Woodman of the World)

Hollomon, Martha R.
Jan. 6, 1889
Apr. 5, 1947

Huffine, Peter
Dec. 25, 1808
May 2, 1882

Huffinies, Rebecca
Oct. 23, 1808
May 29, 1905

Inman, Jo Carolyn
Nov. 29, 1934
Nov. 30, 1934

Jackson, Aaron
July 12, 1899
Apr. 23, 1969
Jackson, Lou Genyer
Feb. 8, 1904
Nov. 5, 1969

Jackson, Sarah A.
1865-1935

Jackson, Solon E.
1867-1942
Jackson, Nancy Ann
1868-1941

Jones, Minnie
wife of Robert J. Jones
July 4, 1882
Aug. 22, 1906

King, Mattie D.
1869-1961

King, Patti Alex
1909-1958

King, W. A. Sr.
1848-1921
King, Mollie
1854-1923

King, William Alex
1872-1953

Ladd, William I.
1876-1935
Ladd. Ora Ethel
1884-1957

Ladd, Willie Maude
1918-1937

Ledbetter, Docia E.
1900-1924

Ledbetter, Mary M.
1903-1922
Ledbetter, Nancy A.
1895-1919

Ledbetter, Reuben P.
1893-1915
Ledbetter, Martha M.
1898-1917

Ledbetter, Robert P.
1854-1929
Ledbetter, Mary Ann
1863-1929

Lemons, Albert
Nov. 30, 1871
June 27, 1969
Lemons, Jessie
Aug. 1905
Jan. 1968
Lemons, Odell
July 18, 1908
Nov. 7, 1964

Lucas, J. D.
Mar. 20, 1881
Apr. 3, 1900

Lucas, Infant Daughter
J. M. & J. C. Lucas
Jan. 8, 1896
Mar. 6, 1897

Lucas, Jehiel (Father)
Nov. 4, 1859
June 5, 1922
Lucas, Ludie (Mother)
Nov. 4, 1859
June 5, 1922

Lucas, John M.
1854-1930
Lucas, Julia C.
1859-1934

Lucas, J. T.
son of J. D. & E. L.
Oct. 4, 1868
July 29, 1895

Magee, B. J.
Aug. 23, 1843
Died
Dec. 25, 1885

Magee, Martha E.
Wife of R. J. Magee
Died
Sept. 12, 1882
33 yrs., 6 mos., 2 days

Magee, S. S.
Jan. 27, 1804
Aug. 22, 1882

Magee, W. R.
Oct. 19, 1811
Aug. 11, 1885

Mason, Dr. F. G.
Sept. 8, 1834
Mar. 19, 1901

Mason, Harriette Ann
Wife of F. G. Mason
Nov. 28, 1844
May 22, 1909

Mason, Jimmy Lee
Son of F. G. and
H. A. Mason
July 2, 1868
Aug. 11, 1890
22 yrs., 23 days

Mason John Franklin
Son of F. G. and H. A. Mason
June 14, 1875
Aug. 12, 1878
3 yrs., 1 mo., 29 days

McCutchen, Infant
Son of R. L. and Minnie
McCutchen
May 3, 1890
Sept. 29, 1890

McCutchen, R. L.
Oct. 10, 1866
Oct. 17, 1892

McKnight, Mrs. M. C.
No Date

Michael, Mrs. M. A. S.
Mar. 26, 1880
Dec. 8, 1900

Michael, R. W.
Jan. 29, 1857
Mar. 9, 1894
37 yrs., 11 mos., 3 days.

Morgan, Annie
Jan. 21, 1866
Jan. 29, 1906

Newsom, Ada Nelle
Oct. 22, 1921
Nov. 1, 1921

Newsom
Infant son of
Mr. and Mrs. E. Newsom

Nolen, Milton Thomas
June 5, 1865
Feb. 21, 1937
Nolen, Callie Hall
Aug. 28, 1885
Feb. 21, 1932

Oliver, Julia Estelle
Mar. 30, 1924
May 24, 1925

O'Neal, Parthena P.
wife of Harvey O'Neal
Aug. 9, 1812
Jan. 8, 1859

Parson, Sallie
Born - 1861
Died - 1940
79 yrs., 13 days

Pierce, Joe H.
Mar. 22, 1892
Mar. 5, 1920
Pierce, Ora
Sept. 30, 1895
Jan. 15, 1920
Son and Daughter of
G. W. and L. E. Pierce

Pierce, William F.
July 25, 1821
April 11, 1858

Pierce, William P.
Died May 26, 1877

Pitt, Allie M.
Wife of O. P. Pitt
Feb. 15, 1872
Feb. 24, 1897
24 yrs., 11 mos., 19 da.

Pitt, Cecil Morgon
July 18, 1896
Dec. 11, 1898

Pitt, George A.
1855-1937

Pitt, J. F.
1872-1908

Pitt, Levi Frances
No Dates

Pitt, Mamie Sue
Daughter of
O. P. and A. M. Pitt
Jan. 27, 1897
Oct. 15, 1897

Pitt, Robert P.
Son of
R. S. and M. A. Pitt
April 14, --
Oct. 27, 1897

Pitt, Tabitha
Wife of G. A. Pitt
1859-1934

Pope, Bartie
Sept. 14, 1852
Mar. 5, 1900

Pope, Bertha Gilmer
Feb. 23, 1900
Oct. 18, 1922

Pope, Brigga
Son of
W. W. and D. E. Pope
July 10, 1882
May 10, 1894
Pope, John
Son of
W. W. and D. E. Pope
May 29, 1867
Sept. 2, 1890

Pope, Cordella
Daughter of
S. and E. Pope
June 7, 1861
Sept. 14, 1876

Pope, Dora
Jan. 0, 1079
Dec. 18, 1906
27 yrs., 11 mos., 5 da.

Pope, Eliza Ann
1827-1898

Pope, Hammie Sr.
Mar. 1886
Oct. 1960
Father of Hammie Jr.

Pope, James Henry
June 26, 1875
Feb. 15, 1908

Pope. Joseph
Aug. 28, 1878
58 yrs.

Pope, J. W.
1841-1925

Pope, Lenora
Daughter of S. and E. Pope
June 5, 1866
Sept. 24, 1875

Pope, Louisa M.
Wife of W. E. Pope
Oct. 11, 1860
Mar. 1, 1887
26 yrs.

Pope, Nancy P.
Daughter of S. and E. Pope
Jan. 15, 1854
July 20, 1872

Pope, Rube A.
1881-1950

Pope, Sandy G.
Jan. 27, 1824
Mar. 31, 1884

Pope. Sarah G.
Daughter of
M. T. Pope
May 23, 1846
Dec. 28, 1892

Pope, Susan
Wife of B. Pope
Died Aug. 20, 1878
53 yrs., 1 mo., 8 da.

Preston, William P.
Broken Stone

Ray, Blanch Lee
Daughter of
G. C. and Susie E. Ray
Dec. 7, 1887
July 16, 1888
7 mos., 9 days

Ray, C. C.
1858-1920

Ray, M. E.
Aug. 14, 1861
May 27, 1912
Ray, H. C.
May 3, 1857
Mar. 15, 1915
Sewell, Elijah
June 16, 1904
April 8, 1906

Ray, Sallie J.
Wife of C. C. Ray
Mar. 12, 1866
Jan. 30, 1908

Ray, Susie G.
Wife of C. C. Ray
Aug. 10, 1868
Sept. 21, 1893
25 yrs., 1 mo., 11 da.

Reynolds, Mary S.
wife of J. H. Reynolds
Died March 7, 1865
45 yrs. old

Roberts, C. L.
Feb. 21, 1877
July 19, 1905

Rose, A. B.
1846-1930

Rose, Eliz abeth G.
Wife of Jas. Rose
Sept. 29, 1838
Aug. 30, 1910

Rose, James
1820-1894

Rose, L. B.
1873-1928
Rose, Ella B.
His wife
1877-1927

Rose, R. R.
Father
June 8, 1842
Sept. 11, 1929
Rose Tempie (His Wife)
Jan. 7, 1842
Oct. 15, 1922

Rose, William A.
1872-1931

Rose, William Stigler
Son of
Mr. and Mrs. Ocie Rose
Born and Died
July 2, 1920

Rose, Sarah Izora
Aug. 30, 1869
Aug. 29, 1946

Sanders, Lenora
Feb. 10, 1869
Sept. 9, 1870
1 yr., 6 mos., 29 days

Sanders, Rev. T. J.
June 26, 1839
Feb. 25, 1915
Father
Sanders, Mary E.
June 20, 1838
Dec. 26, 1910

Sanders, W. A.
July 12, 1864
Aug. 24, 1870

Scott, Nancy
1850-1922

Shackelton, Ernest S.
Son of
R.S. and L.A.
Shackelton
Jan. 3, 1885
Jan. 3, 1886

Shackleton, Matilda Ann
Wife of
C. W. Shackleton
Nov. 13, 1808
May 13, 1858

Simons, Mary Jane
Wife of J. B. Simons
Feb. 2, 1829
Oct. 2, 1885

Skaggs, (Don) A. D.
Son of
J. M. and Martha Skaggs
Mar. 18, 1894
Judy - Finistere, France
Feb. 28, 1918

Skaggs, Ella
1889-1932

Skaggs, Jim
1891-1928

Skaggs, J. M.
1854-1906
Skaggs, Martha
1865-1961

Smith, Charlie A.
May 18, 1871
June 14, 1956
Smith, Matt Shaw
Mar. 9, 1882
Mar. 19, 1959

Smith, John D.
Died Dec. 25, 1903
65 yrs., 10 mos.
Smith, Angeline
Died Jan. 8, 1906
61 yrs., 1 mo., 21 days

Steele, Mary
June 10, 1908
Sept. 1908

Stocton, Mary Grogan
1865-1932
Mother

Thetford, Eva Inez
dau. of A. M. & A. M.
Thetford
Feb. 6, 1907
Mar. 29, 1909

Thompson, L. C.
Died Nov. 26, 1885
47 yrs. 10 mos. 6 da.

Thompson, Sallie J.
Wife of Jarrett Thompson
Oct. 8, 1843
Dec. 31, 1892

Tinkle, Elfida J.
Wife of W. E. Tinkle
Dec. 25, 1851
Apr. 20, 1872
20 yrs., 3 mos., 25 days

Tinkle, W. E.
Died
Jan. 19, 1870
50 yrs. 2 mos.

Tinkle, Walter L.
son of W. E. & E. J.
Tinkle
Died Aug. 8, 1868
4 mos., 3 days

Tinkle, Willie L.
Dec. 18, 1816
May 31, 1876
59 yrs., 5 mos., 13 da.

Vanhoo, Oscar Lee
June 20, 1888
July 3, 1896

Wagster, Dallace
Died Nov. 25, 1905
47 yrs.

Walker, Sophronia E. G.
Wife of J. A. Walker
Daughter of Stephen &
Ellen Milan
Aug. 25, 1845
Nov. 12, 1886

Walters, Alice Geneva
Oct. 19, 1922
June 27, 1924

Walters, Dicie
Aug. 9, 1863
Apr. 1, 1939

Walters, Johnnie W.
1906-1971
Walters, Lorene
1917-

Walters, Joseph
1879-1957
Walters, Mary C.
1890-____

Walters, M. F.
March 12, 1885
June 27, 1891
Walters, A. C.
Sept. 17, 1822
April 15, 1891

Warren, Will B.
1858-1944
Warren, John W,
1860-1931
Warren, Tollie
1876-1952

Watson, Annie
Dec. 16, 1865
Oct. 25, 189?
Broken Stone

Watson, Virgie Leota
Feb. 18, 1893
Aug. 16, 1955

Watson, William Joel
June 13, 1889
Jan. 16, 1925

Webb, Kittie L.
Oct. 19, 1899
Dec. 27, 1900

Webb, Odell
Nov. 17, 1901
Jan. 22, 1919

Webb, T. Hassell
Apr. 28, 1900
May 19, 1911

Webb, Winnie V.
Dec. 10, 1912
Nov. 19, 1918

Wheatley, Jesse B.
1855-1911

Wheatley, Nannie J.
1869-1955

Wilson, Gregory
Aug. 12, 1856
Aged about 93 yrs.

Wilson
Infant Son
J. G. H. & M. W. Wilson
July 30, 1859
5 wks., 4 days

Wilson, Sally
daughter of
J. C. H. & Malinda W.
Wilson
May 5, 185? (Broken Stone)
6 yrs., 9 mos., 31 da.

Williams, Dewitt
1894-19___

Williams, Unia
1898-1925

Williams
Infant of E. C. Williams
Oct. 1915

Williams, F. J. (Hiley)
1867-19___
Williams, Sallie Bell
1870-1929

Williams, Martha
Dec. 15, 1834
Feb. 24, 1910

Williams, Martha E.
daughter of
P.A. & B.A. Williams
Jan. 27, 1869
Aug. 22, 1885
16 yrs., 6 mos., 26 days

Williams, Parlee
wife of Scott Williams
1842-1910

Williams, Tolton F.
Mar. 17, 1836
Nov. 27, 1905
69 yrs., 8 mos., 10 days

Williams, William H.
son of
J. L. & Martha Williams
1854-1898

Williams, Winfield Scott
1849-1932

Williamson, Jane A.
Dec. 31, 1829
Jan. 2, 1881
51 yrs., 1 day

Williamson, John
May 24, 1790
May 8, 1872

Williamson, John Willie
Son of
J. N. & S. E. Williamson
June 28, 1869
Sept. 7, 1870

Woodard, Emiline P.
wife of
W. M. Woodard
May 30, 1829
Jan. 29, 1884

Woodard, William Montgomery
Oct. 4, 1828
Sept. 29, 1888

Woodard, Willie R.
son of
W.M. & E.P. Woodard
Dec. 30, 1861
Mar. 31, 1884

Wright, Finis Leroy
son of
M.L. & O.C. Wright
Jan. 4, 1908
Aug. 23, 1909

Wright, H. B.
Son of G.H. & M.E. Wright
June 22, 1842
July 23, 1857

Wyatt, Alexander
Died Sept. 1, 1882

Wyatt, Eliza
No Dates

Wyatt, Nancy A.
wife of
H. L. Wyatt
Died May 27, 1869

CHURCH GROVE

Church Grove Cemetery is just over a mile from Newbern. Turn right at the red light on Highway 51 South on Main Street. Travel a block, then turn left on the Lanesferry Highway to the end of Haskins Lane. Here turn left and the road will run into Church Grove Cemetery. The 4 1/3 acre plot of ground was purchased from Edward Haskins on January 3, 1860, by A. Harris, A. Enochs, Henry Wynn, Guy Douglass, and Tyre Bell, trustees of the Methodist Episcopal Church Grove for use as a burial ground for the price of $130.00.

Alexander, Flossie
1910-1939

Anderson, Andrew E.
Tennessee
Sgt. 314 Labor BN
July 7, 1931

Arnold, Burin L.
Oct. 13, 1915
March 15, 1973

Barnett, John Asa
Son of
Mr. & Mrs. W. L. Barnett
Nov. 15, 1900
Nov. 7, 1917

Barnett, Millie
Wife of W. L. Barnett
Sept. 28, 1875
Jan. 28, 1902

Bates, Infant Daughter of
C. W. & H. J. Bates
Died March 18, 1888

Beatty, James H.
1878-1935
Beatty, Cora
1892-1943

Benifiel, A. B.
July 17, 1877
June 4, 1898

Bessent, Cora Summers
April 21, 1889
March 8, 1970
Bessent, Will
April 8, 1890
Sept. 24, 1970

Bevis, Mrs. Florence A.
Died April 13, 1972

Bevis, J. W.
1869-1949

Bowen, Robert L.
Dec. 2, 1865
May 19, 1894

Bradshaw, George Jr.
Nov. 1, 1921
Dec. 13, 1922

Bradshaw, C. F.
Nov. 3, 1886
May 9, 1966

Bradshaw, Dossie
Feb. 18, 1884
Oct. 27, 1965

Bradshaw, Jennie
May 26, 1878
June 7, 1930

Bradshaw, W. G.
1868-1952

Brinn, Pennie
Sept. 11, 1861
Aug. 18, 1949

Brinn, W. R.
Feb. 6, 1856
Dec. 27, 1921

Brown, Jettie
Daughter of D.H. & Anna Brown
Oct. 5, 1888
Sept. 13, 1897
Brown, Willie
Daughter of D.H. & Anna Brown
May 20, 1889
July 8, 1890

Burkhead, Ruth
June 5, 1923
Jan. 24, 1929

Burkhead, Tan
Oct. 25, 1876
Nov. 1, 1935

Burp, Mrs. Joe Ella
1914-1942

Burr, James T.
Tennessee
PFC H.Q. & H.Q. Co.
27 Engineer B. N.
March 10, 1942
July 6, 1965

Burr, Rickey Dale
Dec. 19, 1951
April 15, 1963

Butler, Walter Calvin
Son of
Louie & Mattie Butler
1933-1934

Caldwell
Baby of
H.D. & Norelle Caldwell

Caldwell, Hurdle D.
Aug. 25, 1900
Aug. 21, 1967

Caldwell, Norelle Hicks
1905-1940

Callahan, Clarence
Son of F.J. & S.C.
Callahan
Aug. 27, 1881
Aug. 12, 1896

Callahan, Frank J.
Born Jan. 1, 1851
Died _____
Callahan, Susan C.
June 17, 1861
Aug. 26, 1916

Campbell, Alton E.
March 17, 1917
April 8, 1969
Campbell, Lagreta C.
July 7, 1926

Carson, Gurtrude
March 13, 1908
July 17, 1911

Castleman, Lillie
Daughter of Mr. and
Mrs. E. Castleman
Nov. 26, 1901
Nov. 28, 1902

Chamberlin, C. C.
1858-19

Chamberlin, Martha Anne
His Wife
1864-1933

Childress, J. A.
May 12, 1862
April 25, 1929

Childress, Emma Jane
Feb. 4, 1862
Aug. 23, 1900

Clift, Mollie Sue
April 12, 1908
Clift, James L.
Tennessee
PVT U.S. Army
World War I
Aug. 18, 1896
July 24, 1973

Cobb, Charley E.
Jan. 10, 1883
April 5, 1969
Cobb, Lillie B.
Feb. 3, 1876
Oct. 26, 1951

Cobb, Cleophus F.
Sept. 4. 1901
Aug. 19, 1929

Cobb, C. R.
1851-1932
Cobb, Sarah E.
1848-1930

Cobb, Finas
Son of Mr. and Mrs.
G. E. Cobb
Feb. 21, 1907
Jan. 22, 1918

Cobb, John L.
Father
1872-1947
Cobb, Mary E.
Mother
1874-1929

Cobb, John Virl
April 3, 1900
Feb, 7, 1943

Coburn, Sylvester
Son of G.W. & Mary Coburn
Died July 9, 1891
23 years

Cole, G. W.
Son of Andrew Cole
June 23, 1846
March 13, 1868

Cole, H.
Feb. 13, 1842
Dec. 3, 1920

Cole, Mary E.
Nov. 16, 1848
July 18, 1917

Collins, Amanda
1873-1915

Collins, J. B.
1865-1939

Connell, Wesley
1888-1968
Connell, Maggie L.
1892-

Corum, Mrs. A. D.
Nov. 8, 1831
March 9, 1917
Jones, Miss Bob
Sept. 22, 1840
Jan. 24, 1917

Council, Donnell B.
1895-1936
Council, Stratt
1897-1958

Cozart, Earnest
Feb. 5, 1878
Dec. 30, 1948

Cozart, G. E.
Feb. 26, 1949
Feb. 11, 1972

Cozart, Partilla Frances
Died Aug. 7, 1975
95 years, 9 mo. 24 da.

Cozart, R. E.
July 22, 1869
Dec. 19, 1956

Crenshaw, G. J.
Daughter of
W. I. & S. J. Crenshaw
Nov. 25, 1878
Aug. 4, 1879

Crenshaw, Rev. I. I.
Jan. 5, 1819
July 9, 1887

Crenshaw, Jasper Allen
Tennessee
PVT, 161 Inf.
41 Div.
November 29, 1890
July 22, 1935

Crenshaw, Jessica Love
July 6, 1975
5 months and 17 days

Crenshaw, Lettie A.
Wife of W. I. Crenshaw
Dec. 5, 1866
Dec. 17, 1897

Crenshaw, Linnie
1898-19
Crenshaw, Gregg
1896-1957

Crenshaw, Mollie Sue
Nov. 22, 1882
Oct. 23, 1961

Crenshaw, Robert Gregg
Died Dec. 22, 1975
57 years, 6 mos, and 11 days

Crenshaw, Rufus Irvin
Son of W. I. and
L. A. Crenshaw
Nov. 14, 1894
Jan. 30. 1915

Father and Mother
Crenshaw, S. A.
1855-1936
Crenshaw. Elizabeth
(His wife)
1860-1915

Crenshaw, Sallie J.
Wife of W. I. Crenshaw
Daughter of J. T. and
G. E. Montgomery
November 7. 1867
July 6. 1892

Crenshaw. Sallie L.
Oct. 5. 1885
Oct. 14. 1950

Crenshaw. Sam Harris
1935-1954

Davis. Clyde
March 2. 1906
Davis. Lizzy E.
Nov. 16. 1906

Davis. T.
Feb. 15. 1870
March 25. 1891

Davis. W. H.
July 4. 1906
Sept. 12. 1940

Day. Annie May
Dec. 16. 1893
Day. Nathan
Feb. 14. 1902
May 14. 1970

Dennison. James
1867-1954
Dennison. Lizzie
1867-1934

Dennison. May E.
1859-1939

Dennison. W. D.
Jan. 27. 1855
Oct. 27. 1913

Douglas, Guy
Dec. 25, 1826
1912
Douglas, Martha
Sept, 30, 1830
1912

Douglass, Charlie A.
July 18, 1868
6 years, 6 months

Douglass, Reuben
Son of Guy and Martha
Douglas
May 20, 1859
Oct. 8, 1876

Dunahoo, Saphronia I.
1840-1927

Dunevant, Tabitha

Dunivant, Annie Lee
Mother
1890-1955
Dunivant, W. Vernon
Father
1888-1960

Dunivant, Mrs. D. A. B.
Wife of J. M. Dunivant
March 8, 1828
Oct. 10, 1876

Dunivant, Edna T.
Nov. 11, 1879
Sept. 13, 1959

Dunivant, Frankie
oct. 20, 1856
May 14, 1906

Dunivant, George E.
Nov. 15, 1847
Sept. 3, 1878
30 years, 9 mo., 17 da.

Dunivant, J. G.
Died Sept. 4, 1889

Dunivant, Joseph Henry
Jan. 9, 1853
Oct. 13, 1920

Dunivant, Little George W.
Son of W. V. and
Annie Lee Dunivant
Died Feb. 21, 1916
3 years, 2 months, 12 da.

Dunivant, Mary J.
Jan. 14, 1866
July 21, 1949

Dunivant, Patty Lee
Sept. 17, 1931
Sept. 29, 1932

Dunivant, Rosa Tabitha
Died June 10, 1900
Age about 40 years

Dunivant, W. J.
Oct. 22, 1859
Nov. 27, 1915

Dunivant, W. W.
1885-1910

Dycus, John M.
1866-1949
Dycus, M. Emma
1812-19

Enochs, Alfred Jr.
June 19, 1849
Oct. 26, 1911

Enochs, Alfred Sr.
June 15, 1809
Nov. 17, 1879
Enochs, Mary F.
Wife of A. Enochs
Nov. 9, 1813
Aug. 31, 1879

Enochs, George A.
1860-1862

Enochs, J. W.
Aug. 22, 1839
Nov. 12, 1919

Enochs, Matthew P.
1851-1888
Enochs, Mattie Patton
1885-1890
Enochs, Hellen Vaughn
1853-1933

Essary, Doshie Evelyn

Essary, Isabell
June 26, 1871
Aug. 26, 1925

Essary, Mattie Pearl
(No Dates)

Essary, May
(No Dates)

Essary, W. R.
1871-1946

Evans, James H.
Jan. 16, 1857
April 6, 1918
61 years
Evans, Earlene
April 16, 1912
July 8, 1918
5 years

17

Evans, Thomas J.
Dec. 19, 1904
Feb. 13, 1960
Evans, Willie M.
July 17, 1912

Evans, Wm. Larimore
Sept. 20, 1913
Oct. 30, 1917

Flack, C. A.
1851-1934

Flack, J. E.
March 1, 1846
April 26, 1917
Flack, Mrs. Elizabeth
Oct. 20, 1836
April 9, 1929

Flack, Martha
1856-1934

Fowlkes, G. A.
Son of G. J. and
Mattie Fowlkes
Born and Died
Oct. 21, 1912

Frith, A. D.
Sept. 16, 1834
Aug. 24, 1886

Frith, Wesley
March 16, 1837
March 20, 1857

Fuller, Clarence "Rip"
Feb. 12, 1887
April 10, 1973

Fuller, Mary James Ennis
Matthews
Feb. 16, 1888
March 30, 1945

Fuller, Infant Daughter
of Mr. and Mrs.
Clarence Fuller

Fuller, William M.
Oct. 3, 1863
March 1, 1942
Fuller, Sue C.
June 27, 1863
Dec. 8, 1942
Fuller, Sue Lea
Jan. 14, 1902
March 29, 1904

Fuller, W. M.
March 15, 1815
Jan. 17, 1890
Fuller, Mary A.
Jan. 2, 1823
Jan. 6, 1913

Gallahaire, Benjamin F.
June 30, 1890
51 years

Gallahaire, Jimmie
June 11, 1894
Nov. 10, 1916

Gean, James H.
1878-1954
Gean, Ellen H.
1880-1939

Gean, Lela Parlee
July 27, 1885
Sept. 29, 1932

Gelzer, Crafton
1894-1924
Father
Gelzer, Gertie
1899-19
Mother

Gelzer, Crafton F., Jr.
"Freddie"
Dec. 27, 1952
Aug. 26, 1965

Gelzer, J. T.
1858-1912
Gelzer, Ella W.
1866-1921

Gibson, G. W. (Wash)
June 10, 1879
May 2, 1942
Gibson, Lavenia
Jan. 4, 1880
June 18, 1968

Gibson, M. A.
Wife of C. W. Gibson
Dec. 24, 1849
Jan. 27, 1912

Gibson, Mattie B.
June 1, 1908
Oct. 10, 1926

Gibson, Terry Glynn
Aug. 10, 1943

Godwin, Elizabeth Ann
Sept. 13, 1839
Feb. 3, 1913

Gordon, Mrs. Elizabeth Grey
and daughter
Gordon, Ellen

Gray, Velma
Born March 16, 1909
Died Aug. 15, 1939

Green, Duke
Son of S. G. and
L. T. Green
Nov. 23, 1882
Nov. 15, 1904

Green, Owen Thomas
Son of C. C. and
S. E. Green
Jan. 20, 1916
Aug. 26, 1916

Griffin, Clarence C.
Tennessee
PVT World War I
Dec. 15, 1896-
Dec. 31, 1965

Griffin, Thomas J.
Aug. 8, 1861
Feb. 23, 1942

Grimm. Charles J.
June 18, 1814
Oct. 12, 1889

Grimm, Clarence
Feb. 19, 1857
Jan. 16, 1943

Grimm, Madie Enochs
1877-Feb. 22, 1927

Grimm, Nancy Hampton
June 22, 1828
July 6, 1912

Grisham, Thomas A.
1858-1934
Grisham, Missouri J.
1861-1932

Hall, Arvazania B.
Mother
Jan. 31, 1873
Sept. 2, 1918

Hall, Lloyd
1906-1972

Hampton, Howard
1881-1962
Hampton, Josephine
1886-1961

Hampton, J. P.
March 17, 1825
Hampton, Kitty
His Wife
Sept. 17, 1838
Dec. 3, 1903

Haney, John S.
Son of
C.E. and Beulah Haney
1912-1928

Harrington, Sarah Josephine
Wife of
W. W. Harrington
March 2, 1847
May 16, 1884

Harris, Elizabeth J.
Consort of Albert G. Harris
Aug. 30, 1830
June 30, 1859

Harrison, Cora
Aug. 15, 1869
March 13, 1900

Hicks, Dorothy
Dec. 27, 1907
Feb. 1926

Hicks, Effie C.
1866-1894
Wife of Jas. Hicks
28 years

Hicks, James
1854-1947
Hicks, Minnie
1870-1958

Holland, Dollie Rose
Daughter of W. E. and
M. J. Holland
Died March 3, 1877

Holland, Infant Son of
W. F. and M. I. Holland
Born and Died
June 19, 1881

Holland, Mary J.
Dec. 10, 1849
Oct. 4, 1890

Hood, Gurthie
Mother
1893-1962

Hood, L. C.
1915-1918

Hood, Paul Irvin
1913-1914

Howard, Charles A.
March 29, 1838
April 16, 1881

Hudson, Anna Wyatt
Feb. 24, 1896
July 7, 1919

Hunter, Robert L.
June 26, 1936
Nov. 2, 1969

Ingram, Billy Roland
1931-1933

Ingram, Clara J.
Wife of J. L. Ingram
April 18, 1872
Feb. 12, 1901

Ingram, Infant
Daughter of
P. D. and M. Ingram
Still Born
Aug. 20, 1876

Ingram, Infant
Daughter of
P. D. and C. D. Ingram
Born and Died
May 15, 1882

Ingram, Infant
Daughter of
P. D. and C. D. Ingram
Born and Died
Sept. 10, 1884

Ingram, J. L.
May 27, 1868
April 5, 1897

Ingram P.D.
1844-1934
Ingram, Melvina
His Wife
1847-1881
Ingram, Caldona
His Wife
1856-1928

Ingram, Infant of
Roland and Lula Ingram
Born and Died
August 25, 1908

Ingram, Isabella J
Daughter of P. D. and
M. Ingram
Died Nov. 20, 1868
2 years, 1 mo., 5 da.

Ingram, Roland
Dec. 31, 1880
Nov 2, 1912

Jackson, James W.
March 7, 1875
July 18, 1902

Johns, James Robert
Son of J. E. and
Effie Johns
May 10, 1916
Aug. 10, 1920

Johnson, Hattie Agnes
1880-1899

Johnson, Jennie M.
Died 1951

Johnson, Love
1809-1893
Johnson, Polly
His Wife

Johnson, M. Elizabeth
1853-1951

Johnson, Manuel
March 4, 1842
March 8, 1928
Johnson, Mary E.
April 9, 1848
July 29, 1919

Johnson, Mary 1. Ella
1875-1900

Johnson, Sharp
May 29, 1866
Jan. 8, 1913

Johnson, Sherrod
1851-1933

Jones, Infant son of
W. D. and E. A. Jones
Born and Died
March 22, 1899

Jones, Laura Newsom
July 8, 1856
Dec. 12, 1921

Jones, Nathan
Aug. 2, 1799
May 5, 1853
54 yrs., 3 mos., 3 days

Jones, O. A.
July 30, 1845
April 23, 1919
Jones, Susan J.
Aug. 25, 1849
June 25, 1909

Jones, R. S.
1869-1915

Jones, S. A.
Dec. 24, 1803
Aug. 1, 1885

Keen, Lee
Died July 6, 1918
29 yrs., 4 mos., 6 days

Keith, Lillie
Mother
1888-1915

Kennedy, Cantral B.
1913-1970

Kincy, David Almore
Sept. 27, 1874
Oct. 30, 1903

Kincy, Laura A.
Feb. 8, 1834
March 17, 1902
Age 68 years, 1 mo., 9 days

King, Michael O.
July 12, 1818
Sept. 18, 1893

King, Stacy
Wife of M. G. King
Dec. 4, 1806
Sept. 5, 1892

Lamb, B. E.
Daughter of Dr. B. E. and
M. L. Lamb
July 29, 1860
Jan. 12, 1862

Lane, Fannie
Died Dec. 18, 1922

Lay, Docia
May 2, 1825
Jan. 12, 1892

Lowe, Nancy J.
Wife of J. W. Lowe
Sept. 4, 1861
Jan. 10, 1887

Lyon, Emillia
Wife of J. T. Lyon
Died Oct. 5, 1881
Lyon, Infant son
Died Oct. 11, 1881
3 weeks and 3 days

Lyon, J. T.

Marlin, Opal E.
May 9, 1918
Jan. 26, 1919

Marlin, Parlin
May 22, 1834
Feb. 2, 1910

Marlin, Walter
Jan. 30, 1896
Marlin, Allie
May 17, 1898
Aug. 28, 1967

Masterson, Mary M.
Wife of W. A. Masterson
June 26, 1852
Feb. 12, 1893

Matthews, Agnes
April 11, 1854
Nov. 7, 1917

Mauney, Martha E.
Daughter of J. W. & W. H. Mauney
Sept. 24, 1889
July 10, 1890

Maxwell, B. M.
1895-1922

Maxwell, Charles D.
1867-1943
Maxwell, Mary A.
1872-1942

Maxwell, Della
Wife of W. M. Maxwell
Jan. 10, 1881
June 3, 1908

Maxwell, W. M.
1872-1921

McClearn, Joan
Born & Died
Aug. 15, 1939

McCorkle, Alexander Lock
Sept. 28, 1863
Nov. 17, 1948
McCorkle, Margaret Ann
Oct. 26, 1869
Oct. 11, 1922

McCorkle, Margaret Ann
Oct. 25, 1868
Oct. 14, 1936

McDonald, Dewitt
Son of A. H. McDonald
June 9, 1908
Oct. 4, 1912

McDonald, Gladys
1904
McDonald, Robert Sr.
1898-1963

McDonald, Pearl S.
1898
McDonald, Samuel J.
Tennessee
PVT. Btry. C 114 Field Arty,
World War I
Dec. 21, 1891
Mar. 7, 1970

McDonald, Nancy
1865-1947
McDonald, William "Bunk"
1864-1960

McFarland, Minnie
Daughter of M. G. & E. J. Swims
Feb. 6, 1901
June 20, 1919

McGill, Cherry Wilson
Jan. 20, 1919
July 26, 1919

McGill, Soffie
Dec. 17, 1892
Jan. 20, 1919

McKennie, Virginius
1840-1877

McKnight, J. R.
Jan. 20, 1854
May 20, 1911
McKnight, Mrs. R. E.
July 7, 1862
Jan. 22, 1917

McKnight, Mrs. Tennie
1840-1923

Merryman, Arthus R.
1886-1932
Merryman, Mary Lee
1890-1959

Merryman, Dora Lee
Wife of John F
Merryman
1878-1924

Merryman, Mrs. Eula Estella
Died April 10, 1975
66 years, 4 mos., 18 da.

Merryman, Halum 1883-1937
Merryman, Allie
1886-1960

Merryman, John F.
1819-1922

Milliner, N. E., Jr.
July 19, 1925
Sept. 1, 1934

Minor, Katie
Daughter of F. W. &
E.V. Minor
1906-1909

Montgomery, Frankie Dunlap
Daughter of F. T. &
J. H. Montgomery
Apr. 26, 1898
Apr. 26, 1898

Montgomery, John T.
Aug. 22, 1832
Montgomery, China E.
Jan. 16, 1835
Jan. 22, 1908
Montgomery, Dr. William A.
July 20, 1855

Moody, Ollie B.
1905-1971

Moore, George B.
Feb. 20, 1868

Newsome, Soloman
Nov. 1, 1850
July 23, 1899

Nickols, Mary Jane
Wife of J. L. Nockols
Dec. 26, 1854
Aug. 11, 1904

Noel, Floice E.
1901-1964

Oakley, Elizabeth
Mother
1834-1929

Osterholt, Sam Reed
Tennessee
S. Sgt. Tif. B.
7 Cavalry
World War II
Dec. 17, 1915
Oct. 11, 1953

Owen, Our Pet Notie
Daughter of J. M. &
A. E. Owens
Dec. 24, 1889
Jan. 26, 1894

Owens, Mary L.
Daughter of J. M. &
A. E. Owens
July 30, 1867
June 21, 1886

Parker, Lessie Bel
April 2, 1905
July 6, 1905
3 mos., 4 days

Pewett, George M.
1870-1941
Pewett, Jennie L.
1880-1963

Phillips, Dale
July 17, 1909
Oct. 26, 1970

Phillips, Frank
1866-1905

Pilgram, Robert L.
1885-1945

Poor, Addie Beryal
1908-1935

Poor, Arthur M.
Mar. 1, 1868
July 29, 1916
Poor, Jessie L. (His Wife)
July 26, 1878
Jan. 16, 1969

Poor, Cecil C.
April 22, 1899
Jan. 19, 1902

Poor, George W.
Sept. 17, 1834
Aug. 6, 1905

Poor, Mary E.
Wife of G. W. Poor
May 16, 1842
Nov. 24, 1903

Poor, Nuska
1877-1933
Poor, Addie
1881-1951

Poor, "Little" Ruby Arlene
Daughter of A. M. &
J. L. Poor
June 9, 1911
Oct. 28, 1912

Poore, Charles S.
1869-1918
Poore, Emma J.
1871-1918

Price, J. T.
Son of J. T. & S. M.
Price
Oct. 11, 1910
Jan. 27, 1914

Price, Myra B.
Feb. 8, 1888
July 19, 1958
Price, J. T.
Oct. 31, 1879
Aug. 28, 1969

Ragain, Martha N.
Wife of Jas. R. Ragain
Dec. 6, 1851
Dec. 16, 1888

Ragsdale, Charles Green
Dec. 12, 1881
Sept. 4, 1968
Ragsdale, Ida Parten
Feb. 23, 1885
Oct. 10, 1918

Reeves, Artie M.
1849-1931
Reeves, Carol
1850-1919

Reeves, Emma Smith
1879-1929

Reeves, Geneva
Daughter of C. & A.
M. Reeves
April 8, 1876
Mar. 14, 1908

Rice, G. H.
June 1, 1852
Aug. 7, 1928

Rice, Julia Ann
Wife of G. H. Rice
June 28, 1862
Mar. 30, 1908

Riddle, Sam M.
Son of G. B. & S. J. Riddle
Died Sept. 18, 1888
2 years, 7 days

Riddle, Sarah J.
Wife of G. B. Riddle
Aug. 18, 1866
April 19, 1888

Rizley, Robert E.
1868-1921
Rizley, Theresa R.
1870-1927

Robertson, Buddy
1906-1922

Robertson, George J.
1884-1967
Robertson, Lula J.
1883-1951

Runion, Jennie May
Feb. 16, 1910
Sept. 19, 1912

Rush, Henderson Alexander (Bud)
April 15, 1874
Oct. 10, 1959
Rush, Margaret Elizabeth
Aug. 12, 1872
Oct. 7, 1968

Rushing, Betty
Born - 1869
Died - Oct. 21, 1922

Rushing, Jim Allen
Jan. 20, 1975
76 years, 15 days

Rushing, William B.
Tennessee
Pvt. C O 1
World War I
Jan. 23, 1896
Oct. 27, 1972

Sawyer, Minnie
1864-1942

Scates, Ohlen
Son of J. F. & A. L. Scates
April 5, 1902
Oct. 11, 1912

Sewell, Walter O.
Dec. 31, 1894
Feb. 1, 1922

Sharp, Brown
Mar. 21, 1901
June 20, 1970
Sharp, Eva
Oct. 7, 1902

Sharp, Laura Keen
1890-1952

Sharpe, Sue Carolyn
Died Aug. 12, 1975
44 years, 10 mo., 19 days

Shoulders, Bill
1918-1975

Shoulders, Howard
1886-1955

Simons, David
Nov. 23, 1800
April 27, 1894

Smith, C. T.
Jan. 15, 1861
July 15, 1930

Smith, J. N.
1847-1932
Smith, Amanda P.
His Wife
1848-1924

Smith, Joseph
June 5, 1811
June 8, 1814

Smith, Mary
Sept. 26, 1824
Feb. 6, 1887

Smith, P. J.
Daughter of J. W. and
E. E. Smith
May 18, 1831
Sept. 7, 1855

Spence, E. B. "Buck"
1913-197__

Spence, Emma J.
Feb. 17, 1843
Nov. 19, 1903

Spence, John David
Tennessee PVT Co.
4 11 Regt. Tenn
Confederate States Army
Dec. 6, 1844
Oct. 30, 1903

Spence, Nona Green
1879-19__
Spence, John L. "Lem"
1880-1960

Stafford, Lessie
Feb. 14, 1894
Jan. 11, 1913

Sturdivant, (Morgan) H.
Oct. 10, 1839
Aug. 17, 1916

Sturdivant, Margaret J.
Wife of M. H. Sturdivant
Dec. 25, 1844
Jan. 4, 1926

Sturdivant, Andrew J.
Dec. 28, 1883
April 15, 1884

Summers, C. F.
Oct. 23, 1859
Feb. 17, 1893

Summers, Robert Lee
Son of C. F. Summers
April 17, 1887
March 31, 1888

Taylor, Duncan Elzie
July 7, 1881
Nov. 1, 1962

Taylor, Stella
Feb. 21, 1902
April 16, 1966

Taylor, Ezra
Oct. 23, 1889
Feb. 4, 1919

Taylor, Hassie May
Mar. 5, 1917
Feb. 10, 1919
1 year, 11 mos., 5 days

Taylor, Gary Lynn
Feb. 7, 1947
Oct. 12, 1947

Taylor, Holland P.
June 20, 1906
April 26, 1972
Taylor, Clara M.
June 3, 1911

Taylor, James F.
May 14, 1914
Sept. 17, 1969
Taylor, Joe A.
Nov. 19, 1865
Sept. 15, 1949
Taylor, Sarah E.
Sept. 5, 1877
Feb. 17, 1936

Taylor, J. H.
Dec. 3, 1869
July 30, 1905

Taylor, Jimmy Lynn
April 16, 1954
Nov. 4, 1972

Taylor, Vernie
1898-1967

Taylor, William E.
Tennessee
SI US NR
World War I
Sept. 6, 1921
July 6, 1968

Taylor, Wm. E.
1898-1971
Taylor, Vernie D.
1898-1967

Tidwell, Liberty
Father
Nov. 3, 1865
June 3, 1956
Tidwell, Anna
Mother
July 11, 1868
Dec. 2, 1934
Tidwell, Pearly
Daughter
Mar 3, 1889
Feb. 15, 1893

Tidwell, Pearly
Mar. 3, 1889
Feb. 18, 1893

Troy, Annie
Daughter of J. P.
and M. J. Troy
June 10, 1880
Mar. 27, 1896

Troy, Arley Josephine
Daughter of Mr. & Mrs.
M. S. Troy
Dec. 31, 1896
Jan. 29, 1897

Troy, Blanche
Daughter of J. D. & M. J.
Troy
Jan. 26, 1877
Feb. 14, 1884

Troy, Clara Maurine
Daughter of Mr. & Mrs.
M. S. Troy
July 6, 1900
Aug. 1, 1900

Troy, Eunice Anna
Daughter of Mr. & Mrs.
M. S. Troy
Jan. 11, 1906
July 2, 1906

Troy, Jennie M.
Daughter of J. P. and
M. J. Troy
Jan. 29, 1872
Mar. 3, 1884

Troy, John P.
Aug. 4, 1840
Jan. 10, 1886

Troy, Lutie J.
1878-1913

Tucker, Adelene
2nd Daughter of R. W.
and Ella Tucker
Aug. 22, 1856
Oct. 17, 1860

Tucker, J. G.
Sept. 14, 1822
Feb. 1, 1896
Tucker, H. C.
June 27, 1887
Tucker, R. W.
July 13, 1864
Tucker, M. E.
Sept. 28, 1859
Tucker, Infant Son of
J. G. & H. C. Tucker
July 31, 1855
Harper, M. C.
July 30, 1883
Harper, A.
Aug. 14, 1874

Tuten, Imogene
Aug. 26, 1925
Mar. 7, 1929

Tuten, J. W.
Jan. 6, 1854
June 10, 1938

Tuten, Martha June
Wife of J. W. Tuten
Aug. 24, 1857
July 30, 1928

Tuten, Woodrow Wilson
Son of J. T. & J. L. Tuten
March 13, 1913
Oct. 5, 1914

Unfrees, Twity Floyd
Aug. 15, 1893
May 22, 1897

Utley, James A.
May 14, 1819
Feb. 7, 1921

Vires, Jesse H.
1874-1928
Vires, Susie L.
1871-1929

Walker, Nannie
1850-1937
Walker, Frank
1841-1911

Walters, Otis B.
Tennessee
Sgt. U. S. Army
World War II
March 24, 1929
Nov. 4, 1968

Walton, Cora O.
Mar. 15, 1866
Oct. 1, 1868

Walton, Jennie S.
Wife of E. B. Walton
Sept. 30, 1890
Sept. 20, 1914

Walton, Redge May
Tennessee
Cook 321 Inf. 81 dies
March 23, 1932

Walton, T. H.
July 4, 1837
Oct. 29, 1888

Watson, Elizabeth C.
Born 1830
Died Mar. 17, 1903
79 yrs. old

Webb, Robert Luther
Jan. 17, 1871
Nov. 11, 1911

Weedman, Green
Aug. 20, 1833
Jan. 6, 1909

Welch, Elizabeth
Wife of J. C. Welch
May 29, 1813
Jan. 13, 1884

Wilkerson, W. N.
Oct. 14, 1867
May 13, 1913
Wilkerson, T. C.
Son of W. N. & Sallie
Wilkerson
Nov. 4, 1909
Aug. 16, 1910

Williams, A. N.
May 4, 1836
Jan. 20, 1895

Williams, Fannie A.
(Mother)
1842-1918

Williams, James W.
1872-1937

Williams, Martha C.
Wife of A. N. Williams
Born 1838

Wilson. Mrs. Bell
1878-1950

Wilson, Gaylon W.
1905-1927

Wilson, H. Blucher
1886-1959

Wilson, Jas. Timothy
Died June 19, 1887
Age: 34 yrs. old

Wilson, M. Rupert
1876-1964

Williams, R. E.
Aug. 12, 1824
Mar. 14, 1912
Williams, S. M.
Wife of R. E. Williams
May 10, 1853
July 2, 1911

Wood, F. M.
Husband of N. S. Wood
Died Dec. 24, 1899

Wood, N. S.
Wife of F. M. Wood
Died Jan. 9, 1892

Woods, Loraine
Daughter of R. W. &
E. J. Woods
Dec. 7, 1910
Nov. 27, 1911

Wright, Frances
1865-1938

Wright, Guy D.
Tennessee
PVT 46 Infantry
9th Division
Jan. 28, 1925

Wright, J. W.
Nov. 11, 1858
Feb. 15, 1924
Wright, Eliza (his wife)
Sept. 3, 1858

Wynne, Bobie Tarrant
Dec. 11, 1864
May 11, 1948

Wynne, Joseph Walker
Feb. 2, 1869
Sept. 25, 1947

Young, Nannie C.
Wife of W. W. Young
May 20, 1862
July 27, 1897

CLARK CEMETERY

The Clark Cemetery is located on the East Side of the Fairgrounds in Dyersburg just back of the riding ring.

Clark, Amanda C.
Wife of Colonel W. A.
Dawson
June 10, 1831
May 7, 1883
Note: Records of Mrs.
Peter C. Rhea

Clark, Charles P.
December 12, 1821
April 4, 1899

Clark, Henderson
November 10, 1797
January 31, 1883
Clark, Elizabeth Pate
1st Wife of H. Clark
Feb. 10, 1800-1848
Clark, Emeline Mitchell
2nd Wife of H. Clark
October 20, 1860
61 years of age

Cotton, Emma Clark
Wife of Tho's Cotton
July 27, 1836
November 22, 1866

Dawson, Frank
Son of W. P. Dawson
April 28, 1884
July 13, 1884
Note: Records of Mrs.
Peter C. Rhea

Fowlkes, Amanda C.
Born May 14, 1865
Died Jan. 30, 1891

Humphreys, John H.
Oct. 26, 1881
50 years, 11 months, 26 days
Note: Records of Mrs. Peter
C. Rhea

Kirkpatrick, Lou Pate
Wife of J. D.
Kirkpatrick
April 17, 1862
Nov. 23, 1889

Pate, E. C.
September 10, 1830
November 6, 1905
75 years, 1 month, 25 da.

Pate, E. C. Jr.
November 27, 1867
September 14, 1886
Note: Records of Mrs.
Peter Rhea

Pate, Lucy F.
Wife of E. C. Pate
Died May 21, 1874
Age 41 years
Note: Records of
Mrs. Peter C. Rhea

Pate, Stephen D.
July 30, 1820
Mar. 2, 1851
Note: Records of Mrs.
Peter C. Rhea

Summers, Angus Clark
Infant son of Dr. F. and
Dixie Summers
Oct. 19, 1884
Dec. 25, 1884
Summers, Dixie B.
Wife of Dr. F. Summers
May 20, 1863
Nov. 27, 1884

J. L. COBB HOMESTEAD PLOT

Travel Lanesferry Road to Dozier's grocery at Maxey Community. Turn left at Maxey Community Center to third house on right hand side. Husband and wife are buried on homestead.

Cobb, J. L.
Aug. 31, 1827
Oct. 15, 1905

Cobb, C. E.
Wife of J. L. Cobb
May 28, 1826
April 13, 1895

FAIRVIEW CEMETERY

The Fairview Cemetery in Newbern is located approximately one-eighth of a mile from the Illinois Central Railroad at the Jefferson Street intersection. Located on the right side of the street, a road or land on the cemetery's southern border is the southern boundary of the town of Newbern.

Little is known of the early history of the cemetery as deeds were not recorded at the register office in the Courthouse in Dyersburg until 1822. Evidenced from monument inscriptions, burials were made as early as 1801. So the land purchased for the initial cemetery probably dates to 1800.

3.28 acres of additional land was purchased for the cemetery by the City of Newbern on December 11, 1937 from Mrs. Ann Stoner for the price of $328.00. There are approximately 11 acres in the entire cemetery.

Abernathy, Kings S.
1905-1969
Abernathy, Jarmine L.
1907-_____
Abernathy, Jerry Allen
1941-1942

Adams, G. W.
May 2, 1856
Dec. 8, 1928

Adams, Howard R.
1908-1974
Adams, Ola A.
1908-_____

Adams, Nona B.
July 14, 1925
Adams, Bennie E. "Boots"
Dec. 17, 1920
Feb. 4, 1971
Tennessee
Sgt. U. S. Army
World War II

Adams, Rome
1894-1953
Adams, Ruby
1896-19__

Adams, William Cody
1891-19__
Adams, Mary Augusta
1891-1955

Adkins, Joseph B.
June 18, 1902
June 10, 1971
Adkins, Carrie M.
June 12, 1912

Agee, Jack
1898-1950
Agee, Willie
1902-

Akin, Edna Earl
Nov. 14, 1900
Jan. 29, 1963

Akin, Aaron Burnie
Tennessee
PVT. U.S. Marine Corps
World War I
April 8, 1900
Dec. 29, 1960

Allen, Pearlie Lee
Jan. 16, 1976
81 years old

Alsup, Joe A.
Oct. 26, 1913
Oct. 19, 1935

Anderson, Ezra A.
March 27, 1904
Feb. 13, 1971
Anderson, Mora P.
No Dates

Anderson, Grady
May 22, 1901
Dec. 17, 1973
Anderson, Tamsie
Aug. 28, 1902
No Date

Anderson, John F.
Jan. 11, 1863
Dec. 1, 1940

Applewhite, Carol
July 4, 1897
Sept. 9, 1898

Applewhite, E. F. "Chunk"
Nov. 28, 1875
Feb. 25, 1956
Applewhite, Evie E.
June 13, 1893
June 16, 1967

Applewhite, Mattie
Sept. 17, 1867
May 28, 1938
Applewhite, Thomas R.
Jan. 1, 1860
April 10, 1913

Applewhite, Micheal Lynn
1949-1955

Armstrong, Albert Via
Sept. 12, 1886
July 1, 1958

Armstrong, Edith Marzell
Sept. 10, 1912
June 1, 1974

Armstrong, J. N.
Jan. 2, 1891
Age 57

Armstrong, Mary Bell
July 31, 1894
Dec. 17, 1924

Arnett, Alton B.
1904-___
Arnett, Alton B., Jr.
1945-1971
Arnett, Lillie S.
1903-___

Arnett, Comp
1874-1969
Arnett, Fannie
1875-1936

Arnett, Jeff
1862-1937
Arnett, Emma
1856-1939

Arnett, Joseph E.
1882-1961
Arnett, Katherine E.
1884-19___

Arnett, Lynn
1902-1971
Arnett, Erin

_____

Arnett
Infant Daughter of Lynn &
Erin Arnett
Aug. 18, 1930

Arnett, R. T.
Dec. 19, 1900
Aug. 30, 1910

Arnett, Sr. Elmo
1867-1947
Arnett, Sarah Elizabeth
1866-1946

Arnold, John G.
1844-1884
Arnold, Almira J.
1854-1933

Arnold, Oliver J.
1844-1904

Ary, Arlie
Nov. 14, 1920
Jan. 14, 1937

Ashley, Daniel W.
Feb. 12, 1910
June 27, 1968
Ashley, Lyda M.
Feb. 21, 1912
No Date

Ashley, Theresa Diane
June 28, 1964
June 28, 1964

Ashcraft, Addie Fowlkes
1878-1941
Ashcraft, Harris Cas
1873-1952

Ashcraft, Callie
March 22, 1848
June 13, 1901

Ashcraft, Glenn
1900-1956
Ashcraft, Dixie
1908-___

Ashcraft, Guy
Feb. 15, 1877
Oct. 13, 1891

Ashcraft, John W.
1847-1932

Ashcraft, Mrs. Lettie Vaughn
Oct. 21, 1870
June 23, 1966

Ashcraft, Sallie M.
May 9, 1892
Feb. 14, 1897

Ashcraft, Tom Calvin
1878-1935
Ashcraft, Pearl Weakley
1872-1958

Ashcraft, Winnie D.
Jan. 21, 1907
Sept. 2, 1907

Atkins, A. A.
Oct. 12, 1848
May 30, 1928
Atkins, M. M.
Dec. 11, 1849
March 30, 1936
Wife of A. A. Atkins

Atkins, E. C.
Feb. 22, 1860
May 18, 1907
47 years, 3 mos., 26 days
Atkins, M. E.
Jan. 3, 1863
Sept. 6, 1933

Atkins, J.D.C. "Clint"
1885-1956
Atkins, Mamie Cawthon
-----1964

Atkins, James S.
1879-1944

Atkins, Dr. R. L.
May 11, 1864
Feb. 19, 1916
Atkins, Hattie
Wife of Dr. R. L.
Atkins
Dec. 29, 1874
May 27, 1912

Atkins, William J.
1862-1935

Austin, Babe
1895-1958

Austin, Gerald Don
1931-**1945**

Austin, Frances E.
1922-1956

Austin, Philip Glen
Son of Wayne and Lois
Austin
Nov. 18, 1952

Austin, R. C.
Feb. 27, 1893
Nov. 28, 1973
Austin, Vivian Smith
Feb. 14, 1900

Austin, Tillman A.
1882-1961
Austin, Bertha J.
1888-19__

Austin, William
Sept. 29, 1901
Feb. 5, 1965
Austin, Corrine
Born Sept. 11, 1912

Ayers, Alice
1857-19__
Ayers, Add
1855-1935

Ayers___
Infant of Alice & Add Ayers

Ayers, Bessie Pierce
1884-1941
Ayers, Claude
1882-1934

Ayers, Eva
Daughter of Rod and Alice
April 15, 1904
17 years, 7 months 15 days

Ayers, Galen
Son of Add and Alice Ayers
Dec. 15, 1903
25 years, 2 mos., 5 days

Ayers, Galen, Jr.
1931-1940

Ayers, Grover
Son of Add and Alice
Sept. 14, 1890
Mar. 19, 1900

Ayers, Jere Gene
1936-1954

Baker, Byron Glen
Jan. 10, 1923

Baker, Nettie
June 14, 1895
Baker, Gentry
July5, 1893
Sept. 27, 1963

Baker, Oscar G.
1862-1941
Baker, Martha Ann
1865-1944

Baker, Quincy M.
1881-1946
Baker, Allie
1887-1964

Baker, William
Feb. 1, 1830
May 18, 1910
Baker, Loucinda
Dec. 4, 1838

Baldridge, Byron
Oct. 20, 1922
June 11, 1937

Baldridge, Charles W.
Mar. 31, 1886
April 22, 1965

Baldridge, Elizabeth C.
April 18, 1973
Baldridge, Earl C.

Balthrop, Allen Edward
July 9, 1898
Aug. 14, 1972
Balthrop, Gladys Brown
Oct. 5, 1899

Banks, Avie P.
1880-1954

Banks, Jim
1892-1928

Barger, C. A.
Nov. 27, 1834
Apr. 1, 1892

Barger, S. A.
Wife of C. A. Barger
Aug. 7, 1830
Nov. 2, 1892

Barger, G. A.
Son of C. A. & S. A.
Barger
Aug. 1, 1866
July 5, 1889

Barham, Florence E.
Wife of Gordon Barham
Aug. 21, 1868
July 28, 1900

Barham, John
Nov. 17, 1837
Aug. 12, 1894

Barker, Ben W.
1884-1966
Barker, Cora A.
1892-1970

Barker, Emma K.
1869-1945

Barker, James H.
1876-1943

Barnett, Mallie M.
1880-19__
Barnett, T. L.
1877-1962

Bass, Jimmie Wallace
1922-1939

Beasley, Earnest F.
1879-1961
Beasley, Myrtle
1888 1943

Beasley, Pamela Jay
April 8, 1959
July 29, 1960

Beatty, James T.
July 24, 1922
Married May 7, 1949
Beatty, Martha Ann
Jan. 23, 1919
Apr. 20, 1974

Beaty, James W.
Tennessee
PFC HQ Far East
Comd. AAF
World War II
May 1, 1916
Dec. 20, 1959

Biffle, Bobbie
Wife of N. A. Biffle
1874-1913

Biffle, Martha Leach Shelton
Wife of W. M. Biffle
Jan. 24, 1837
Jan. 23, 1907

Biffle, Nat A.
1867-1939

Biffle, Solon I.
1858-1938

Biffle, W. M.
Mar. 3, 1828
Nov. 16, 1897

Bird, Barbara Wittmer
Wife of J. K. Bird
1874-1928

Bird, J. K.
1869-1929

Blankenship, Arthur
1883-1955
Blankenship, Belle
1881-1945

Blankenship, William
1862-1951
Blankenship, Sarah
Elizabeth (Bettie)
1862-1940

Blank, Mattie Idell
Wife of George Blank
Jan. 11, 1868
Dec. 11, 1895

Blessing, Dennis Mason
Dec. 27, 1956
Apr. 30, 1957

Blessing, James H.
Oct. 11, 1889
Sept. 9, 1958
Blessing, Lillie L.
April 10, 1896

Bloodworth, Harold S.
Jan. 18, 1916
July 7, 1958

Bloodworth, Harvey H.
1885-1940
Bloodworth, Gertrude P.

Bloodworth, Sibyl Pope
1908-1910

Boatright, Malissa
1877-1951
Boatright, Billie
1875-1947

Bone, W. D.
July 14, 1859
Mar. 6, 1901

Borden, Ozell
Jan. 8, 1910
Oct. 20, 1974
Borden, Lavina
Nov. 8, 1908

Boren, Bertha Scobey
1881-1969

Bouldin, John M.
1889-1964
Bouldin, Irene
1892-1972

Bradford, Ruth
1897-19__
Bradford, R. E.
1901-1954

Bradshaw, Scrappie Light
1852-1927
Wife of Thomas E.
Bradshaw

Bradshaw, Thomas E.
1851-1893

Bradshaw, Topsie
Jan. 27, 1887
July 23, 1887

Brake, Joe L.
1883-1971
Brake, Bessie Glenn
1888-1965

Brake, Paul M.
Sept. 25, 1910
March 25, 1974
Brake, Addie M.
Jan. 8, 1911

Brake, Vernon E.
1923-1969

Braly, Margaret Malvina
"Mallie"
Daughter of Rev. S. H. and
Fannie Braly
Sept. 1, 1890
Dec. 14, 1892

Brammer, Lenos H.
Feb. 4, 1897
Brammer, Edgar L.
Sept. 30, 1900
Apr. 14, 1874

Brasfield, Eber
1887-1959
Brasfield, Florence
1881-1968

Brewer, Lara
Daughter of T. A. and
Mannie Brewer
Oct. 28, 1890
Oct. 22, 1895

Bridges, Claude
July 28, 1901
Aug. 1, 1975

Bridges, Joseph H.
Nov. 21, 1876
Mar. 9, 1963
Bridges, Ada Alma
Jan. 10, 1881
Nov. 17, 1938

Brinkley, Jno H.
Jan. 6, 1886
26 yrs., 8 mo., 28 da.

Brinn, William J.
Tennessee
Pvt. U. S. Army
World War I
Sept. 4, 1896
Mar. 30, 1970
Brinn, Lola C.
1898-19__

Broadous, Algernom
1864-1935

Broadous, H. I.
1827-1918

Bromley, Dennis Lee
Apr. 17, 1951

Bromley, Jeff
1889-1949
Bromley, Flaudie
1892-19__

Bromley, William E.
Tennessee
PFC. 1 Station Comp.
World War II
Nov. 4, 1914
Aug. 9, 1971
Bromley, Helen
1918-19___

Brown, Basil Walton
Sept. 6, 1860
July 5, 1937
Brown, Mattie McConnell
Apr. 13, 1868
Feb. 26, 1923

Brown, George
1862-1936
Brown, Mattie
1870-1939

Brown, H. Joe
1905-19__
Brown, Jewell Cobb
1905-___

Brown, Littia
1858-1940
Brown, C. Frank
1852-1938

Brown, Estelle
Daughter of C. Frank Brown

Brown, Lula Jones
Nov. 28, 1878
Mar. 16, 1966
Brown, Joseph Lee
Mar. 28, 1864
Sept. 1, 1928

Brown, Mamie Jones
1878-1967
Wife of Will Brown

Brown, May Rainey
1877-1970
Brown, John
1875-1959

Brown, Millard V.
1907-1935

Brown, Thelma
1898-1923
Daughter of Will and
Mamie Jones Brown

Brown, Will
Husband of Mamie
Jones Brown
1873-1939

Bryan, A. Rupert
1885-1952
Bryan, Emma M.
1886-1956

Bryan, Earnest
Son of F. B. & M. E.
Bryan
Nov. 16, 1890
Sept. 18, 1891

Bryan, Jerry
1939-1940

Bryan, Maggie L.
Daughter of F. B. Bryan
Sept. 14, 1863
Aug. 12, 1891

Bryant, A. E., "Dick"
World War 1 Vet. Co. K
119th Inf.

Bryant, Ethel Steelle
1891-1973

Bryant, Floy Keith
Jan. 21, 1894
Sept. 23, 1973

Bryant, Ivan
1891-1934
Bryant, Minnie Farris
1886-1953

Bryant, James A.
Apr. 23, 1888
Apr. 24, 1972

Bryant, Lillian
1891-1923

Bryant, Minnie
Nov. 30, 1889
Aug. 9, 1929

Bryant, William E.
1864-1958
Bryant, Dora Annett
1860-1938

Bunn, Minnie Becton
1859-1945
Father
Bunn, Isral Gulecu
1847-1920

Infant Son of Becton and
Hattie Bunn
Dec. 28, 1928

Bunn, J. N.
Oct. 25, 1866
May 18, 1905

Bunn, Lula E.
Feb. 10, 1867

Bunn, W. T.
Feb. 21, 1833
Dec. 22, 1916
Bunn, Matilda E.
Wife of W. T. Bunn
Aug. 22, 1827
Dec. 17, 1905

Birch, Charlie R
July 8, 1878
May 30, 1971
Birch, Willie P.
Oct. 2, 1884
Dec. 9, 1971

Burch, Ella
1887-1959

Burch, Jessie B.
1918-1958

Burkeen, Betty Ferguson
April 7, 1883
Jan. 23, 1950

Burkeen, Charles Gentry
1871-1947

Burkeen, Geneva
Oct. 18, 1913
Burkeen, James E.
POR. U.S. Army
May 1, 1913
Sept. 22, 1974

Burkeen, Guy
Oct. 17, 1889
Oct. 1, 1965

Burkeen, J. H.
1867-1946

Burkeen, James J.
Tennessee
PFC. Co. E 16 Inf.
World War 1
May 9, 1898
Nov. 7, 1969

Burkeen, Jodie
1896-1969
Burkeen, Berlie V.
1900-1971

Burkeen, Vandelia
1854-1928

Burkett, Allen A.
1897-1947
Burkett, M. Otis
1898-19__

Burkett, Infant Son of
Mr. & Mrs. A. A. Burkett

Burkett, Bernice J.
Nov. 28, 1907
June 23, 1963

Burkett, Bert
1906-19__
Burkett, Marie
1905-19__

Burkett, Bob L.
1875-1921
Burkett, Perry
1914-1924
Burkett, Mattie
1882-19__

Burkett, Kenneth Bryon
1951-1970

Burkett, L. G.
Oct. 16, 1873
Mar. 22, 1954
Burkett, Jennie
Feb. 14, 1875
May 27, 1927

Burkett, Robert
1871-1945
Burkett, Pennie
1875-19__

Burns, James A.
1890-19__

Burns, Zula, V.
1894-1948

Bush, Edna
1899-19__

Bush, John
1875-1964

Butler, Delia H.
Nov. 22, 1904
Butler, Elizia
Dec. 1, 1902
Mar. 22, 1972

Butler, Harvey B.
1895-19__
Butler, Parlee S.
1897-1955

Butler, Jonathon
Jan. 10, 1975
Jan. 10, 1975

Butler, Matthew J.
1895-1946
Butler, Sarah Bell
1895-1970

Butler, Minnie B.
1875-1959
Grandmother
Pollack, Jimmie B.
1943-1954

Butler, Willie S.
1885-19__
Butler, John C.
1876-1946

Byars, Ernest E.
Feb. 11, 1893
May 12, 1968
Byars, Lillian G.
Sept. 17, 1893

Byrn, Minnesota
Wife of J. W. Byrn
Aug. 12, 1870
Aug. 30, 1895

Byrns, Richman L.
1892-1933

Callis, Mary B.
Feb. 21, 1905
Callis, Felix, Dale
Aug. 31, 1903
June 28, 1974

Campbell, Arther
1882-1967

Campbell, Leona
1885-1964

Campbell, Nancy
1890-19__
Campbell, Jake
Arkansas
PFC 313 CD & Fire Co., QMC
World War I
July 13, 1890
March 3, 1970

Campbell, R. S. (Bob)
1854-1937
Campbell, Mary S.
1862-1947

Canada, Janie
1863-1943

Capelle, Callie Rodgers
April 25, 1865
Feb. 6, 1933

Capelle, Little Callie
Aug. 9, 1899
Nov. 9, 1899

Capelle, Little Girlie
Dec. 5, 1883
Oct. 9, 1884

Capelle, Essie
Died Sept. 4, 1936

Capelle, Grace J.
Died Aug. 12, 1964

Capelle, Roger S.
June 2, 1891
May 24, 1966

Capelle, Sannie
Died May 12, 1946

Capelle, William Henry
June 11, 1850
Sept. 5, 1910

Capelle, William H.
Apr. 27, 1889
Feb. 13, 1967

Carman, Reuben E.
Tennessee
CPL 268 Coast Duty
World War II
April 4, 1912
Sept. 17, 1968

Carman, William Thomas
Aug. 25, 1870
Nov. 28, 1958

Carnell, John Luther
1852-1940

Carnell, John Robert (Jr.)
1917-1939

Carnell, Robert B.
1890-19__
Carnell, Lora M.
1892-19__

Carpenter, Emma Viola
1873-1926

Carpenter, John B.
1875-1923

Carpenter, Maggie L.
1878-19__

Carpenter, Maggie F.
1893-1954

Carpenter, W. A.
Feb, 5, 1871
Aug. 10, 1934

Carpenter, William L.
Dec. 5, 1900
Carpenter, Octa B.
Nov. 5, 1902

Carnell, Abner Frazier
Nov. 4, 1902
April 11, 1967
Carnell, Edith Rose
Born Jan. 6, 1905

Carrell, Janice
Oct. 20, 1947
Dec. 2, 1968

Carrell, Otha Bernal
1882-1957
Carrell, Sallie Irene
1887-1965

Carroll, Aaron
Feb. 23, 1910
Carroll, Girzelle
Mar 25, 1912

Carson, James Edgar
Apr. 29, 1900
Mar. 30, 1971
Married Feb. 21, 1919
Carson, Mirl Hicks
July 16, 1900

Cavender, George W.
Apr. 28, 1882
July 21, 1941

Cawthon, E. J.
Wife of J. L. Cawthon
Feb. 12, 1859
Feb. 12, 1888
Cawthon, Bettie Love
Dau. of J. L. & E. J.
Cawthon
Feb. 5, 1888
July 5, 1888

Cawthon, Baby
No Dates

Cawthon, John L.
April 15, 1847
Dec. 30, 1893

Chalker, Lexie D., Jr.
May 4, 1930
July 7, 1930

Chalker, Mary Sue
Sept. 29, 1926

Chamberlin, Edd Columbus
Died May 11, 1975
75 years, 3 months 0 days

Champion, Emmet A.
1878-1940

Champion, Samuel
1918-1922

Cherry, Eunice Fuller
1864-1950

Cherry, Dr. E. O.
Husband of Eunice
Fuller Cherry
1862-1927

Childress, Jerrell
1921-1939

Churchwell, Brown,
1915-1955
Churchwell, Winnie Bell
1917-1958

Churchwell, Katie
July 29, 1878
Mar. 26, 1926

Churchwell, Paul
Son of J. A. and Katie
Churchwell
Feb. 25, 1908
Jan. 30, 1921

Churchwell, S. E. "Bo"
1897-1947
Churchwell, Verna M.
1898-

Clanton, Roy
1878-1966
Clanton, Julia M.
1884-19__

Clift, Celina Johns
1839-1907

Clift, Rev. H. D.
1844-1920

Clift, Mattie Snead
1881-1968

Cobb, Eural R.
1896-1964
Cobb, Ida F.
1897-1960

Cole, James Hamilton
Feb. 22, 1915
Feb. 23, 1915

Coleman, Norma Belle
Aug. 12, 1894
Jan. 21, 1904

Collins, James W.
Feb. 11, 1896
Feb. 15, 1931

Combs, Edward M.
May 16, 1907
Combs, Eudora L.
Nov. 17, 1915
Nov. 16, 1957

Combs, Halbert C.
April 5, 1878
Aug. 2, 1959
Combs, Josie L.
Dec. 3, 1880

Combs, Ronnie
Son of Fred & Esther
Aug. 31, 1940
May 5, 1942

Combs, Willie S.
Tennessee
PFC BTRYB 539 FA BN
World War II
Feb. 17, 1922
Nov. 1, 1971

Cook, Cordie A.
May 31, 1891
June 26, 1970
Married June 9, 1912
Cook, G. Louis
Aug. 19, 1884
Feb. 4, 1968

Cook, Finis
1906-__
Cook, Thelma
1909-__

Cook, George A.
1882-1953
Cook, Velma V.
1889-1974

Cook, James M.
Mar. 12, 1932
Sept. 30, 1972

Cook, John W.. "Jack"
1890-1952
Cook, Allie B.
1894-19__

Cook, Lutie
1870-1949
Cook, Walter
1872-1965

Cooley, Clarence
Tennessee
PFR COB 309 Field
Sig BN
World War I
May 16, 1891
May 7, 1954

Cooper, J. M.
1871-19__
Cooper, P. M.
His Wife
1871-1941

Copeland, W. E.
Died April 8, 1897

Cornell, Harry E.
1854-1941
Cornell, Susie F.
1866-1949

Cotton, Lillie
1864-1946

Cottrell, Velva F.
Feb. 15, 1921
Mother
Cottrell, George H.
April 19, 1916
June 12, 1966
Father

Covilli, Domonica Giovanelli
1892-1975

Cowart, William Perry
"Bill"
1947-1975

Cox, Bryant
1847-1924
Cox, Sallie R.
1847-1891

Cozart, Earl
Sept. 11, 1908
April 24, 1971
Cozart Clara M.
Nov. 28, 1912

Cozart, Sarah E. D.
1848-1932

Crawford, Andrew Beuran, Jr.
Aug. 17, 1917
April 12, 1926

Crawford, A. B.
1888-1968
Crawford, Corinne
1888-1958

Crawford, Gladis Lucile
Dau. of A. B. &
Corinne Crawford
Feb. 21, 1914
Nov. 28, 1918

Crawford, Robert F.
Aug. 15, 1891
Feb. 26, 1958
Crawford, Allie F.
Feb. 22, 1889
Jan. 20, 1958

Crawford, Sam
1897-1964

Crenshaw, Jettie Bush
July 4, 1872
Jan. 14, 1947
Crenshaw, John Allen
Sept. 12, 1850
Aug. 22, 1922

Crenshaw, John Bush
1895-1968
Crenshaw, Gladyes K.
1895

Crenshaw, Robert Irwin
Son of J. A. & Ida
Crenshaw
Feb. 27, 1890
May 26, 1890

Crenshaw, Ida M. Townsend
Wife of J. A. Crenshaw
Feb. 3, 1867
July 17, 1890

Creson, Vianna E.
1917

Crisp, Luem Enochs
1890-1943

Crosthwait, Martha E.
1915-1928

Crosthwait, W. F.
1876-1949
Crosthwait, Daisy
1890-19__

Crouson, Lena Pearl
1892-19__
Crouson, Elias L.
1889-1956

Crouson, Mary Dale
Infant Dau. of
Cecil & Sonia Crouson
Feb. 10, 1946
Nov. 12, 1947

Crowder, Richard B.
1830-1929
Crowder, Mary E.
18__-1919

Cryer, Lillie E.
1899-1972

Culp, Bettve Sue
Sept. 26, 1932
May 29, 1935

Curtis, James H.
1900-1956
Curtis, Neller S.
1901-1976

Curtis, Joe F.
1870-1949
Curtis, Dora
1874-1951

Daniel, Joseph Lee
Tennessee
S N US NR
April 1, 1931
Dec. 19, 1966

Daniel, Luvern
1922-1946

Daughtry, Carmon W.
April 28, 1975
73 years 9 mos., 2 da.

Daughtry, Willie Jean Champean
1892-1960

Davis, A. J. (Jay)
Jan. 14, 1887
Apr. 16, 1950
Davis, Georgia
Sept. 8, 1892

Davis, Claude
1898-1974
Davis, Frances
1914-___

Davis, Ernest Lee
1859-1885

Davis, Ernest Lee Jr.
1882-1918

Davis, E. M. E.
1858-1933

Davis, Eula R.
Dau. of G. W. &
N. A. Davis
July 5, 1884
Oct. 13, 1902

Davis, George E.
March 14, 1880

Davis, George Emery
Tennessee
PVT U.S. Army
World War I
March 14, 1890
June 5, 1972

Davis, George W.
1849-1924
Davis, Nancy A.
1859-1934

Davis, Herbert Harold Jr.
Infant Son of
Mr. & Mrs. Harold Davis
Jan. 9, 1952

Davis, Leila Frances
1856-1924

Davis, M. B.
Nov. 20, 1899
Dec. 30, 1914

Davis, Martha B.
1886-1958

Davis, Mary Jane
1886-1944

Davis, Samuel H.
1889-1960

Davis, Tracy Neil
Aug. 28, 1967
Aug. 19, 1975

Davis, Trudie Lee Cobb
Wife of Geo. Davis
Feb. 25, 1894
Sept. 5, 1922

Davis, W. J.
Died Sept. 2, 1893

Davis, Willard M.
1884-1937

Davidson, Pattye Evelyn
1949-1949
Davidson, Perry Wilson
1949-1949

Dennison, Earl
Father
1889-1968
Dennison, Lola
Mother
1893-19

Dennison, Euble U.
1903-
Dennison, Mary Whitson
1904-1905

Dennison, Jenora Smith
1879-1965

Dennison, John Weldon
1877-1938

Dickey, Anderson
July 31, 1820
Jan. 31, 1867
Dickey, Joanna
July 28, 1820
Mar. 28, 1889
Dickey, George Stephen
Son of A. & J. Dickey
B. Sept. 16, 1845
June 18, 1853

Dickey, Anderson
Died Sept. 27, 1897

Dickey, Boiseau
Feb. 9, 1875
June 30, 1876

Dickey, Edna
June 3, 1881
May 12, 1888
Dickey, Neola
D. Oct. 24, 1942

Dickey, Robert J.
D. Jan. 14, 1916

Dickey, Rosa Lee
Wife of Asa Dickey
Oct. 30, 1861
April 28, 1898
Dickey, Louise
Dau. of Asa & Rosa L.
Dickey
April 12, 1897
Aug. 4, 1897

Dickey, Sallie Boiseau
D. Oct. 29, 1933

Dickey, William C.
Jan. 5, 1848
July 16, 1888

Dickson, A. E.
Dec. 19, 1831
Jan. 15, 1908
Dickson, L. A.
Aug. 11, 1847
Oct. 5, 1910

Dillon, John Maurice
1874-1947
Dillon, Ruby Browder
1885-1969

Dinwiddle, Bessie, Grisham
Died June 27, 1956

Ditmore, Aline Crenshaw
Oct. 17, 1893
October 25, 1969

Ditmore, E. R.
May 8, 1861
Aug. 8, 1935

Ditmore, Mrs. Martha E.
July 8, 1849
Feb. 8, 1928

Ditmore, Oscar
1887-1939

Ditmore, Parker
1890-1926

Dixon, Thomas J.
Dec. 26, 1867
Nov. 14, 1918
Dixon, Ella Frances
June 9, 1876
Oct. 23, 1917

Dodds, John S.
Nov. 14, 1898

Dodds, May H.
May 21, 1900
Nov. 27, 1967

Dopf, Thelma Featherson
Nov. 13, 1906

Dotson, Mary Lynn
March 16, 1871
Sept. 27, 1955

Dotson, William James
Mar. 19, 1867

Doss, Bessie
1892-1973
Doss, George O.
Tennessee
PVT Medical Dept.
World War I
March 16, 1893
Aug. 9, 1964

Douglas, Amanda V.
Dec. 13, 1897
Oct. 17, 1970
Douglas, Arthur L.
Dec. 1, 1894
Sept. 2, 1969

Douglas, Robert W.
1872-1966

Dowland, Billy Gene
July 27, 1928
Dec. 26, 1969
Dowland, Daisy, Tharp
Aug. 17, 1928

Drane, John M.
Born July 28, 1882
Died Sept. 18, 1974

Drane, Lillie Wilson
Mar. 19, 1888
July 28, 1968
Wife of John M. Drane

Drane, Robert W.
Jan. 25, 1850
July 12, 1888

Drewry, Charlie C.
Tennessee
PFC 16 Engres
World War I
July 15, 1894
Jan. 4, 1948

Drewry, Charles N.
1855-1900
Drewry, Etta E.
1856-1943

Dunahoo, Ervin
Dec. 4, 1898
May 4, 1970
Dunahoo, Irene
June 17, 1904

Dunahoo, Harell Cole
Dec. 4, 1910
Mar. 22, 1969
Dunahoo, Ruby Lee
Sept. 11, 1910

Dunahoo, Mary Ethel
1894-19
Dunahoo, Walter Othel
1895-1956

Duncan, Charlie
Aug. 20, 1880
May 4, 1884

Duncan, Ennis
Son of L. P. & L. L.
Duncan
Dec. 20, 1895
Aug. 10, 1896

Dunivant, Jessie McKinley
Died June 15, 1974
78 years 4 mos. 4 da.

Durham, Ernest Earl
1901-1936

Duncan, Fannie M.
1906-1965
Duncan, Ernest D.
1893-1960

Duncan, Lavern L.
Jan. 4, 1842
July 6, 1885

Duncan, L. P.
Jan. 25, 1841
May 1, 1881

Dunlap, A. C.
Dec. 22, 1868
Feb. 2, 1906
Dunlap, John Ed
June 9, 1898
Mar. 11, 1904

Dunlap, Finis Ewing
Jan. 23, 1844
Sept. 15, 1891
Dunlap, Sarah Frances
July 29, 1851
Nov. 26, 1937

Dunlap, Infant son of
F. E. and S. F. Dunlap
No Date.

Dunlap, Mary C.
His Wife
1847-1930
Dunlap, Rev. J. A.
1841-1897

Dunlap, Noah G.
1906-___
Dunlap, Pauline M.
1915-1970

Dunlap, Infant daughter
J. C. & M. M.
May 14, 1897
July 9, 1897

Dycus, James W.
July 23, 1909
Jan. 21, 1970
Dycus, Clara B.
March 22, 1903
July 18, 1961

Dycus, Oneda Tharp
Sept. 20, 1915
Jan. 4, 1938

Dyer, Paul B.
Tennessee
Sgt. 902 Training
GPAAF
World War II
Sept. 17, 1920
Apr. 30, 1956

Eason, Ivor A.
1887-1915

Eason, Julia
1865-1920

Eason, J. F.
1844-1920

Edwards, Ernest M.
May 24, 1851
Feb. 11, 1883

Edwards, Herbert G.
Son of Ernest and Alice
Edwards
April 12, 1880
Nov. 28, 1880

Edwards, Teresa Carol
Oct. 8, 1966
Oct. 12, 1967

Edwards, Willie Ernest
Son of Alice and
Ernest Edwards
Sept. 11, 1881
Mar. 15, 1883

Edmiston, Roy Fay
Gunner Mate 1st Class
Nov. 8, 1919
Dec. 28, 1943
Died in Trinided
British West Indies

Ellis, Ava Goforth
Jan. 12, 1895
Nov. 17, 1969

Ellis, J. R.
1875-19__
Ellis, Izora
His Wife
1875-1930

Ellis, James Thomas
Tennessee
Staff Sgt. 385 Inf.
76 Inf. Div.
Mar. 28, 1918
Jan. 27, 1945

Ellis, John T.
1887-1963
Ellis, Evelyn E.
No Dates

Ellis, Sara F.
Oct. 27, 1866
Sept. 17, 1947

Elkins, James D.
1863-1947
Elkins, Sarah E.
1873-1944

Elkins, Monroe S.
1891-19
Elkins, Hattie
1891-1967

English, Eva
Wife of Dr. A. Q. English
No Dates

English, Floyd
Son of A. D. and K. W.
July 28, 1887
Aug. 21, 1887

Enochs, Beatrice J.
Oct. 20, 1887
Enochs, Joe M.
May 6, 1888
Jan. 19, 1967

Enochs, Belle
Mar. 13, 1856
Jan. 21, 1922

Enochs, Joseph Robertson
Aug. 28, 1882
Aug. 11, 1967
Enochs, Mary Jones
Dec. 24, 1886
July 5, 1966

Ervin, Jeremy Paul
Died Sept 28, 1975
11 days old

Evans, A. T.
No Date

Evans, Lillie W.
No Date

Evans, Benjamin H.
Pfr HQ 294 Mil
Police Co., World War 1
June 28, 1888
June 10, 1966

Evans, Clarence
Tennessee
S Sgt. HO Col Army
World War II
May 12, 1923
Mar. 6, 1950

Evans, Dempsey W.
Tennessee
PFC Med Dept. 44
Armd Inf BN
World War II BSM
Feb. 17, 1923
Mar 23, 1964

Evans, George G.
1864-1931

Evans, James S.
Tennessee
S SGT 59 QM Base Depot
World War II
Mar. 18, 1918
Feb. 26, 1966

Evans, Jesse T.
Tennessee
WAGR 105 SN Train
30 Div.
World War I
Aug. 19, 1886
June 28, 1944

Evans, Lewis A.
1846-1918
Evans, Sarah J.
1847-1930

Evans, Mary
1869-1954

Evans, Mary F.
1888-19
Evans, Charlie
1881-1960

Evans, R. T.
1892-
Evans, Flora L.
1896-1970

Evans, Robert "Tommy" Jr.
Jan 8, 1942
Mar. 24, 1973

Evans, W. B. "Mark"
1899-
Evans, Celia J.
1903-1970

Faircloth, Elizabeth H.
1843-1923

Faircloth, James H.
1832-1898

Farris, Allene
Feb. 5, 1922
Dec. 20, 1941

Farris, Louise
Aug. 16, 1913
Farris, Allen
Tennessee
PVT Co. 2 Inf.
Tenn. NG
World War I
Nov. 29, 1898
Dec. 10, 1965

Faulkner, Jim W.
Aug. 2, 1871
Aug. 22, 1936
Faulkner, Minnie Brown
Dec. 16, 1869
Jan. 8, 1957

Featherston, Faustine Idella
Daughter
1903-___

Featherston, Melda Ann
1937-1961

Featherston, Orlande Edward
Nov. 9, 1877
June 3, 1949

Ferguson, Elaine
1914-___
Ferguson, Meadows
1913-___

Ferguson, Doneta
Dec. 12, 1964
Apr. 17, 1967

Ferguson, J. Albert
1847-1937
Ferguson, -Bob
1885-1951

Ferguson, Lon
Mar. 29, 1878
Nov. 23, 1953

Ferrell, Samuel Isaac
1860-1941
Ferrell, Mary Frances
1869-19__

Fielder, William
Kentucky
2nd Lt. U.S. Army
World War II
July 26, 1893
Sept. 9, 1970

Finch, Fern
1891-1969
Finch, George
1879-1931

Fitzgerald, Jennie May
1884-1964

Fitzgerald, Velma Lucille
No Date

Fitzgerald, Herbert
Mar. 10, 1895
Jan. 14, 1972

Flack, B. M.
1915-1939

Flack, Charlie S.
1869-1948

Flack, Ida Jane
1873-1931

Flack, Finis
1912-1971
Flack, Irene
1914-

Flatt, Bettie
1870-1940

Flatt, Clara Jane
1942-1927
Grandmother

Flatt, Donna
May 20, 1962
May 20, 1962

Flatt, Jon Athyln
(Infant)
Sept. 5, 1948

Flatt, John Hugh
Mar. 19, 1899
Dec. 17, 1920

Flatt, W. J.
Nov. 1, 1861
Nov. 21, 1923

Flowers, Kittie Bell
1904-1928

Flowers, Walker E.
1886-1955
Floers, Ola Oates
1890-1968

Forrester, A. G.
1851-1943
Forrester, Lotty
1857-193-

Forrester, Eula
1880-1925
Forrester, J. M.
1875-1947

Forrester, Ophelia
1889-1964
Mother
Forrester, Ira
1882-1960
Father

Forrester, Edward
1909-1944
Son

Forrester, Thomas
Tennessee
Sgt. 807 Mil.
Police Co.
World War II
Aug. 4, 1918
Apr. 30, 1970

Forister, Rubie Jewel
Jan. 2, 1919
Aug. 2, 1951

Fowler, Glen
Tennessee
Sgt. U. S. Army
Korea Vietnam
BSM & OLC
June 12, 1927
March 12, 1973

Fowler, George H.
Dec. 18, 1895
June 21, 1965
Fowler, Mary Duncan
Jan. 28, 1896
Mar. 22, 1965

Fowlkes, A. B.
1867-1919

Fowlkes, Aubrey M.
1882-1959
Fowlkes, Virginia
Carroll
1894-19

Fowlkes, Dorris
Oct. 13, 1910
Mother
Fowlkes, Ersie M.
Feb. 17, 1892
Feb. 16, 1974

Fowlkes, Eudora L.
April 14, 1860
June 22, 1940

Fowlkes, Evie L.
1897-1961

Fowlkes, Parsha L.
1900-1937

Fowlkes, Harriet M.
1859-1934

Fowlkes, James W.
1854-1916

Fowlkes, M. F.
Dec. 15, 1859
Aug. 9, 1913

Fowlkes, M. L.
Feb. 26, 1850
Sept. 30, 1908

Fowlkes, Parsha L.
1853-1885

Fowlkes, "Little" Scrappe
Dau. of Parsha & Scrappie
Fowlkes
June 22, 1883
July 26, 1883

Fowlkes, "Little" Topsie
Dau. of Parsha & Scrappie
Fowlkes
June 22, 1883
July 26, 1883

Fowlkes, Mrs. Sallie Bingham
Dau. of J. S. &
Elizabeth Bingham
March 22, 1855
Nov. 17, 1920

Fowlkes, Sam L.
1883-1936
Fowlkes, Blanche
1892-19

Fowlkes, Valeria Gladys
Sept. 3, 1891
Mar. 3, 1908

Fowlkes, William R.
1880-1954

Fowlkes, Wood
1803-1860

Frame, Dixie Ashcraft
Oct. 21, 1906
April 20, 1958

Franks, Laurie Annie
Daughter
July 12, 1964
July 21, 1964

Freeman, Frances Atkins
1890-1971

Freeman, Martha Edward
1911-1912

Freeman, Nora M.
1861-1937
Freeman, C. B.
1847-1930

Fulghum, Albert Leon
1844-1896
Fulghum, Mary Senter
1848-1916

Fulghum, Annie McCutchen
1878-1958

Fulghum, Charlie
1877-1961

Fulghum, Docia Jones Taylor
1878-1918

Fulghum, Elizabeth Taylor
Oct. 28, 1918

Fulghum, James Lamb
1892-1972
Fulghum, William S.
Pvt. MG Co. SO. Inf.
World War II
June 8, 1891
Oct. 21, 1968

Fulghum, Laura Eva
1882-1965

Fulghum, Leon
1902-1949

Fulghum, Lonnie
1875-1921

Fulghum, Murray
1871-1921

Fulghum, Murray H.
Feb. 11, 1913
Feb. 22, 1914

Fuller, Nancy L.
Feb. 20, 1817
June 12, 1888
Fuller, Hezekiah
Aug. 9, 1811
Aug. 19, 1887

Fulghum, Robert Leroy
Tennessee
TECS Co. D 129 Inf.
ENG. BN
Dec. 1, 1908
Nov. 23, 1965

Fulghum, Norvellia
Apr. 30, 1876
July 28, 1901
Fulghum, Ealy
Mar. 16, 1842
Apr. 26, 1896
Fulghum, Emery R.
Dec. 2, 1834
Nov. 16, 1911

Fulghum, Sara Ann
Dec. 22, 1948
Feb. 5, 1966

Fulghum, Tobe
1866-1955
Fulghum, Margie
1887-19

Fuller, S. E.
1845-1889

Fuller, E. J.
Mother
1845-1920

Fuller, George B.
Jan. 24, 1824
July 28, 1885

Fuller, Georgia Hurt
Wife of B. F. Fuller
July 7, 1885
Feb. 29, 1920

Fuller, George Timothy
Feb. 17, 1868
July 3, 1898

Fuller, George W.
Mar. 20, 1837
Apr. 13, 1878

Fuller, Hattie L.
Dau. of H. & N. Fuller
June 22, 1862
Mar 21, 1877

Fuller, Nancy L.
Feb. 20, 1817
June 12, 1888
Fuller, Hezekiah
Aug. 9, 1811
Aug 19, 1887

Fuller, Willard P.
Son of H. N. Fuller
Nov. 7, 1852
July 22, 1853
8 mo. 22 days

Fultz, Lela A.
1908
Fultz, Jim A.
1897-1956

Fultz, Nancy J.
1868-1946
Fultz, Joseph C.
1857-1944

Fultz, Will
1892-1965
Fultz, Lala
1897-19

Fry, Macie D.
Dec. 15, 1891
Fry, Lulie V.
Feb. 4, 1895
Sept. 26, 1956

Fryer, Bettie G. Weakley
Oct. 9, 1851
Apr. 8, 1929
Fryer, Robert Lee
Feb. 19, 1871
Oct. 7, 1880

Fryer, Dr. R. N.
Mar. 5, 1831
Apr. 7, 1915

Fryer, Martha Ann Weakley
His wife
Jan 13, 1839
June 2, 1885

Gambill, Arch P.
1871-1943
Gambill, Missouri
1869-19

Gatlin, Louise D.
Aug. 5, 1911
Gatlin, James A.
June 24, 1924
Oct. 27, 1973

Garner, S. Jane
May 23, 1882
May 20, 1906

Gauldin, Mattie Capelle
Oct. 3, 1845
Oct. 14, 1900

Gentry, Belle S.
1853-1940

Gentry, Joseph H.
1882-1960

Gentry, Nathan Blythe
1884-1964

Gentry, Richard Collins
1881-1961

Gibbons, Porter
1894-1968
Father
Gibbons, Seicle
1900-
Mother

Gibbons, Will
1891-19
Gibbons, Lora
1899-1965

Gibbs, Martha G.
Nov. 22, 1942

Gibson, Mattie
1884-19
Gibson, Oscar
1869-1961

Gifford, John F.
July 5, 1897
Mar. 25, 1969
Gifford, (No first name)
Wife of John F. Gifford
1894-1940

Gill, Alice E.
Mother
1856-1921

Gill, Basil C., Brother
1891-1894

Gill, Robert S.
Father
1858-1909

Gilliam, James H.
Mar. 17, 1869
Mar. 17, 1948
Gilliam, Ida D.
Nov. 22, 1873

Gillmore, Lillian
Died Aug. 1, 1889
Age 24 years

Gilmore, Robert
Son of R. M. & E. A.
Jones
July 20, 1883
May 20, 1897

Glasgow, Erma A.
July 19, 1910
Nov. 10, 1959
Glasgow, Howard
May 25, 1903

Glass, E. B.
Mar. 12, 1858
Dec. 28, 1886

Glass, Nannie Campbell
Wife of W. W. Glass
1867-1934

Glass, W. W.
1858-1917

Glidewell, Johnnie
Mar. 29, 1902
Glidewell, Verda
July 14, 1891
Sept. 5, 1968

Godwin, Esther
Aug. 4, 1888
Jan. 15, 1965
Godwin, Ditzel
Mar. 17, 1895
Aug. 16, 1971

Godwin, George Thomas
Sept. 14, 1875
Mar. 24, 1958
Godwin, Martha Nolen
Feb. 11, 1884
June 7, 1948

Godwin, James W.
Oct. 23, 1877
Mar. 1, 1957
Godwin, Mary E.
July 1, 1892
May 26, 1962

Godwin, William E.
1905-1955
Godwin, Vernelle
1913-19

Goodrum, J. T.
Dec. 9, 1849
May 23, 1920

Goss, Angelia Frances
Daughter of Joe M. &
Maxine Goss
Mar. 4, 1959
Mar. 7, 1959

Gourley, George McMude
Aug. 20, 1902
Sept. 26, 1974

Graves, Carl Monroe
Mar. 18, 1910
Dec. 17, 1971
Graves, Jessie Fowler
Feb. 25, 1917

Grayson, L. F.
Died Nov. 27, 1922
Wife
Grayson, Jane
Died Feb. 22, 1930

Green, Carter, Roulac
1877-1935

Green, Charles F.
1901-1974
Green, Elizabeth P.
1909-

Greer, John Allen
1873-1941
Greer, Mary Elizabeth
1868-19

Greer, Jones
1901-1958

Gregory, E. W.
1857-1943
Gregory, Bettie H.
1859-1921

Gregory, G. W.
July 4, 184
Sept. 20, 1899
Gregory, Eva E.
Wife of G. W. Gregory
Nov. 18, 1863
Feb. 3, 1889

Gregory, Marlin W.
1883-19

Grey, Hugh McCullough
Son of J. P. &
Margaret M. Grey
Died June 24, 1891

Griffin, Baby Brother
Oct. 5, 1965

Grimm, Goldye
1907-1954

Grimm, Charlie
1909-

Grisham, Benjamin Franklin
1875-1951

Grisham, Blain Gentry
1880-1966

Grisham, Clarence
1886-1933

Grisham, George W.
April 25, 1838
Sept. 27, 1911
Grisham, Rebecca
His Wife
Aug. 13, 1848
Feb. 5, 1908

Grisham, Maggie T.
1885-1973

Gullett, Clarence
1892-1935
Gullett, Ilda
1894-1959

Gullett, Daniel B.
1858-1942
Gullett, Lou E.
1865-1944

Gullett, Eddie Vern
Tennessee
Sgt. 97 AAF Bonb G P
Mar 29, 1924
Nov. 11, 1944

Gullett, Tinnie T.
April 17, 1873
April 29, 1887

Gunter, Polkie
1892-1969

Hale, Albert T.
Jan. 7, 1871
Aug. 29, 1957
Hale, Pnolar Prence
June 21, 1886
Feb. 22, 1957

Hale, Guy Fulghum
Tennessee
Pvt. 302 Engrs.
April 9, 1922

Hale, Maurice G.
Tennessee
Cook US Army
World War I
July 7, 1898
April 6, 1962

Hall, Ada
Wife of J. E. Hall
April 27, 1868
Mar. 7, 1918

Hall, Albert Victor
Jan. 24, 1900
Jan. 9, 1902

Hall, Clarence Richard
1898-1971

Hall, Dora Hildreth
1863-1940

Hall, Elizabeth
Wife of Alfred F. Hall
Dec. 17, 1844
Aug. 26, 1886

Hall, Emerson Ethridge
Father
1859-1941
Hall, Jennie Eliza Pope
Mother
1863-1941

Hall, E. M.
1820-1902
Hall, Sara
1st wife of E. M. Hall
1821-1885
Hall, Margaret L.
2nd wife of E. M. Hall
1837-1887

Hall, Etta R.
1866-1953
Hall, John A.
1862-1907

Hall, Etta T.
Wife of J. A. Hall
June 29, 1859
Mar. 21, 1932

Hall, Evie
1874-1960

Hall, Infant boy of
J. E. & Ada Hall
Born and Died
July 1, 1896

Hall, Infant girl of
J. E. & Ada Hall
Born and Died
Mar. 8, 1893

Hall, J. A.
Nov. 13, 1842
Aug. 8, 1922

Hall, J. A.
Wife of W. H. Hall
July 21, 1873
Oct. 11, 1908

Hall, W. H.
Aug. 14, 1867
Apr. 20, 1934

Hall, J. E.
June 1, 1869
Sept. 4, 1945

Hall, Lizzy H.
Oct. 28, 1882
May 23, 1963

Hall, Lola Forrester
1879-1955

Hall, Dr. Luther B.
1878-1959

Hall, Mary E.
Wife of J. A. Hall
July 8, 1847
Feb. 13, 1881

Hall, Missia
Daughter of J. A. &
M. F. Hall
July 6, 1874
Aug. 27, 1875

Hall, Rubie
Daughter of Mr & Mrs.
S. R. Hall
Mar. 5, 1904
July 9, 1904

Hall, S. R.
1872-1936

Hall, Thelma
1897-1941

Hall, William
Jan. 21, 1870
Oct. 31, 1958

Hallum, Bertha E.
June 27, 1906
Aug. 3, 1944

Hallum, Hubert
Apr. 27, 1902
June 18, 1951

Hambrick, Hattie A.
1875-1938
Hambrick, Dave Dickson
1859-1939

Hambrick, Minnie Merle
Mar. 9, 1895
June 29, 1918

Hamilton, ____
May 2, 1861
Aug. 1938

Hamilton, Annie B.
1865-1931

Hamilton, Bifle B.
1888-1941

Hamilton, Calvin
Aug. 11, 1894
Aug. 15, 1896
Hamilton, Hettie
Aug. 21, 1873
Hamilton, Hickman
June 2, 1871
Mar. 25, 1910

Hamilton, Emerson
Jan. 12, 1857
May 2, 1904

Hamilton, Gentry
1875-1925

Hamilton, J. C.
1880-1910
Hamilton, Florence W.
Wife of J. C. Hamilton

Hamilton, J. H.
Died May 16, 1910
Age 79 years

Hamilton, Jake
July 22, 1855
April 22, 1913

Hamilton, Jane
Wife of J. H. Hamilton
Died June 15, 1903
Age 89 years

Hamilton, Jennie
Nov. 28, 1858
Nov. 7, 1937

Hamilton, M. C.
1855-1925
(Large Hamilton Stone)

Hamilton, Mallie
Died Oct. 1, 1905
Age 43 years

Hamilton, Mollie
Wife of Marion C.
Hamilton
Sept. 22, 1858
May 4, 1887

Hammer, Frank Powell
May 26, 1886
July 19, 1888

Harden, Jimmie
1925-1943

Harden, Jimmie
1925-1943

Hardin, Florance
1885-1966
Mother

Hardin, Lee
1888-1966
Father

Hardin, Paul H.
June 12, 1893
Apr. 26, 1969
Hardin, Vennie W.
Mar. 28, 1890
Nov. 18, 1973

Hardison, Alice
1850-1873

Hargrove, Fronie James
1894-1963

Hargrove, Sherman F.
1894-1941

Harper, David Koffman
Died April 1, 1975
70 years 4 mos. 3 days

Harper, Dona Z.
Wife of A. M. Harper
Mar. 28, 1878
Oct. 8, 1904

Harper, William H.
Tennessee
CPL 6835 QM Remarent Depot
World War II
May 7, 1926
Aug. 19, 1960

Harrell, Manie Clay
Feb. 7, 1858
Feb. 14, 1888

Harrington, Dorothey M.
Sept. 23, 1910
Aug. 17, 1967

Harrington, Elmer Wilson
1878-1947
Harrington, Kittie McCutchen
1883-1947

Harrington, Margie H.
1907-19
Harrington, Wilson B.
1889-1966

Harrington, Mary
1885-1950
Harrington, J. B.
1881-1932

Harrington, Sabrina E.
Dec. 25, 1885
Dec. 11, 1961
Harrington, Robert P.
Nov. 10, 1871
June 10, 1954

Harrington, Wayne H.
1912-1969

Harrington, Helen P.
1915-

Harris, Dr. Allen
Oct. 20, 1821
Jan. 20, 1884

Harris, Albert G. (Pop)
1874-1941

Harris, Albert G., Jr.
Tennessee
Wagoner Btry E
312 Fld Arty
World War I
July 8, 1896
Nov. 26, 1958

Harris, Mrs. Albert G.
"Ducky"
1873-1951

Harris, Amabell Williams
Mar. 7, 1906
Harris, Milam King
Tennessee
U. S. Army
World War II
Oct. 29, 1910
April 18, 1973

Harris, Carolyn Frances
Jan. 19, 1916
Nov. 14, 1916
Harris, Eva Lucille
Jan., 1898
Sept. 1898

Harris, Charles W.
Tennessee
PFC Medical Dept
World War I
July 26, 1901
Aug. 31, 1959

Harris, Daniel P.
Sept. 26, 1860
Jan. 8, 1880

Harris, Issac A.
Aug. 13, 1852
Aug. 9, 1882

Harris, Issac A.
Son of L. A. &
I. A. Harris
Apr. 11, 1881
Mar. 11, 1896

Harris, Issac A. B.
Dec. 18, 1867
July 30, 1871

Harris, Dr. Hubert W.
1894-1926

Harris, James Palk
Apr. 11, 1847
Sept. 27, 1900

Harris, James L.
1878-1944

Harris, Mrs. Jennie T.
1852-1923

Harris, Lee Webb
Died Oct. 14, 1956

Harris, Mary Ann
July 29, 1829
Dec. 25, 1901

Harris, Mary E.
Wife of J. P. Harris
Oct. 1, 1851
Aug. 3, 1874

Harris, Mellie Welborn
1879-1973

Harris, Stonewall J.
Oct. 30, 1863
Nov. 10, 1926

Harris, T. H.
Nov. 3, 1869
Jan. 18, 1944

Harrison, Mrs. Mamie
July 13, 1975
63 yrs, 5 mos. 11 days

Hart, Issac C.
Nov. 22, 1907
Sept. 24, 1965
Hart, Mary Frances
Nov. 14, 1908

Hart, Leonard H.
1884-1935

Hartsfield, Ada Bell
Apr. 25, 1923
Feb. 18, 1960

Haskins, Dr. A. B.
Apr. 15, 1852
Jan. 14, 1892

Haskins, Dr. Edward T.
1874-1945
Haskins, Myra Rainey
1879-19

Haskins, Guy Douglass
1884-1946

Haskins, Guy Douglass
1906-1968

Haskins, J. C.
1846-1898
Haskins, A. E.
1849-1933

Haskins, John Christopher
1890-1937

Haskins, Martha Yvonne
D. Aug. 8, 1942

Haskins, Verda Ritchey
1908-1961

Hathaway, Claude
1914-1958

Hathaway, Mattie
1878-1954
Hathaway, William C.
1879-1931

Hathaway, Ruth F.
1917-1956

Harvey, Belle Akin
Wife of W. A. Harvey
Oct. 18, 1866
Nov. 16, 1920

Hawks, Evelyn A.
Aug. 31, 1955
Oct. 5, 1973

Head, Caldonia
1866-1942

Head, Herbert N.
1904-1967

Head, James H.
1933-1969

Head, James M.
1851-1940

Head, Lorain H.
1903-

Heathcott, Hobert V.
Sept. 9, 1903
Heathcott, Martha E.
Sept. 1, 1903
Sept. 13, 1968

Hendrix, Grover C.
1895-1964

Hendrix, Lucille L.
Wife of Grover C.
Hendrix
1901-19

Hensley, Byrd Clark
Son of C. & M. M.
Hensley
Mar. 5, 1883
Mar. 31, 1887

Hensley, Mozella Manly
Oct. 27, 1855
Oct. 20, 1935

Hicks, Lorain
1897-1918

Hicks, Marvin F.
1888-1957
Hicks, Mallie R.
1895-1962

Hicks, R. Carl
1899-1954
Hicks, Winnie Cole
1900-19

Hildreth, Mary M.
Feb. 14, 1875
June 19, 1901

Hildreth, Nancy G.
Wife of W. W. Hildreth
May 28, 1828
July 23, 1901

Hill, Hugh A.
1831-1862
Hill, Jane I.
Wife of H. A. Hill
1834-1915

Hilliard, Beverly L.
May 10, 1948
Dec. 3, 1953

Hines, Pattie
1880-1956
Hines, Will T.
1871-1961

Hinson, Edward Meeks
1901-1958

Hinson, Milt
1880-19
Hinson, Rosie
1883-1961

Hinson, Dr. S. F.
1872-1936
Hinson, Ardellar
1874-1936

Holman, Franklin W.
Tennessee
Tec 5 Med Det
283 Engr. C. B. N.
World War II BSM
Jan. 10, 1917
Sept. 7, 1958

Holman, Leona B.
1871-1943

Holland, DeWitt T. Dr.
1891-1960
Holland, Violet King
1906-19

Holland, Elton
July 17, 1904
June 8, 1974
Holland, Isabel C.
March 1, 1906

Holland, Everett S.
Cpt. U. S. Army
Oct. 12, 1893
July 4, 1974

Holland, Harvey Ferrell
Sept. 23, 1882
Apr. 8, 1885
2 years 6 months 15 days

Holland, Ida Mai
Wife of W. F. Holland
Mar. 11, 1875
Dec. 23, 1928
Holland, W. F.
July 10, 1842
April 13, 1918

Holland, Miss Mamie
"My Sister"
Sister of Dr. Dewitt
Holland and Everett S.
Holland
(No Dates)

Hollingsworth, James L.
1860-1941
Hollingsworth, Pearl
1875-1945

Hollister, Elsie May
Feb. 5, 1888
Jan. 24, 1918

Hollister, Elsie May
Feb. 5, 1889
Jan. 24, 1916

Hollister, Maie Gibbons
1889-
Hollister, Walter Dale
1884-

Hollister, Vivian Lucille
(No Dates)

Holloway, Lena
July 15, 1889
Sept. 23, 1971
Holloway, S. W. "Boss"
Aug. 15, 1889
May 23, 1952

Holloway, Norbert N.
MSGT U.S. Army
Jan. 7, 1910
May 25, 1975

Hooper, Mattie F.
1879-1953

Hooper, Harold
1914-
Hopper, Lula Mae
1913-1975

Hornbeak, Samuel M.
Jan. 1, 1914
Sept. 19, 1969

Hornbeak, Della B.
(No Dates)

House, Andrew Richman Dr.
Nov. 7, 1916
Feb. 5, 1970
House, Anna Frances Johnson
Oct. 22, 1915
April 22, 1969

House, George W.
1874-1940
House, Dollie V.
1880-1953

House, Mary
April 27, 1906
House, Ben Allen
Sept. 16, 1902
June 6, 1964

Howell, Elbert F.
Aug. 29, 1901
Jan. 25, 1970
Howell, Navie L.
Aug. 14, 1903

Howell, Laverne
1923-1930

Howell, Ray E. Jr.
Jan. 30, 1917
Jan. 27, 1919

Hufstedler, Pinkney C.
1897-1967

Hufstedler, Travis H.
1934-195.

Hughey, Mary
1903-19
Hughey, Harm
1898-1961

Hugueley, R. W.
1879-1963
Hugueley, Eunice
1886-1967

Huie, Maury Adolphus
Tennessee
Cpl. U.S. Army
World War I
Oct. 31, 1896
Aug. 22, 1965

Huie, Nell Campbell
Oct. 31, 1896
Aug. 22, 1965

Huie, Joe Howard
1929-1937

Hulme, F. E. P.
Dec. 14, 1876
Jan. 22, 1949
Hulme, Lula F.
Oct. 6, 1887

Hulme, Robert C.
Sept. 24, 1824
Dec. 20, 1914
Hulme, Emily J.
Dec. 9, 1835
Aug. 28, 1920

Hunt, Jackson L.
Son of J. T. & S. Hunt
May 29, 1904
Aug. 10, 1904

Hurley, Infant
Son of M. P. &
E. A. Hurley
Born & Died
Aug. 4, 1897

Hurley, Martha
Wife of M. P. Hurley
Oct. 15, 1826
Oct. 30, 1886

Hurley, Mitchell Figret
Son of M. P. &
E. H. Hurley
Feb. 4, 1891
Aug. 8, 1895

Hurly, Andrew D.
Dec. 14, 1867
Mar. 4, 1931
Hurly, Emma A.
July 25, 1874

Hurly, Eliza
1862-1898

Hurt, Amanda
Wife of James F. Hurt
Mar. 7, 1851
June 9, 1896

Hurt, Irene Davis
Mother
1867-1941

Hurt, James F.
Jan. 19, 1881
Mar. 16, 1908

Huston, Eugene E.
1876-1947
Huston, Beatrice
1874-1942

Huston, Sara Anne
June 26, 1906
May 21, 1970

Hutcherson, Charles E.
Oct. 14, 1930
Oct. 23, 1930

Ingram, J. D.
1912-1958
Ingram, Exie
1915-

Ingram, Mattie
July 22, 1873
July 20, 1950
Ingram, A. Q.
Dec. 26, 1871
Oct. 24, 1961

Ingram, Rebecca F.
Sept. 6, 1872
Jan. 29, 1968
Ingram, Will C.
Sept. 28, 1874
Aug. 15, 1967

Inman, C. F.
1856-1927

Inman, George
Tennessee
Pfc. Motor Transport Corp.
World War I.
Nov. 30, 1894
Oct. 4, 1957

Inman, Joe
1866-1939
Inman, Esther G.
1874-1963

Inman, Margaret C.
1870-1963

Inman, Robert M.
1872-1939

Inman, Sterling Price
May 16, 1862
Jan. 31, 1932
Inman, Erma Turner
Feb. 17, 1879

Jacobs, Martin Luther
Tennessee
Sgt. Btry A 27 Arty CAC
World War I
March 12, 1895
Apr. 22, 1956

Jacobs, Ross A.
Feb. 8, 1893
May 11, 1958
Jacobs, Lucille M.
Feb. 17, 1906

Jacobs, Vera Townsend
Aug. 28, 1889
Dec. 13, 1961

Jackson, John A.
1885-1937
Jackson, Evie D.
1886-1971

Jackson, Lon B.
1896-1943

Jackson, Maggie
1878-19

Jackson, George
1866-1937

Jackson, Wyatt
1906-1974
Jackson, Nellie
1906-
Married July 31, 1926

Jannings, Ruby T.
1910-
Jannings, Russell R.
1903-

Jenkins, Martin Allen
1888-1956
Jenkins, Mary Hull
1889-19

Johns, Tennie H.
1892-19
Johns, Lee D.
1890-1962

Johnson, Alma Troy
1880-1973

Johnson, Betty L.
1886-1971
Johnson, Luther L.
1885-1969

Johnston, Dollie H.
1898-19
Johnston, Ganes
1898-1950

Johnson, Eva Mai
1902-1956
Johnson, Byrl
    -1965

Johnson, Everett
1884-1968
Johnson, Pearl
1889-

Johnson, Lizzy Hurt
Aug. 6, 1878
Aug. 6, 1969
Johnson, Ernest L.
May 2, 1876
Feb. 24, 1957

Johnson, Loy J.
Tennessee
Pvt. 45 Depot SVC
World War I
Feb. 20, 1894
Feb. 20, 1967

Johnson, Ollie
Feb. 4, 1890
Dec. 15, 1973
Johnson, Willie W.
July 5, 1894

Johnson, Samuel Lee
Jan. 15, 1855
July 7, 1941
Johnson, Martha E.
July 12, 1857
Apr. 5, 1935

Johnson, Tom
1883-19
Johnson, Donna M.
1889-1959

Johnston, Robert Palmer
Son of James &
Pattie Johnston
Oct. 26, 1870
April 5, 1872

Johnston, Robert Wilson
Infant Son of
W. E. & L. M. Johnston
Nov. 29, 1881
July 3, 1882

Johnston, Robert
Son of D. B. &
M. J. Johnston
Aug. 26, 1889
Oct. 24, 1890

Johnston, Robert E.
Jan. 25, 1816
July 26, 1890
Johnston, Lucy M.
Wife of R. E. Johnston
Feb. 16, 1825
Dec. 15, 1902

Johnston, Dr. William E.
Mar. 9, 1847
July 28, 1888
Johnston, Laura M.
Wife of W. E. Johnston
Sept. 26, 1853
Jan. 27, 1895

Jones, Adelle G.
1860-1940

Jones, Almira Virginia
June 21 to
July 26, 1910

Jones, Annie H.
1874-19
Jones, Robert G.
1873-1943

Jones, J. Blake, Son
1898-1920
Jones, James G., Father
1874-1960

Jones, Jack
1893-1963
Jones, Beulah
1898-1970

Jones, Jack W.
1921-1945

Jones, James A.
1872-1948
Jones, Laura B.
1875-1955

Jones, James Ira
1842-1922
Jones, Iola Clay
1849-1932

Jones, John S.
Tennessee
Pvt. Co. 1 323 Inf.
July 29, 1890
Mar. 10, 1969

Jones, Minnie B.
1878-1964
Jones, Wiley T.
1875-1956

Jones, Minnie C.
April 8, 1893
Jan. 6, 1975

Jones, Ola Mae
Sept. 6, 1883
Aug. 8, 1969

Jones, Robbie Scobey
Feb. 25, 1892
Mar. 24, 1958

Jones, Sue Council
1927-1965

Jones, Thomas A.
1883-1965
Jones, Ella Arnold
1881-19

Jones, William Edward
Mar. 13, 1880
Oct. 24, 1963

Jones, Wiley T.
1875-1956
Jones, Minnie
1878-1964

Jordon, Liliam May
Daughter of
Callie Jordon
D. June 25, 1898

Joslin, J. H.
1856-1933
Joslin, Martha
His Wife
1855-1930

Joslin, Mary Allen
Oct. 10, 1895
June 6, 1922

Joslin, Robert D.
June 14, 1886
Apr. 14, 1929

Joslin, Ruth
Nov. 5, 1899
Joslin, Clay
Oct 20, 1895
Mar. 15, 1971

Joslin, Thomas Augustus
Feb. 22, 1865
July 1, 1957
Joslin, Hattie Carpenter
July 12, 1876
Jan. 6, 1959

Kee, Marvin C.
1898-1955

Keith, Ben Anna
Oct. 29, 1873
Jan. 21, 1944

Keith, Marion
June 22, 1870
May 19, 1904

Kelly, Inez Jane
Apr. 17, 1896
Apr. 2, 1972

Kelso, Martha T.
1911-
Kelso, Albert L.
1910-1952

Kenny, Allie Beech
Nov. 22, 1871
Dec. 2, 1929

Kenney, David A.
May 22, 1872
May 16, 1935

Kenney, Fleur
D. 1923

Kenney, Lydia
1903-1946
Kenney, Geraldine
1900-1948

Kenney Phylis Marie
D. 1924

Kennon, Bev. H. L.
Mar. 14, 1802
Mar. 14, 1870

Kepley, Sophronia J.
Wife of J. M. Kepley
1856-1943
Kepley, Margaret L.
Daughter of S. J. &
J. M. Kepley
1885-1958

Kilzer, James Calhoun
(Cal)
Aug. 11, 1955
Feb. 1, 1974

King, Ben Davis
May 13, 1887
Jan. 18, 1968
King, Birdie B.
Feb. 1, 1892
May 2, 1970

King, Charlie H.
Tennessee
Pfc 197 Medical
Amb Set
World War II
June 12, 1912
Aug. 3, 1953

King, Coley T.
Jan. 5, 1885
Apr. 4, 1962
King, Laura Ingram
June 27, 1887
Apr. 11, 1966

King, James H.
Oct. 4, 1862
Sept. 28, 1939

King, James Mecham
1878-1935
King, Lillian Scott
1884-1964

King, Kate M.
1868-1950

King, Keith E.
May 30, 1958
Jan. 21, 1974
King, Kenneth E.
May 30, 1958
July 6, 1959

King, Murray
Son of J. H. & Kate M.
Mar. 3, 1904
June 14, 1906

Kiser, Sue Ernestine
Feb. 12, 1907
March 3, 1954

Kizer, Carrie Pearl
1927-1948

Knight, A. J. "Jack"
(No Dates)
Knight, Elizabeth M.
1885-1967

Ladd, James Earl
Sept. 13, 1906
Nov. 24, 1971
Ladd, Camille
Chitwood
Nov. 1, 1908

Ladd, Noble A.
1866-1939
Ladd, Mallie Lee
1882-1954

Ladd, Rice R.
1912-1939

Lambert, Carlene
1913-1920

Lambert, Clennie Q.
June 5, 1883
Sept. 30, 1962

Lambert, Geneva Blankenship
1901-1971

Lambert, J. C.
Sept. 10, 1829
Feb. 1, 1905
Lambert, M. J.
His Wife
Mar. 6, 1831
Jan. 24, 1909

Lambert, James S.
June 7, 1857
Feb. 8, 1892
Lambert, Fannie E.
His Wife
Aug. 27, 1862
July 8, 1916

Lambert, Jimmy C.
Father
1891-1918

Lambert, Robert Lee
July 21, 1871
June 11, 1966
Lambert, Tinnie Huguley
Mar. 18, 1877
Feb. 26, 1971

Lambert, Samuel C.
1898-1928

Lancaster, Homer W.
1889-1934

Lancaster, J. G.
1867-1927
Lancaster, Martha K.
1871-1952

Lancaster, James L.
1860-1944
Lancaster, Electie
1872-1929

Lancaster, John A.
1839-1912
Lancaster, Dora E.
1860-1938

Lancaster, John Henry, Father
July 18, 1867
Nov. 4, 1903

Lancaster, Kittie Hampton
Mother
Jan. 8, 1873
Aug. 21, 1955

Langley, L. V. (Dunk)
1889-1963
Langley, Mattie E.
1890-

Lanier, Bosie
May 1, 1894
April 7, 1966
Lanier, Minnie Baker
Dec. 11, 1895
Nov. 22, 1960

Lanier, Brady
1889-1965
Lanier, Lona
1896-19

Lanier, Elba B.
1913-1930

Lanier, Emma
1891-1929

Lanier, Infant Son of
P. T. & N. A. Lanier
Oct. 28, 1876
Oct. 29, 1876
Lanier, Infant Son of
P. T. & N. A. Lanier
Born and Died
Aug. 24, 1884

Lanier, Infant Son of
P. & Laura Lanier
April 9, 1880
July 20, 1884

Lanier, Joan Ann
Nov. 19, 1964
Nov. 20, 1964

Lanier, Millard D.
1895-1968
Lanier, Modie B.
1898-1964

Lanier, P. T.
Feb. 2, 1854
Nov. 26, 1907

Lanier, Robbye Anne
Nov. 21, 1954
Oct. 9, 1957

Lanier, Robbye Sullivan
1911-1953

Lanier Vergie
Feb. 14, 1801
Sept. 21, 1801

Lanier, William H.
July 1, 1805
Nov. 6, 1880

Largent, Mrs. Kyle H.
Died Mar. 24, 1974
87 years 3 mos. 28 days

Laton, Grace Marie
Mother
June 20, 1924
Oct. 9, 1955

Laton, Olivia Ann
Sister
Sept. 27, 1949
Jan. 23, 1953

Layman, Albert A.
1882-1962
Married Aug. 3, 1903
Layman, Linnie M.
1888-1966

Ledsinger, Hattie A.
1881-1959
Ledsinger, Robert H.
1877-1935

Leek, William N.
1858-1928

Leek, William W.
Tennessee
Pvt. Co. B 141 Inf.
World War I
Jan. 19, 1894
Feb. 21, 1961

Lewellyng, Charles H.
1881-1963
Lewellyng, Ora Hunt
1879-1967

Lewis, Joe J. Pope
(No Dates)
Lewis, Talmage K.
1990-1956

Light, Mary S.
Wife of Palmer Light
July 16, 1822
April 27, 1883

Lindsey, Joseph
1918-1927

Lingenfelter, Ray Edward
Son
May 10, 1946
Lingenfelter, Mai Belle
Mother
May 17, 1911

Link, Porter
1876-1957
Link, Mammie J.
1882-1965

Lockhart, Chester
July 22, 1881
Nov. 17, 1881

Lockhart, Remington
Aug. 12, 1886
Aug. 25, 1887

Long, Mrs. Mollie
Dec. 16, 1974
93 yrs. 6 mo. 20 days

Lucas, Arnie B.
1916-1941

Lucas, Audrey Balthrop
Dec. 8, 1890
Lucas, Joseph A.
Feb. 2, 1880
Mar. 4, 1956

Lucas, James I.
April 3, 1877
Oct. 9, 1959

Lucas, John Qnice
April 3, 1888
Jan. 17, 1969
Lucas, Irene Taylor
July 12, 1905

Lucas, Joseph Bennett
Sept. 17, 1883

Lucas, Effie Porter
Dec. 19, 1892
Feb. 5, 1963

Lucas, Myrtie P.
Oct. 23, 1881
Aug. 2, 1963

Lucas, Otho, Father
Nov. 14, 1890
Oct. 19, 1966
Lucas, Mary, Mother
Nov. 29, 1896

Lucas, Peggy Ann, Daughter
Mar. 11, 1931

Lucas, W. S. "Buddy"
1885-1963
Lucas, Dona Ray
1890-19

Lyon, Elizabeth B.
Sept. 2, 1880
Dec. 24, 1956

Magee, Dave F.
1873-1951
Magee, Lutie A.
1880-19

Magee, Mattie
1879-1938

Magee, Rufus B.
1882-1950
Magee, Nannie
1882-1941

Malcomb, Hattie
Daughter of S. C. &
Ethel Malcomb
Feb. 12, 1904
May 26, 1910

Mallard, A. T.
1914-1959
Mallard, Willie Mai
1920

Mallard, Allen
Aug. 8, 1878
Oct. 11, 1936
Mallard, Lula
Sept. 2, 1884
May 6, 1975

Mallard, Freda B.
Son of J. F. &
Josie Mallard
Apr. 13, 1897
Feb. 12, 1899

Mallard, Mrs. Hattie Lula Pope
Died May 6, 1975
90 yrs. 2 mo. 22 days

Mallard, James Wesley
Dec. 9, 1974
79 yrs. 2 mo. 22 days

Manly, J. A.
Mar. 3, 1824
Jan. 3, 1872

Manon, Melinda
1963-1967

Maxedon, Mollie Barker
July 29, 1882
May 30, 1908

Maxwell, Robert Lee
Jan. 12, 1872
July 10, 1890
Maxwell, M. Y.
Mar. 5, 1843
Feb. 16, 1911

Meadows, Ben F.
Oct. 4, 1857
Feb. 23, 1891

Meadows, Bernie F.
Tennessee
Pfc. HQ. Co. 118 Inf.
30 Div.
World War I
May 4, 1893
Jan. 11, 1953

Meadows, Mattie
1862-1933
Meadows, Oliver
1864-1903

Meadows, W. Lawton
1885-1954

Medearis, Mamie Bell
1892-19
Medearis, Ben W.
1891-1956

Medling, Stephen Vernon
Father
1889-1953
Medling, Mary Scobey
Mother
1890-1956
Medling, Steve
Son
1918-1942
Medling, Steve
T. Sgt. U. S. Air Force
Missing in Action over
Med. Sea

Menzies, Finis E.
1868-1934
Menzies, Belle E.
1874-1957

Menzies, W. C.
Aug. 2, 1835
Aug. 12, 1897

Merideth, Mattie Lee
June 1, 1892
May 22, 1961

Merideth, William P.
1881-1954

Merlin, George
No Dates)

Michael, Emma E.
1886-1943
Michael, Adolphus J.
1869-1944

Milan, Fannie Bell
Wife of William F. Milan
Oct. 24, 1869
Apr. 25, 1901

Milan, Franklin
1901-
Milan, Martha J.
1907-19-

Milan, Mary B.
1873-1964
Milan, William F.
1862-1943

McAlilley, James Edward
Nov. 6, 1861
June 9, 1933
McAlilley, Mary Ruth
Nov. 3, 1869
Jan. 30, 1950

McCorkle, Edd A.
1873-1950
McCorkle, Donna M.
1877-1967

McCorkle, Elizabeth Hall
1856-1935
"Miss Betty"

McCorkle, Dr. J. S.
1837-1904
McCorkle, E. O.
1843-1919

McCullough, Benana
Wife of J. W. McCullough
June 25, 1877
July 25, 1906

McCullough, Infant daughter
No Dates

McCullough, Infant son
No Dates

McCullough, J. W.
1872-1941

McCullough, Jim
1884-1951
McCullough, Maude
1890-19

McCullough, John B.
Tennessee
PFC 3310 Air Base GP AF
World War II
May 16, 1928
May 25, 1970

McCullough, V. E.
Wife of W. W. McCullough
April 12, 1837
Feb. 14, 1921

McCutchen, Elmora
Dau. of J. N. &
A. L. McCutchen
Oct. 1, 1876
Jan. 28, 1898

McCutchen, Hettie Tatum
No Dates

McCutchen, J. N.
1850-1922

McCutchen, Jennifer Denice
May 28, 1971

McCutchen, Louella W.
1856-19

McCutchen, Robert N.
1889-1918

McCutchen, Tom
1852-1923

McCutchen, W. A. "Mac"
1893-1968

McCutchen, Mrs. W. T.
1854-1929

McDaniel, Ella Smith
1873-1948
McDaniel, Walter Scott
1870-1951

McDavid, Bittie
1887-1922
McDavid, Victoria
1845-1900
McDavid, J. L.
1845-1911

McDavid, Gertrude
1880-1967

McFarland, Roy
1902-1968
McFarland, Margaret W.
1902-

McGhee, Ella Mae Brasfield
Feb. 20, 1914
Nov. 22, 1962

McIntosh, Claude L.
July 22, 1898
June 23, 1975
McIntosh, Bettye A.
July 31, 1909
Oct. 24, 1975

McIntosh, Robert Glenn
Feb. 20, 1962
Feb. 22, 1962

McKee, Elry E. "Red"
1901-1969
McKee, Annie N.
1906-

McKee. Steve
June 2, 1953
Feb. 14, 1969

McKnight, Gertie
1899-
McKnight, Joe Herbert
Tennessee
Engl. U.S. Navy
World War I
Dec. 25, 1897
May 28, 1959

McKnight, Hattie Mai
Feb. 6, 1876
Feb. 1, 1928
McKnight, Charlie Clyde
Aug. 12, 1874
Feb. 26, 1937

McKnight, Homer Russell
Feb. 8, 1903
Feb. 16, 1972

McWhirter, Jerald W.
1907-
McWhirter, Artie Mai
1902-1962

Meter, Della
Died Mar. 6, 1962

Miller, Carl M.
Sept. 5, 1922
June 12, 1975

Miller, Carl Melton
June 12, 1975
52 years 9 mos. 7 days

Miller, Clara P.
1894-1948

Miller, Lark M.
1882-1964

Miller, Sallie F.
Nov. 13, 1974
71 yrs. 1 mo. 10 days

Miller, Sarah Carpenter
May 19, 1903
Miller, William Henry
May 18, 1904
Aug. 1, 1966

Miller, W. G.
1871-1948
Miller, Ella
1882-19

Milner, John E.
1882-1953
Milner, Bertha M.
1886-1959

Montgomery, Ethel May
Oct. 26, 1893
May 18, 1902

Montgomery, Frank T.
1869 1943

Montgomery, Hettie Pate
1873-1947
(Note: Wife of F. T.
Montgomery)

Montgomery, Infant Daughter
of M. & R. N. Montgomery
Died 1903

Montgomery, Jennie
Wife of F. T. Montgomery
Aug. 5, 1871
Oct. 16, 1911

Montgomery, Margaret Herring
1846-1936

Montgomery, Martha
1883-1961
Montgomery, Robert N.
1871-1951

Montgomery, Robert N., Jr.
1911-1974
Montgomery, Mary E.
1917-

Montgomery, Thelma
Dau. of F. T. &
Oct. 26, 1899
May 18, 1903

Montgomery, W. E.
1883-1937
Montgomery, Margarette
Henley
1888-1955

Moody, Joe Asa
Jan. 14, 1884
Apr. 17, 1950
Moody, Florence
Jan. 8, 1889
    --

Moore, Beatrice M.
1911-
Moore, Buford C.
1907-1970

Moore, Elizabeth
Wife of Captain W. A. Moore
1849-1939

Moore, J. S.
Nov. 30, 1854
Apr. 21, 1936
Moore, Lela I.
July 21, 1858
July 6, 1953

Moore, Kirby Edward
1889-
Moore, Linnie Lee
1894-1971

Moore, Kirby Edward Jr.
1916-1924

Moore, S. McDavid
1894-1894

Moore, Sammie E.
Wife of William Moore
April 7, 1871
July 18, 1894

Moore, Sammie R.
Son of W. L. &
S. E. Moore
April 7, 1894
Aug. 4, 1894

Moore, W. A.
May 13, 1837
Sept. 13, 1917
Cap. of Co. A
50 Tennessee Inf.

Moore, William
1853-1928

Moore, V.
1870-1936

Mooring, Mrs. Kate Craig
Dec. 7, 1831
Mar. 13, 1919
Mother

Mulherin, Dr. Charles L.
1886-1944
Mulherin, Flora C.
1890-1972

Mulherin, Pat B.
Sept. 22, 1890
Dec. 18, 1973
Mulherin, Irene L.
Sept. 16, 1891
Jan. 4, 1971

Mullins, Annie Clara
1891-19
Mullins, Claggett R.
1885-1960

Murray, Loyd
1928-1968
Murray, Annie Sue
1932-1967

Murray, Minnie Lee A.
1893-1968
Murray, William
1901-19

Murray, William P.
Died Oct. 10, 1975
71 years 11 mos. 9 days

Myracle, P. H.
Dec. 6, 1874
May 6, 1923
Father

Myracle, Patra Reed
Jan. 4, 1879
Feb. 10, 1951
Mother

Myracle, Philip R.
Dec. 23, 1912
Apr. 3, 1973

Newhouse, Emma L.
1885-1958

Newhouse, L. T.
1875-1930

Newman, Ary Washington
Son of Paton &
Rebecca Newman
Feb. 23, 1877
Mar. 13, 1901

Newman, Bennie
1869-19
Newman, D. E.
1861-1930

Newman, James B.
Brother
1884-1940

Newman, Octava
Dau. of Paton &
Rebecca Newman
Dec. 13, 1879
Nov. 28, 1902

Newman, Paton
Dec. 20, 1844
Apr. 30, 1917
Newman, Rebecca
His Wife
July 8, 1849
July 20, 1926

Newsom, Alicia Frances
Infant dau. of
Mr. and Mrs. Clark Newsom
Dec. 19, 1954

Newsom, G. S.
Mar. 23, 1862
Jan. 21, 1926
Newsom, S. D.
His wife
May 8, 1866
Apr. 13, 1924

Newsom, Lexie D.
1888-19
Newsom, Mamie J.
1892-19

Newsom, Mozelle G.
B. June 28, 1903
Newsom, Hubbard C.
Tennessee
PVT. Co. B
307 Mil. Police
World War I
Jan. 29, 1895
June 29, 1971

Newsome, Dotyre
1896-1952
Newsome, Wyatt
1885-1949

Newsome, Jennie Mae Hambrick
1892-1972
Newsome, Roy Edward
1887-1964

Newsome, L. C.
Tec 5
16 Calvary Recon Sq.
April 16, 1915
Sept. 3, 1941

Newton, Louis
1887-1919

Nicks, Charles Edward
Son
Jan. 11, 1956
June 22, 1975
Age 19 yrs. 5 mos. 11 days
Nicks, Morene
Mother
Oct. 25, 1918
May 1, 1968

Nicks, Cora Mae
June 17, 1878
Jan. 9, 1968

Nicks, Cora Mae
June 17, 1878
Jan. 9, 1968

Nicks, Frank E.
1904-1973

Norman, Gladys, Bridges
1909-1963

Norsworthy, Ola Mai
Mother
1893-1969

Norvell, Illa Belle
July 24, 1966

Norvell, L. G., Sr.
Died Sept. 15, 1911

Norvell, L. G., Jr.
Feb. 19, 1902
Dec. 9, 1959

Nunn, Earl
Died Aug. 21, 1925

Nunn, Elmer E.
1004-1928

Nunn, Irene
Died Cec. 21, 1887

Nunn, Laura
1858-1928

Nunn, Nannie
1879-1973

Nunn, Nathan W.
Jan. 4, 1846
Nov. 27, 1927

Nunn, Newton J.
1843-1911

Nunn, Newton J., Jr.
1889-1949

Nunn, Robert R.
Died Jan. 1, 1923

Nunn, Sarah E.
July 23, 1850
Sept. 28, 1928
Nunn, Nathan W.
Jan. 4, 1846
Nov. 27, 1927

O'Guinn, Fred Ray
Oct. 22, 1902
O'Guinn, Alene Gilmer
July 8, 1902

O'Guinn, Theodore
1894-1968
O'Guinn, Mable V.
1900-19

Oliver, Oscar B.
1887-1959
Oliver, Lata W.
1885-1969

Oliver, Will F.
1892-1971
Oliver, Zora M.

Owen, Annie
Mother
1847-1925
Owen, J. M.
Father
1847-1926

Owen, J. Bunyan
1879-1949
Owen, Myrtle R.
1887-1918

Owen, Mertie
1880-19
Owen, Frank
1884-1958

Owens, Annie Belle
1896-1900

Owens, Rev. Charles L.
1929-1973
Owens, Joy Corinne
1931

Owens, Charles O.
Died April 29, 1975
67 years 0 mos. 18 days

Owens, Joe T.
1881-1952
Owens, Hattie R.
1877-1953

Owens, Lula
1868-1944
Owens, E. R.
1868-1939

Owens, Mattie Lou
1906-1907

Owens, Robert C.
Father
1875-1961
Owens, Mary S.
Mother
1880-1967

Osborne, Thomas Pinkston
Tennessee
Carpenters Mate 2CL
U. S. Navy
April 25, 1936

Pace, A. Ivie
Son of A. R. &
Lucy A. Pace
March 14, 1880
Jan. 24, 1915

Pace, A. R.
1854-1931
Pace, Lucy A.
1857-1928

Pace, Berl
1904-1968
Pace, Julia
1906-
Pace, James
1936-

Pace, Bob
1875-1935

Pace, H. C. "Bill"
May 12, 1908
Dec. 22, 1966

Pace, H. J.
July 6, 1850
Feb. 6, 1892

Pace, Harold
Born Feb. 11, 1912
Pace, Allie L
Born Apr. 13, 1911

Pace, James T.
June 9, 1889
Apr. 30, 1972
Pace, Bessie B.
Oct. 7, 1890

Pace, Joe B.
1899-19
Pace, Irene
1897-19

Pace, Mrs. Kate
1878-1969

Pace, Mattie F.
Wife of H. J. Pace
July 30, 1856
Nov. 20, 1900

Pack, Dorothy - Sister
1927-1963

Pack, Evie - Mother
1901-
Pack, Sam - Father
1891-1972
Tennessee
PFC HQ 46 Infantry
World War I
Aug. 20, 1891
Mar. 1, 1972

Page, Hattie Lou
1901-

Page, William Henry
1865-1951

Pannell, Virginia Kelso
1907-1963

Parker, Chester Allen
Cpl. 2480 QM Truck Co.
World War II
May 31, 1922
Nov. 21, 1967

Parker, Frances Elizabeth
1888-1961
Parker, Walter Bedford
1886-1959

Parker, G. W.
July 9, 1845
Jan. 3, 1916

Parker, James M
Feb. 21, 1916
Jan. 16, 1967
Parker, Frances Ruth
July 19, 1917

Parker, Roland L.
Tennessee
Sgt. 304 Inf.
World War II
Oct. 12, 1924
April 21, 1945

Parks, Earl S.
Sept. 8, 1888
Feb. 23, 1946
Parks, Alma Hall
Dec. 30, 1891
Aug. 8, 1973

Parks, Georgia Fowler
July 2, 1922

Parks, Infant dau. of
Earl S & Alma H. Parks
May 18, 1912
May 22, 1912

Parks, Lewis Hollomon
Nov. 1, 1903
Oct. 23, 1964

Parks, Nettie Ann
Wife of H. Parks
Dau. of John G. &
Adline A. Williams
Dec. 20, 1871
June 20, 1954

Parnell, James Franklin
Father
1909-
Parnell, Dixie Johnson
Mother
1910-
Parnell, Jere Johnson
Son
1932-1933

Parnell, Lessie
1902-
Parnell, Welthy
1901-1969

Parnell, Robbie
1893-1970
Parnell, Dewitt
1894-1973

Parnell, Wiley
1886-1974

Parnell, Willie Pace
Sept. 24, 1882
July 8, 1966
Parnell, Smith
Dec. 18, 1882
July 24, 1951

Pate, Glen W.
1880-1933
Pate, Beulah H.
1880-1921

Pate, Infant of
Glen W. & Beulah Pate
1904

Pate, Joe Calvin
Sept. 2, 1907
May 7, 1962

Pate, John Calvin
1846-1928
Pate, Millie H.
1852-1919

Pate, Wava
1892-1899

Patterson, Aaron E.
Oklahoma
Bugler MG Co 156 Inf.
World War I
Nov. 11, 1895
Nov. 28, 1964

Patterson, Ben E.
1875-1963
Patterson, Julia S.
1880-1959

Patterson, J. W.
1904-1930

Patterson, Lucy
Sister
1870-1949
Patterson, Charles H.
1872-1958

Payne, Marcus
Son of F. W. & S. P.
Jan. 23, 1863
May 15, 1878

Payne, Robert W.
Son of F. W. &
S. P. Payne
Mar. 30, 1868
Sept. 4, 1876

Payne, William
Jan. 11, 1804
Sept. 11, 1884
Payne, Sarah H.
Dec. 10, 1804
Aug. 6, 1886

Paynter, H. H.
No Dates

Peacock, Henry M.
1846-1929
Peacock, Georgia
1854-1936

Peacock, Tip
July 17, 1878
Sept. 8, 1904

Peevyhouse, Ida
Oct. 6, 1898
Peevyhouse, Robert H.
Tennessee
Pvt. U. S. Army
World War I
June 5, 1894
July 28, 1972

Perry, Gerald W.
July 4, 1952
Sept. 8, 1967

Phebus, Anna Kate
Died Mar. 18, 1935

Phebus, John Lankford
1858-1934

Phebus, Lillian Lucile
1897-1898

Phebus, Margaret Ann
1860-1937

Phebus, Margaret Edith
1900-1955

Phelan, Mrs. R. E.
Wife of L. N. Phelan
Oct. 1, 1845
Feb. 2, 1888

Phillips, Edward W.
Jan. 13, 1883
Feb. 8, 1967
Phillips, Florence
Mar. 13, 1886
Dec. 19, 1968

Phillips, Sgt. Verney E.
Nov. 3, 1919
May 22, 1949

Pierce, Emeral L.
1887-1962
Pierce, Johnie A.
1888-19

Pierce, Frances Helen
Daughter
1924-

Pierce, Georgia Wyatt
Born 1905
Died 1935

Pierce, John L.
April 3, 1918
Sept. 28, 1920

Pierce, Maggie Davis
1875-1942

Pierce, Raymond McCoy
Son
1927-1954

Pierce, Robbie Lee
1900-
Pierce, Brice J.
Tennessee
Pvt. Co. A
107 Mach Gun Bn
World War I
May 6, 1895
June 3, 1969

Pierce, Sallie D.
Wife of Martin L. Pierce
1877-1948

Pierce, Sallie D.
Wife of Martin L. Pierce
1877-1948

Pinner, Loda B.
Nov. 24, 1878
Nov. 27, 1959

Pitt, Donald L.
Nov. 18, 1934
Oct. 6, 1967

Pitt, Doyle Evelyn
1912-1966

Pitt, Pierce
1908-

Pitt, Minnie
1877-19
Pitt, W. F. Edd
1869-1956

Pittman, Wade H.
1878-19
Pittman, Nannie E.
1881-1960

Pledge, Robert E.
Dad
1885-1954
Pledge, Lela E.
Mama
1890-
Pledge, Robert L.
1912-
Pledge, Tommye J.
1910-

Plew, Elbert Earl
1919-1966

Poole, Orville Jacob
Mar. 15, 1886
Mar. 31, 1941
Husband of Margaret K.
Poole

Pope, Albert L.
July 11, 1881
Mar. 27, 1921

Pope, Albert Ross
May 31, 1901
Feb. 2, 1973
Pope, Mary Tharpe
Dec. 8, 1903

Pope, Alse
Oct. 18, 1853
Pope, Malinda
Mar. 6, 1845
Dec. 6, 1923

Pope, Dewitt T.
1891-1968
Pope, Minnie H.
1895-19

Pope, Doshia Emeline
Mother
Oct. 21, 1844
Mar. 27, 1931

Pope, Eunice J.
Sept. 19, 1922
Sept. 12, 1974
Pope, Pauline
Apr. 21, 1926

Pope, Homer B.
1879-1961

Pope, Emma L.
1884-1961

Pope, John S.
Tennessee
Pvt. Inf.
World War I.
Jan. 14, 1895
April 8, 1971
Pope, Ann Belsha
Aug. 3, 1898

Pope, Joseph A.
1849-1926
Pope, Lucy F.
1846-1931

Pope, Lex
Oct. 8, 1874
Mar. 7, 1942

Pope, Mary Frances
Dau. of Lex & Nancy Pope
Sept. 16-Nov. 1, 1908

Pope, Nancy C.
Sept. 19, 1884
Feb. 26, 1968

Pope, W. B.
July 30, 1861
May 11, 1899

Pope, W. W.
Dec. 24, 1831
Feb. 16, 1910

Poor, George A.
1901-
Poor, Roslyn P.
1906-1974

Poor, Grady M. I.
1898-1958
Poor, Tula J.
1902-19

Poor, Robert E.
1886-1949
Poor, Adeline E.
1888-1941

Poore, Robert Aaron
Father
1905-1968
Poore, Esther Arnette
Mother 1907-

Poore, William Irvin
Died June 27, 1949

Poore, William J.
1865-1950
Poore, Martha E.
1869-1956

Porter, H. C.
Nov. 7, 1843
Oct. 24, 1904
Porter, Katie M.
1873-1928

Porter, John Nathaniel
1888-1965
Porter, Lelia Frieberg
1894-

Porter, Robert L.
Apr. 22, 1903
Sept. 18, 1959
Married July 27, 1926
Porter, Catherine T.
No Dates

Porter, Sallie Hampton
1863-1938

Porter, Sheffer
1896-1964
Porter, Blanche
1900-19

Porter, Tobitha P.
June 26, 1853
July 6, 1906

Porter, William Douglass
1890-1954
Porter, Lucy McDonald
1890-19

Poteet, Bennie
1893-1945
Poteet, Drury
1903-19

Poteet, Edward "Bud"
Father
1902-1966
Poteet, Oma Jewell
Mother
1906-

Poteet, Edward Mack
1863-1943
Poteet, L. Frances
1867-1942

Poteet, Onie
Mar. 7, 1906
Nov. 23, 1974
Poteet, Bilma
April 9, 1909

Poteet, Rosa Ella
1895-19
Poteet, Jim G.
Tennessee
Pvt. U. S. Army
World War I
April 15, 1891
Mar. 8, 1968

Pritchard, J. W.
May 8, 1843
Aug. 25, 1911
Pritchard, Bernie E.
Sept. 14, 1880
Feb. 26, 1904
Pritchard, Maggie M.
Feb. 3, 1857
Apr. 28, 1919

Purcell, Marian L.
1913-1974

Pursley, Aaron T.
Apr. 25, 1863
Dec. 3, 1909

Purvis, Robert R.
Father
Nov. 4, 1865
Feb. 28, 1941
Purvis, Ada Idell
Mother
June 23, 1873
Jan. 6, 1944

Purvis, Virginia Ruth
Oct. 17, 1924
Sept. 28, 1942

Purvis, Whitlow H.
Tennessee
CCM USNR
World War II
July 28, 1911
Dec. 5, 1957

Pryor, Emaline
1855-1942

Radford, Edna Avery
Wife of J. S. Radford
Aug. 29, 1872
Sept. 15, 1900

Radford, Edward M.
Mar. 5, 1891
July 1, 1954

Radford, James S.
Father
1873-1936

Radford, S.
July 17, 1849
Aug. 8, 1898

Ragsdale, Flora
Mother
Nov. 13, 1880
Sept. 6, 1969
Terry, Hazel
Sister
Sept. 30, 1910
Mar. 17, 1955

Rainey, Armonde B.
Dec. 13, 1881
July 26, 1945

Rainey, Beulah
1883-1934
Rainey, Alva
1875-1947

Rainey, R. M.
1848-1935
Rainey, Nancy
1856-1930

Ramsey, Donna Fulghum
Died April 18, 1957

Rasberry, Wm. Thomas (Billy)
Nov. 18, 1934
Dec. 20, 1963

Ray, Alexander L.
June 14, 1868
Oct. 29, 1939
Ray, Estella Ann
Nov. 11, 1869
May 21, 1952

Ray, Cora Burkeen
1876-1959

Ray, Connie J.
Feb. 20, 1903
Jan. 20, 1962

Ray, Eddie Farris
1915-1974

Ray, Elsie Henry
Dau. of A. L &
E. A. Ray
Oct. 2, 1893
June 16, 1902

Ray, Infant Dau. of
A. L. & E. A. Ray
Born & Died
Sept. 9, 1903

Ray, John D.
Dec. 21, 1880
Feb. 28, 1968

Reaves, George N.
Nov. 3, 1885
Mar. 4, 1972
Reaves, Mary M.
Nov. 29, 1903

Reece, J. W.
1865-1958
Reece, S. M.
1866-1935

Reece, Lulu
1882-19

Reed, Osce Ola
1884-1954

Reeves, Effie Hambrick
Dec. 28, 1890
Nov. 1, 1959

Rice, A. G.
Sept. 1, 1859
Apr. 21, 1890

Rice, Ida Earlie
Sept. 2, 1893
Rice, Archie N.
Dec. 20, 1885
Dec. 22, 1951

Rice, Michael
Son
Mar. 21, 1949
Jan. 20, 1965

Rice, Walter, H.
1883-1958
Rice, Millie J.
1896-19

Ridens, W. F.
1867-1889

Ridens, W. W.
1887-1926

Ridens, William Samuel
1876-1942

Ridens, Calvin
1904-1924

Ridens, Dollie C.
1887-1922

Ridens, Dora
1861-1935

Ridens, Elizabeth H.
1872-1960

Ridens, G. H.
1855-1903

Ridens, J. R.
1880-1900

Ridens, J. W.
Dec. 18, 1858
May 9, 1903

Ridens, Lee
Born 1880

Ridens, Nancy M.
1858-1924

Ridens, Ollie P.
1882-1947

Richardson, Otis E.
1893-1953
Richardson, Leslie R.
1899-19

Riley, Virgie M.
1902-1954
Riley, Henry W.
1900-19

Rizley, Rena
1895-1945

Robbins, Joseph Ezra
Born April 7, 1901
Died Jan. 28, 1974
Robbins, Cammie Baker
Born Oct. 18, 1904

Roberts, Bertie
Feb. 6, 1888
Mar. 27, 1951
Wife of W. F. Roberts

Roberts, W. F.
Oct. 13, 1880
June 5, 1961

Robertson, Lura C.
1874-1968
Robertson, Elisha A.
1870-1957

Robertson, Moody Elisha
July 31, 1903
Aug. 22, 1964

Robertson, Richard
Dec. 18, 1916
Oct. 28, 1930

Robeson, Vera
1903-
Robeson, Arthur
1888-1970

Rodgers, Albert - Father
1863-1931
Rodgers, Willie M. - Mother
1869-1907

Rodgers, George M.
1861-1941
Rodgers, Mary Ada
1868-19

Rodgers, James
Son of A. L. &
W. C. Rodgers
Died 1887
Stone Broken

Rodgers, Nancy Emma
Jan. 15, 1976
69 years

Rodgers, Willie C.
Tennessee
Tec 5 32 Armd Regt.
3 Armd Div.
World War II
March 7, 1920
Aug. 28, 1944

Rogers, H. Nelson
Nov. 26, 1902
Apr. 9, 1969

Rogers, Jimmie
Died Aug. 4, 1886

Rooks, Nettie
Mother
1873-1947

Roop, Henry Adrian
1875-1957

Roop, Laura D.
Jan. 22, 1877
Apr. 24, 1947

Rose, Alvin C.
1918-1966

Rose, Ernie
1908-1936

Rose, Minnie
1880-1967

Rose, Ogie
Aug. 20, 1884
Jan. 14, 1964
Rose, Zona Austin
Oct. 27, 1886
Jan. 27, 1968

Rose, William R. "Yink"
1919
Father
Rose, Edna Faye
1916-
Mother
Rose, William Ernie
1943-1962
Son

Rose, Wilton
July 12, 1898
Sept. 21, 1959
Rose, Vera
Jan. 3, 1898

Ross, Harry F.
1881-1959
Ross, Annie Jones
1875-1929

Rudolph, Abb
1883-1953
Rudolph, Elizabeth M.
1884-1972

Rudolph, Hooper H.
Tennessee
PFC 207 Co MIL POL Corp.
World War I
Aug. 9, 1892
Oct. 31, 1949

Rudolph, J. C.
1858-1934

Rudolph, Minnie
1862-19

Rudolph, Lenoard C.
1903-
Rudolph, Saline A.
1904-

Rudolph, Neal
1910-1912

Rudolph, William Ray
May 29, 1890
May 31, 1970
Rudolph, Maggie Lee
Mar. 16, 1899
Mar. 24, 1971

Rush, Thelma I.
1935-
Rush, Lessie May
1899-1957
Rush, Charlie G.
1921-
Rush, Bill
1925-
Rush, Jewell
1925-

Ryan, Ada Ridens
Wife of R. J. Ryan
1879-1949

Ryan, R. J.
1874-1916

Salisbury, Allie M.
Wife of A. D. Salisbury
Jan. 29, 1891
April 6, 1919

Sammons, Miss Georgia
Aug. 28, 1974
82 yrs. 11 mos. 20 days

Sanders, Irene Voss
Mother
1898-1973

Scobey, Edna Earl
Daughter
1913-1938

Scobey, John A.
1873-1953
Scobey, May
His Wife
1879-19

Scobey, M. Ella Williams
1912-
Scobey, George Ezra
1905-1969

Scobey, Minnie
1888-19
Scobey, Luney
1881-1958

Scobey, Ruby Virgil
Aug. 23, 1898
Dec. 9, 1967
Scobey, Annie Mai
Sept. 9, 1902
Apr. 2, 1971

Scobey, Winfred Harold
Son
1911-1944

Scobey, William B.
1884-1943
Scobey, Willie A.
1888-1972

Scott, Benjamin C.
1887-1949
Scott, Hattie B.
1888-1949

Scott, Emma Clay
Dec. 15, 1868
Jan. 4, 1950

Scott, Manuel C.
(Blount)
1907-1939

Scott, Neely, F.
1902-1970
Scott, Bertha M.
1907-1971

Scott, Nell
1913-1944

Seat, Annie Lea Brown
1903-1945
(Note: Dau. of Will
and Mamie Jones Brown)

Seigfried, Vergie A.
Wife of John Seigfried
Dec. 6, 1878
Feb. 19, 1910

Self, Eula Dickey
Mar. 23, 1948
Wife of Marvin Self

Self, Gussie M.
1906-
Self, George M.
1898-1952

Self, Jessie E.
1900-1955
Self, Blanche E.
1900-

Self, Marvin
Died Nov. 5, 1931

Sewell, Lois T.
July 28, 1916
Dec. 22, 1970

Shackleton, Joel F.
July 19-
Aug. 15, 1936

Shaw, Annie A.
May 25, 1907
May 2, 1915

Shaw, Inez
Mother
1872-1953
Shaw, Fount L.
Daddy
1867-1940

Shaw, George Erman
No Date)
Shaw, Ollie Holman
1890-1955

Shaw, S. E.
Aug. 28, 1880
Sept. 14, 1933
Shaw, E. O.
Mar. 6, 1841
Jan. 2, 1917

Sherrell, Jim H.
1877-19
Sherrell, Nannie A.
1884-1951

Sherrill, David Hall
Nov. 16, 1899
Jan. 13, 1971

Sherrill, J. F.
Oct. 10, 1822
Aug. 10, 1890

Sherrill, Mamie G.
Died July 1, 1922
Sherrill, William H.
Died Dec. 10, 1922

Sherrill, Nona M.
April 20, 1870
Jan. 26, 1935
Sherrill, Dr. David A.
Mar. 4, 1858
Feb. 29, 1947

Sherrill, Sarah Malvina
Dau. of D. A. & Nona
Sherrill
Aug. 31, 1889
Oct. 22, 1897

Sherrod, Icebinder L.
Wife of J. M. Sherrod
Nov. 6, 1825
Jan. 13, 1884
Sherrod, John B.
Son of J. M &
I. L. Sherrod
July 4, 1849
June 18, 1887

Ship, Allen
Son of Allen M. & Estella Ship
July 19, 1893
Aug. 12, 1896

Shoffner, Mary E.
Wife of M. L. Shoffner
Aug. 29, 1847
Shoffner, Martin L.
May 27, 1848
Feb. 14, 1906
Shoffner, Mary B.
Aug. 3, 1877
Jan. 29, 1902
Shoffner, Martin L. Jr.
Mar. 12, 1896
Aug. 6, 1919
Shoffner, Martin L. III
No Date

Shuck, Evelyn Farror Holman
Died Feb. 23, 1975
66 years, 9 mos. 21 days

Shuckm Mary Beth
June 4, 1956
Sept. 29, 1956

Simmons, Alvin M.
PFC U. S. Army
July 18, 1912
April 28, 1975

Simmons, Bingham B.
Father
1906-
Simmons, Josie J.
1909-1965

Simmons, Era
Tennessee
Sgt. 306 MBL Ord. Rep. Shop
World War I
Sept. 10, 1891
Sept. 8, 1959
Simmons, Alma
1896-
Simmons, John Henry
Father
1888-1970
Simmons, Claudie May
Mother
1889-1972

Simpson, J. Vernon
Jan. 12, 1972
July 25, 1923
Simpson, Jean Troutt
June 3, 1948
Simpson, J. Vernon
July 9, 1945

Simrell, Robert Darryl
Oct. 15, 1939
July 20, 1967

Sims, Dewey A.
1899-1959

Sims, W. J.
1885-1973

Smith, Clyde Allen
1892-1970
Smith, Cynthia Quinn
1897-1955

Smith, Elizabeth Azalia Spear
June 9, 1870
July 3, 1953

Smith, Elizabeth Leftwich
July 24, 1827
Feb. 28, 1902

Smith, Enoch B.
July 8, 1882
Oct. 22, 1958
Smith, Donnie L.
May 16, 1887
Jan. 3, 1972

Smith, J. Frank
1880-1970
Smith, Addie E.
1880-1970
Smith, Hugh de Graffen Reid
Sept. 7, 1846
Jan. 11, 1926

Smith, Jessie M.
Mother
Aug. 8, 1886
      --
Smith, Joseph D.
Father
Sept. 1, 1879
July 18, 1973

Smith, Joan
June 29, 1940
Jan. 21, 1941

Smith, Joe Huie
Sept. 17, 1907
Aug. 19, 1968

Smith, Joseph Luther
Oct. 25, 1879
June 8, 1966
Smith, Josie Ethridge
Sept. 1, 1885

Smith, Madge McCorkle
July 21, 1901
Oct. 25, 1972
Wife of Richard F. Smith

Smith, Marguerite Abigail
Oct. 8, 1911
Oct. 22, 1911

Smith, Mary F.
1862-1945

Smith, Mat
Feb. 2, 1846
Apr. 4, 1919

Smith, Richard F.
April 5, 1900
Aug. 29, 1967

Smith, Robert M.
1849-1929

Smith, Sadie A.
Died Aug. 10, 1974
73 yrs. 3 mo, 14 days

Smith, Shirley N.
May 28, 1923
Smith, Fred Sr.
June 5, 1920
Sept. 1, 1960

Smith, Sidney J.
1900-1925

Smith, Thomasella
1912

Spain, Robert E.
1930-1937
Spain, James W.
1910-1961
Spain, Myrtle E.
1911-

Stalkup, Nancy J.
Wife of B. S. Stalkup
Died Aug. 16, 1876
20 years 20 mos and 2 days

Stanfield, Chester Eugene
1883-1966
Stanfield, Carra E.
1887-19

Stanfield, David Eugene
Son of
Ed & Olivia Stanfield
Nov. 28-Nov. 30, 1950

Stanfield, Gladys G.
Sept. 30, 1917
Feb. 23, 1958

Stanfield, John L.
1905-1972
Stanfield, Maxine S.
1923-

Stanfield, Shelby Thomas
Son of S. E. &
Gladys Stanfield
Nov. 21, 1945
Mar. 20, 1946

Steele, Cherry
Tennessee
2nd Lt. Co. B 371 Inf.
World War I
Oct. 24, 1895
Feb. 11, 1956

Steele, Frank
Died Aug. 2, 1949

Steele, George M.
1860-1948

Steele, Florence
1871-1953

Steele, J. A.
Aug. 26, 1855
Aug. 23, 1894
Steele, Allie
Died Feb. 25, 1927

Steele, Johnnie
1894-

Steele, Mabel
1893-1971

Steele, Marcus
Died Dec. 18, 1925

Stephens, Guy
1898-1962
Stephens, Maude
1901-1975

Stockton, Jimmy Lee
Tennessee
PFC U. S. Army
Jan. 3, 1934
Aug. 24, 1968

Stockton, Robert T. Jr.
Tennessee
PFC Infantry
World War II
April 4, 1924
April 3, 1948

Stribling, Charlie Andrew
Tennessee
PVT. 309 Inft. 78 Div.
World War I
Jan. 16, 1897
Oct. 7, 1948

Stribling, Elbert
June 29, 1902
--
Stribling, Alma
Feb. 5, 1917
--

Sturdivant, Mary Ann
Waddy
Feb. 7, 1870
June 23, 1936

Sullivan, Dr. W. O.
1874-1928
Sullivan, Annie Claiborne
1882-1944

Summers, Lee Clinton
Aug. 15, 1880
Jan. 4, 1970

Summers, Lener Bell
Dec. 3, 1890
June 6, 1973

Sutton, Charlie M.
Dec. 25, 1878
Nov. 30, 1966
Sutton, Sallie M.
Nov. 10, 1880
Feb. 26, 1957

Sutton, Lela Eva
May 26, 1903
Aug. 10, 1920

Swims, Adolph
Father
1896-
Swims, Ollie
Mother
1904-

Swims, Jasper N.
Nov. 20, 1890
Mar. 6, 1953
Swims, Willie M.
Born Feb. 27, 1896

Swims, Jessie G.
Oct. 6, 1904
May 19, 1973
Swims, Gladys K.
July 17, 1909

Swindler, Henry J.
Apr. 3, 1865
Feb. 13, 1933

Swindler, Laura May
Daughter of
H. J. Swindler
May 22, 1866
Apr. 12, 1902

Swindler, Mable
Aug. 12, 1889
May 26, 1913

Swindler, Mary Elizabeth
Dau. of J. M. &
Neely Swindler
1902-1904

Swindler, Nancy J.
Dec. 26, 1891
Oct. 27, 1934

Swindler, Nina L.
Daughter
19 -
Swindler, Neely H.
Mother
1877-19
Swindler, Jeptha M.
Father
1868-1948

Tabor, Doris L.
Died Nov. 7, 1975
55 yrs. 0 mos. 26 days

Tabor, Ophelia
Daughter
June 30, 1922
Feb. 6, 1965

Tabor, T. G.
1883-1942
Tabor, Kate
1892-

Tackett, William A.
July 25, 1879
Jan. 23, 1949
Tackett, Ida L.
Feb. 5, 1879
Mar. 15, 1967

Taggart, Leonel T.
Feb. 28, 1904
May 30, 1957
Taggart, Anna L.
Sept. 14, 1908

Sisters
Tanner, Mollie Crawford
1896-1921
Tibbs, Pirlie Crawford
1900-1932
Crawford, Finnie Eveline
1885-1935

Tarrant, Chas. R.
1906-1940

Tarrant, Evelyn H.
1908-1960

Tatum, Hub
No Dates
Tatum, Martha

Tatum, Martha Ann
Dec. 2, 1874
Nov. 13, 1956

Taylor, Basil Manuel
1870-1924

Taylor, Bob
Son
1895-1918

Taylor, Bobbie Wayne
1937-1941

Taylor, Ethel Emma
Aug. 26, 1902
Oct. 18, 1969

Taylor, John W.
1865-1953
Taylor, Emma B.
1876-19

Taylor, Martha Haskins
Dau. of J. C. &
A. E. Haskins
1883-1937

Taylor, Thomas L. Sr.
1890-1956
Taylor, Mattie L.
1906

Taylor, William Riley
1915-1952

Tharp, Alice P.
Oct. 18, 1913
April 9, 1964
Tharp, John A.
Jan. 23, 1900

Tharp, Lilliam
1899-19
Tharp, Willie C.
1885-1942

Thomason, Freeda
1919
Mother
Thomason, Joffre
1918-
Father

Thomasson, Rose Blackwood
1874-1931

Thompson, Arch
1894-1952
Thompson, Pearl
1896-19

Thompson, Bobbie B.
Feb. 12, 1936
Nov. 30, 1946

Thompson, Ernest B.
Pvt. 520 Air Tec. GPAAF
World War II
Dec. 25, 1906
April 2, 1966
Thompson, Loma C.
1910-

Thompson, Fred L.
1911-1962
Thompson, Opal L
1916-

Thompson, Harriet
1918-1947
Thompson, J. D.
1918-

Thompson, J. M.
Aug. 23, 1867
July 19, 1893

Thompson, James Mack
Sept. 18, 1878
Jan. 8, 1943
Thompson, Nancy Hickman
July 3, 1804
Jan. 11, 1943

Thompson, John R.
April 14, 1879
Oct. 26, 1968
Thompson, Hessie B.
April 13, 1886
Mar. 8, 1963

Thompson, John S.
May 31, 1841
Jan. 8, 1900

Thompson, Julia E.
Jan. 3, 1859
Jan. 8, 1900

Thompson, June Nine
1900-1967
Thomspon, Sam
1897-1942

Thompson, Luther David
June 26, 1975
63 years 4 mos. 5 days

Thompson, Paula Gean
July 10, 1936

Thompson, Will A.
Aug. 22, 1885
April 23, 1965
Thompson, Irene J.
Nov. 20, 1890

Tigrett, Hamilton Parks
Oct. 27, 1875
Nov. 14, 1958
Tigrett, Sara Nunn
Nov. 8, 1881
Mar. 16, 1971

Tigrett, Issac
1912-1970

Tilford, Robert B.
1890-1960
Tilford, Ivy
1893-1969

Tillman, Ollie Joe
Oct. 5, 1909
Mar. 14, 1957
Tillman, Evie C.
Nov. 29, 1910

Tillman, Ralph B.
1887-1958
Tillman, Virginia R.
1888-1960

Tipps, Shellie Gene
June 16, 1974
26 years 2 mos. 0 days

Todd, May Pewett
1907-
Todd, Paul Wesson
1907-1974

Todd, Walter A.
1883-1942
Todd, Anie Y.
1887-1967

Towns, Green
1891-1937
Towns, Sula
1893-1969

Towns, Richard L.
1863-1945
Towns, Senia S.
1872-1940

Townsend, Baby
July 9, 1887
Aug. 12, 1887

Townsend, Beauregard
Age 30 years

Townsend, Clyde
1908-1968

Townsend, J. Thomas
1865-1938
Townsend, Anna Beck
1869-1938

Townsend, Little Cora
Age 6 months

Townsend, Robert W.
June 13, 1835
Apr. 30, 1895

Troutt, Willie G.
1888-19
Troutt, Clara B.
1892-1972

Tully, Bea
1912-

Tully, Dock P.
1878-1968

Tully, Floyd C.
1901-

Tully, Kate
1881-1966

Tupman, Mary Wyatt
May 12, 1890
May 7, 1969

Turner, Virgil S.
1846-1897
Turner, Ida Dorgas Gaither
1855-1924

Turner, Winnie V.
1891-1972

VanEaton, Arthur
1883-1956

VanEaton, Bertha
1892-1975

VanEaton, Lloyd
1920-1966
VanEaton, Laverne
1919-

Van Vickle, William Eddie
Aug. 31, 1948
Jan. 15, 1971

Vann, Mary S. Fuller
Wife of J. C. Vann
June 10, 1840
Sept. 13, 1877

Voight, Jo Evelyn
June 10, 1938
--
Voight, Roger L.
Apr. 24, 1937
June 29, 1972
Voight, Roger L.
Minnesota
ADJC U. S. Navy
Vietnam
Apr. 24, 1937
June 29, 1972

Voltermann, Fred Henry
May 17, 1870
April 21, 1937
Voltermann, Enola D. Prichard
Feb. 12, 1877
Dec. 8, 1945

Voltermann, Sarah Agnes
Daughter
Nov. 17, 1903
Oct. 15, 1918

Voss, Clarence R.
1888-1963

Waddy, Joe K.
January 20, 1868
December 16, 1896

Wadlington, Sallie Bennetta
Dau. of B. C. &
M. A. Wadlington
Jan. 11, 1878
Sept. 8, 1882

Wadsworth, Mary M.
1886-1964

Wagster, Hester L.
Mother
1892-1954
Wagster, Luther W.
Father
1880-19

Waldran, Mary H.
No Dates

Walker, Edward B.
1905-1956

Walker, James H.
July 4, 1896
Walker, Fannie
Mar. 5, 1898
May 21, 1969

Walker, Robert L.
1876-1931
Walker, Winnie B.
1881-1966

Walton, Ernest B.
Mar. 29, 1886
--
Father
Walton, Maud
Jan. 16, 1895
Sept. 2, 1972
Mother
Walton, Louise
Jan. 4, 1922
--
Daughter

Walton, Jennifer Leigh
Inf. Dau. of Mike and
Lana Walton
Nov. 19, 1971
Our Baby

Walton, Robbie W.
1896-19
Walton, Oliver P.
1891-1948

Ward, Benjamin F.
Jan. 28, 1890
--
Ward, Bernice E.
Feb. 24, 1892
May 23, 1968

Ward, Nannie Mae
July 21, 1922
Nov. 11, 1957

Warden, Josie L.
Mar. 9, 1893
Jan. 25, 1973
Warden, James F.
Tennessee
Pvt. Co. B 46 Inf.
World War I
Mar. 31, 1895
Nov. 23, 1956

Watlington, J. Frank
1861-1946
Watlington, Rosa Lee
1877-1938

Watlington, John W.
1860-1935

Watlington, Martha A. Sherrod
1860-1927

Watson, R. Z.
Dec. 28, 1829
March 8, 1908

Watts, Nannie A.
Sept. 22, 1852
May 12, 1864
Mother
Watts, William M.
Feb. 12, 1882
Mar. 9, 1885
Brother

Watts, Susie B.
1890-1932
Mother
Weakley, Mary Anne
1854-1917

Weakley, Mary Fryer
Dau. of D. M &
K. L. Weakley
April 4, 1903
Sept. 20, 1906

Webb, Lawerence N.
1894-
Webb, Bessie J.
1896
Married Aug. 2, 1914

Webb, Milford R.
1915-1975
Webb, Martha Lee
1915-
Married Oct. 29, 1932

Webb, Paschal T.
1874-1958
Webb, Lou Ella
1875-1955

Weddington, James M.
1860-1934
Weddington, Mollie Arkins
1858-1935

Wesson, J. D.
Died July 19, 1908

West, Albert
Sept. 7, 1910
Dec. 22, 1925

West, Daniel
Co. G.
2 Tennessee Inf
Spanish Am. War
1877-1922

West, J. D.
Aug. 2, 1897
West, Maurine
Sept. 27, 1907
Nov. 22, 1969

West, James H.
1871-1957
West, Mattie E.
1887-19

West, Shirley Ann
Dau. of O. L. &
Doll West
Sept. 5, 1935
April 27, 1937

Westbrooke, Dr. John Robert
Aug. 4, 1822
July 8, 1899
Westbrooke, Martha Ann
Feb. 11, 1827
Westbrooke, William Ivie
Mar. 31, 1868
Mar. 15, 1886
Westbrooke, Kate Grey
Mar. 5, 1858
Apr. 1, 1887
Westbrooke, Andrew Jackson, Jr.
Nov. 5, 1859
Sept. 8, 1861
Westbrooke, Alvin Caldwell
Feb. 5, 1891
Oct. 4, 1890
Westbrooke, Infant Son of
J. R. Westbrooke, Jr.
and Lucie H. Westbrooke

White, Alma
Mother
1895-1936

White, Augustus B.
1873-1950
White, Luna P.
1879-1948

White, C. M.
1866-1893

White, Infant Son of
L. C. & S. P. White
Dec. 1, 1882
Aug. 12, 1883

White, Jefferson L.
Tennessee
Waggoner U. S. Army
World War I
Jan. 19, 1890
Mar. 24, 1959

White, L. A.
1868-1897

White, Lemuel C.
Jan. 11, 1834
May 23, 1906
White, Sarah P.
Dec. 12, 1841
July 12, 1916

Whitson, Avie A.
1875-1962

Whitson, Brank Newton
Died Nov. 28, 1975
77 years 7 mos. 27 days

Whitson, George N.
Tennessee
PFC 805 Mil Pol. Co.
World War II
Sept. 27, 1916
June 19, 1959

Whitson, Ollie Meadows
Sept. 5, 1901
Feb. 29, 1968

Whitson, Patsy Jane
1936-
Whitson, Martin Samuel
1929-1971

Whitson, Sam T.
1893-19
Whitson, Virgie S.
1897-1951

Whitson, W. M.
1874-1923

Whitwell, Miss Lee
April 7, 1871
Aug. 7, 1953

Whitwell, Thomas D.
Jan. 1, 1859
May 20, 1945

Whitworth, Harry
1890-1965
Whitworth, Grace
1904-19

Widdis, Patrick B.
1917-1969
Widdis, Patrick B.
Tennessee
Lieutenant U. S. Navy
World War II
Oct. 24, 1917
July 2, 1969
Widdis, Linda L.
1918-1970

Wilkerson, Asa
1892-1971
Wilkerson, Sannie
1895-1968

Williams, Alfred L.
1888-19
Williams, Edith S.
His wife
1892-1957

Williams, Allie
1843-1915

Williams, Annie
1887-19

Williams, James W.
1869-1945

Williams, Carrie A.
1875-1937
Williams, Granville O.
1865-1941

Williams, Curtis
1904-1943

Williams, D. V.
1834-1870

Williams, Ed E.
1858-1932

Williams, Elmer H.
1880-1951
Williams, Elva B.
1880-1967

Williams, Elmer H. Jr.
1918-1919

Williams, Floyd
June 9, 1910
--
Williams, Ruth
Nov. 17, 1914
--

Williams, Frances K.
1882-1931

Williams, Harry J.
1900-1956

Williams, Haywood
1899-
Father
Williams, Lois Jones
1899
Mother
Williams, Joe E.
1934-
Son

Williams, Horace C.
Oct. 5, 1898
Feb. 10, 1974
Williams, Tommie L.
June 30, 1905

Williams, Issac McLeod
Infant
June 21, 1921
June 24, 1921

Williams, Ira G.
1887-1964
Williams, Mattie Lou
1890-1963

Williams, Issac N.
1853-1934
Williams, Elizabeth G.
His Wife
1868-1956

Williams, James Anthony
May 11, 1964
May 12, 1964

Williams, Jennie
Dau. of John G. &
Adline Williams
May 20, 1877
Jan. 20, 1955

Williams, Kathleen Stout
1864-1932

Williams, Capt. L. M.
1831-1900

Williams, Lay A.
1901-1964
Williams, Katherine B.
1924-

Williams, Lay V.
1873-1961
Williams, Lillian S.
1883-1966

Williams, Mary Jane
Wife of Thos. W.
May 27, 1832
Oct. 15, 1886

Williams, "Little" Margaret
May 31, 1918
Nov. 28, 1921

Williams, Otis Cherry
1914-1917

Williams, R. E.
1870-1958
Williams, Mary L.
1874-1951

Williams, Safford S.
1891-1958
Williams, Nell W.
1901-1962

Williams, Samuel U.
1874-1957
Williams,
1878-1965

Williams, Susan L.
April 11, 1842
April 21, 1866

Williams, T. Hardy
1864-1910

Williams, Thos. J.
Feb. 17, 1830
Sept. 23, 1887
Aged
57 yrs. 7 mos 6 days

Williams, Virginia
1869-1874

Williams, Walter A.
1878-1936
Williams, Melissa Ann
1878-1964

Williamson, Mrs. M. A.
Wife of S. E. Williamson
May 6, 1851
Jan. 11, 1891

Wilson, Bobby Lynn
Nov. 7, 1938
Nov. 10, 1957

Wilson, Eddie Eryl
Mother
1891-1947

Wilson, Evie
1874-1960

Wilson, Flora Fuller
1865-1942

Wilson, Franklin R.
ARM 2/c
1920-1945

Wilson, Johnnie W.
1895-19
Wilson, Mattie Lee
1893-1973

Wilson, Melven V.
1868-1930

Wilson, Mickey Louis
July 12, 1948
May 10, 1971
Wilson, Mickey Louis
Texas
Sp 5 Co. B 6 BN 27 Arty
Vietnam Arcom
July 12, 1948
May 10, 1971

Wilson, Nannie Jean
April 24, 1888
July 3, 1941

Wilson, Nora Nunn
No Dates
Wilson, George Otis
1892-1963

Wilson, Oliver E.
1911-1937

Wilson, Paralee T.
Aug. 12, 1843
May 10, 1939

Wilson, Samuel D.
July 26, 1835
Mar. 8, 1908

Willis, Lawrence W.
Tennessee
Pfc. 12 Inf
World War I
June 21, 1923
Aug. 12, 1944
Willis, Mary P.
1891-1961

Wofford, Inez F.
1869-1951

Wright, Jess
Tennessee
Pvt. Hq. Co. 46 Inf.
World War I
Aug. 24, 1891
Mar. 18, 1965
Wright, Beulah
Jan. 24, 1892
Oct. 12, 1972

Wyatt, Annie Biffle
No Dates

Wyatt, Eugene Ripley
1876-1951
Wyatt, Minnie Taylor
18 -19

Wyatt, J. Otis
1926

Wyatt, James N. (DDS)
Sept. 15, 1893
Feb. 16, 1953
Wyatt, Eva Hurley
Mar. 9, 1897
Jan. 10, 1972

Wyatt, Martha G.
Apr. 15, 1867
May 31, 1942
Wyatt, Joseph H.
Dec. 19, 1865
Dec. 6, 1924

Wyatt, Wilbur Carl
Mar. 8, 1874
Mar. 13, 1957
Married June 24, 1896
Wyatt, Vada Gregory
Oct. 12, 1875
Apr. 14, 1959

Wynne, B. F.
Dec. 23, 1845
Nov. 11, 1929
Wynne, Anne A.
Oct. 28, 1843
June 27, 1924

Wynne, Emma J.
1855-1895

Wynne, Infant Twins
1901
Twins of Mr. and Mrs.
John G. Wynne

Wynne, John G.
Died Nov. 4, 1929

Wynne, Johnnie Mae
1902-1910

Wynne, Ora Mae
1874-1966

Youree, Frank
Feb. 8, 1876
Sept. 2, 1899

Youree, Thomas J.
Aug. 21, 1837
Jan. 24, 1904
Youree, S. B.
Wife of T. J. Youree
Mar. 31, 1842
July 4, 1897

Zarecor, Belle
1866-1945
Zarecor, J. J.
1859-1923

Zarecor, Herman L.
1906-1972

FISHER FAMILY PLOT

The Fisher burial plot is located about five miles directly north of Newbern on Highway 51 N. The home is on a high hill on the left side of the road, and the grave site is back of the house.

Fisher, Cloye Baker
Oct. 15, 1900
Jan. 2, 1950

FOWLKES CEMETERY

The Fowlkes Cemetery is located six miles from Newbern on Highway 51 S. The Cemetery is on the old H. L. Fowlkes farm. The homeplace burned and the family plot is located in the pasture behind the barn.

Fowlkes, Georgia
Dau. of P. T. & Jennie Fowlkes
1887-1888

Fowlkes, Henry
Oct. 4, 1789
Feb. 12, 1865

Fowlkes, H. L.
Oct. 26, 1827
Nov. 12, 1899

Fowlkes, Laura E.
Dau. of H. L & Marya Fowlkes
Sept. 7, 1851
Oct. 18, 1866

Fowlkes, Mrs. Marya
Wife of H. L Fowlkes
Nov. 4, 1827
Dec. 3, 1906

GAULDIN CEMETERY

The Gauldin Cemetery is located approximately one-half mile west of the Roellen-Newbern county road at a point 2.5 miles south of U. S. 51. It was initiated on the home yard of the Michael Olive Branch Gauldin family after their settlement in Dyer County in 1847.

Dickerson, James Sider
Son of Archer &
Margaret Dickerson
Feb. 18, 1859
Oct. 18, 1864

Dickerson, Margaret A.
Sept. 16, 1833
March 1, 1895
Dickerson, Archer A.
Sept. 16, 1823
April 12, 1898

Gauldin, Algernon S.
March 12, 1846
July 2, 1858

Gauldin, Cleopatra F.
Dau. of J. W. &
L. A. Gauldin
Nov. 28, 1858
Dec. 6, 1872

Gauldin, D. W.
Feb. 7, 1828
Jan. 6, 1896
Gauldin, E. B.
Oct. 20, 1867
Oct. 26, 1895

Gauldin, Eunice Ann
Dau. of J. W. and
M. A. Gauldin
Nov. 21, 1869
March 3, 1877

Gauldin, Eunice A.
Nov. 21, 1869
March 3, 1877
Gauldin, R. K.
Oct. 10, 1866
Jan. 18, 1901

Gauldin, J. W.
Sept. 7, 1831
May 30, 1895
Gauldin, M. A.
His Wife
Aug. 28, 1839
Nov. 22, 1905
Gauldin, L. A.
His Wife
Nov. 17, 1835
July 23, 1860

Gauldin, Lucinda A.
Consort of J. W.
Gauldin
Nov. 11, 1835
July 23, 1860

Gauldin, M. O B.
June 29, 1801
Jan. 11, 1886
Gauldin, Margaret P.
Wife of M. O B. Gauldin
Feb. 7, 1802
Jan. 7, 1897
Gauldin, Agnes T.
Dau. of M. O. B. &
M. P. Gauldin
Nov. 8, 1829
Feb. 10, 1880

Newbill, Emma
Wife of J. S. Newbill
Nov. 26, 1865
May 10, 1884
Newbill, J. S.
Husband of Emma Newbill
April 22, 1862
April 29, 1884

Roney, Addie V.
Wife of A. L. Roney
Feb. 6, 1860
July 29, 1921
Roney, Alexis L.
Oct. 13, 1838
Feb. 28, 1907

Scott, H. P.
May 8, 1826
May 14, 1891
Scott, Mary J.
Wife of H. P. Scott
July 14, 1824
March 8, 1908
Scott, Sarah L.
Dau. of H. P. & M. J. Scott
April 18, 1858
July 3, 1881

HICKS CEMETERY

Hicks Cemetery is located six miles from Dyersburg off of Highway 20 at Finley. Turn at the Methodist Chruch and go north for one-tenth of a mile, or five houses, past the church on the right side of the road.

Hicks, Ella E.
Dau. of J. H. & T. C. Hicks
Dec. 5, 1863
Jan. 29, 1887

Hicks, John
Father
March 28, 1839
Feb. 11, 1916
Hicks, T. C.
His Wife   Mother
Aug. 12, 1839
Nov. 1, 1924

Raine, Maude I.
Wife of Charles Raine
Jan. 7, 1873
Jan. 26, 1901

Rawles, Irvin G.
1887-1929

Heard A. E.
July 7, 1891 Died
31 years of age

HURRICANE HILL CEMETERY

Hurricane Hill Cemetery is located about four and one-half miles from Dyersburg. Travel north on the Lanesferry Highway for three miles. Then take a right turn on the Hurricane Hill Road. Go about a mile to the first blacktop road and turn to the right for about three hundred yards. The cemetery joins the Hurricane Hill Cumberland Presbyterian Church, and they are located on the west side of the road.

Adams, Maudie
Born & Died 1942

Ames, Dennis
1898-1960
Ames, Eva R.
1888-1959

Apple, Edgar
1871-1957
Apple, Lillian
1876-1963

Apple, Estey Clide
Son of F. P. & H. N.
Apple
Feb. 24, 1884
Jan. 17, 1885
Aged 1 yr. 1 mo. 3 days

Apple, F. P.
Aug. 12, 1852
Apr. 7, 1924
Apple. H. N.
Dec. 26, 1853
Apr. 25, 1939

Apple (Infant)
Son of F. P. & H. N.
Apple
Born & Died Oct. 11, 1898

Apple, Katherine E.
Oct. 6, 1845
April 5, 1917

Apple, Macon Van Buren
Jan. 30, 1841
Nov. 28, 1918

Arnold, Bessie
July 31, 1902
July 29, 1904

Arnold, Elizabeth Jane
Aug. 14, 1828
Dec. 7, 1904

Arnold, William C.
1880-1953
Arnold, Louise
1893-19

Autry, Dennis A.
Aug. 3, 1887

Autry, Polly J.
Mar. 7, 1884
Feb. 24, 1966

Barnett, E. M.
Jan 2, 1880
July 7, 1916

Barnett, Elma
May 25, 1888
March 16, 1915

Boon, Henry E.
Jan. 4, 1877
Mar. 5, 1888

Boon, Mary M.
Nov. 22, 1839
June 12, 1900

Bowen, Eliza J.
Born --
Died Sept. 12, 1878

Bowie, J. T.
Oct. 9, 1844
Jan. 28, 1894

Bradley, James M.
1877-1945
Bradley, Leona I.
1880-1939

Bradley, Jessie M.
Tennessee
Cook Co G 323 Inf
World War I
Dec. 28, 1894
June 10, 1969

Bradley, John H
Aug. 14, 1902

Bradley, Alma S.
Aug. 31, 1902
June 3, 1970

Bradley, Luther R.
Tennessee
Pvt. U. S. Army
World War I
Dec. 21, 1900
April 24, 1973

Bradley, Muriell Delouris
Jan. 14, 1933
Jan. 28, 1933

Bradley, Robert Jefferson
April 11, 1906
Oct. 19, 1937

Bradley, W. H.
Nov. 28, 1892
June 19, 1968

Carson, Alfred W.
1877-1958
Carson, Hettie J.
1882-1968

Carson, Chester C.
July 23, 1893
April 11, 1965
Carson, Iva
Jan. 5, 1894
Aug. 1, 1971

Carson, James Durl
1868-1940
Carson, Mattie E.
1871-1943

Claiborne
Son of R. F. &
E. F. Claiborne
June 1, 1870
Oct. 27, 1882

Claiborne, Eugenia F.
Wife of Robert E.
Claiborne
June 18, 1843
Apr. 27, 1920

Claiborne, R. F.
Aug. 8, 1839
June 20, 1907

Cobb, A. J.
Jan. 14, 1852
Feb. 12, 1891

Cobb, Allie R.
July 23, 1870
Aug. 15, 1904

Cobb, Jacob
Feb. 18, 1832
Sept. 17, 1906
Cobb, Martha
Mar. 1, 1843
June 5, 1919

Cobb, John Hester
Dau. of John H. &
Josiephene Cobb
Jan. 7, 1895
July 26, 1895

Cobb, Joseph Covington
Son of John H. &
Josephene Cobb
Aug. 15, 1899
June 4, 1901

Cobb, Josephene Covington
Aug. 20, 1868
Jul 16, 1906

Cobb, Robert Lee
July 27, 1864
June 4, 1939

Cobb, Sola Biffle
Feb. 5, 1908
May 30, 1928

Cobb, William
July 19, 1827
Mar. 21, 1905

Crenshaw, J. H.
Dec. 8, 1830
May 6, 1895

Davis, Amanda Gayle
Died Dec. 13, 1966

Davis, Clifford Pursell
1889-1926

Davis, Edmond O.
1891-1955

Davis Elease
1928-1929

Davis, J. D.
1915-1935

Davis, Jeff
Born Aug. 17, 1861
Died Feb. 6, 1885

Davis, Jess Byars
Dec. 6, 1911
May 28, 1965
Davis, Gladys
June 12, 1915

Davis, Joseph A.
Oct. 27, 1881
July 20, 1956

Davis, Walter
1904-1956

Davis, William C.
1872-1946
Davis, Martha L.
1870-19

Dobbs, J. Claude
Oct. 9, 1910
April 11, 1974
Dobbs, Gladys M.
Sept 2, 1921

Drane, Nattie E.
Wife of R. W. Drane
Born Nov. 14, 1854
Died Dec. 23, 1879

Duke, "Baby Boy"
Died May 28, 1971
- years, 0 mos., 0 days

Duke, Frances L.
Oct. 3, 1920
Mar. 15, 1968

Duke, Jess Thomas Jr.
Tennessee
Pvt. 894 Tank Destroyer BN
World War II
Feb. 15, 1908 - Feb. 11, 1957
Duke, Fern B
Aug. 5, 1908

Duke, Jessee T., Sr.
1875-1965
Duke, Rosie G.
1886-1965

Duke, Noah W.
Jan. 26, 1915
Feb 13, 1937

Duke, Roy
1906-1959

Earnhart, Eliza
July 23, 1839
Sept. 8, 1903

Fair, J. Henry
1905-1965
Fair, Susie E.
1912-1945

Fields, Julia A.
April 21, 1795
Oct. 17, 1872
Wife of James Fields

Fields, Peter G.
Aug. 31, 1825
June 20, 1855
Aged 29 yrs., 9 mo. 20 da.

Fields, Robert A.
Aug. 8, 1835
Feb. 28, 1856

Fields, Sallie V.
Wife of R. H. Molloy
Born: Aug. 14, 1832
Died: Sept. 22, 1889

Fowlkes, Annie Lou
Wife of S. P. Fowlkes
1869-1903

Fowlkes, Asa
Mar. 6, 1809
April 16, 1901

Fowlkes, Brice
Aged 10 months, 10 days

Fowlkes, Dick
1880-19
Fowlkes, Nellie
1881-1940

Fowlkes, Ella Katherine
Jan. 22, 1851
July 19, 1920

Fowlkes, Ernest
Son of
Wm & Lizzie D. Fowlkes
Born in May 17, 1870
Died in July 19, 1876

Fowlkes, J. H.
Born Aug. 27, 1803
Died June 1, 1837

Fowlkes, John Robert Lafayette
Son of S. A. & Martha
Fowlkes
July 8, 1848
Sept. 13, 1855

Fowlkes, Martha A.
Wife of Asa Fowlkes
June 22, 1818
Sept. 17, 1892
74 years 2 mos 22 days

Fowlkes, Minnie Wood
Oct. 3, 1873
Dec. 10, 1873
Inf. dau. of J. A. & A. D. Fowlkes

Fowlkes, Ruby Pearl
Born Aug. 1, 1893
Died May 24, 1895

Fowlkes, S. O. H.
Wife of Jas. H. Fowlkes
Died August 16, 1884
Aged
46 years 9 mo. 19 days

Fowlkes, Viola
Dau. of Asa & Martha Fowlkes
Mar. 23, 1859
Feb. 18, 1870
10 years 10 mos 25 days

Fowlkes, W. A.
1842-1907
Fowlkes, Lizzie H.
His Wife
1844-1912

Frazier, W. I.
May 16, 1860
Oct. 20, 1904

Fumbanks, Al
Aug. 29, 1837
Sept. 24, 1921
Fumbanks, Elizabeth F.
June 24, 1841
July 31, 1930

Fumbanks, Ivy Lucille
Nov. 1899
Nov. 1915

Fumbanks, Infant
Son of Guy & Ivy
Fumbanks
Nov. 24, 1897
Nov. 24, 1897

Fumbanks, Ivy Maude
Born July 8, 1870
Died Nov. 24, 1899

Fumbanks, J. C.
Jan. 31, 1846
Aug. 27, 1886
46 years 6 mos. 26 days

Fumbanks, Mabel
Dau. of Cry & Ivy
Fumbanks
Oct. 22, 1895
Jan. 14, 1896

Fumbanks, Watkins
Son of A. L & E. F.
Fumbanks
Dec. 7, 1867
Aug. 2, 1869
1 yr. 7 mos. 23 days

Gibson, Mary
Dau. of T. F. & A.
Gibson
Sept. 21, 1830
Sept. 10, 1893

Hall, William Ernest
Oct. 15, 1891
Jan. 29, 1920

Hammonds, Lurlene
Oct. 27, 1934
Oct. 18, 1936

Hardin, Perlie J.
No Dates

Harness, Nathan Norman
Son of C. C. & D. E.
Harness
Oct. 27, 1912
Oct. 27, 1912

Harris, T. J.
July 10, 1881
Dec. 22, 1940
Harris, Donnie
May 3, 1879
Mar. 2, 1958

Harrison, Joseph
Dec. 2, 1823
Feb. 27, 1877

Harrison, Marthy
Wife of Joseph Harrison
Jan. 11, 1825
Oct. 29, 1891

Hawkes, James E.
Son of J. W. & S. B.
Hawkes
Mar. 2, 1899
Apr. 28, 1899
Aged 1 mo. 26 days

Hawkes, W. J.
1840-1921
Hawkes, M. M.
1837-1901

Hawkes, William H.
Son of J. W. & S. B.
Hawkes
Jan. 20, 1893
April 9, 1893
Aged 2 mo, 19 days

Hilliard, Bobby Brown
Feb. 19, 1935
Jan. 29, 1950

Hilliard, Pearl R.
Jan. 9, 1896
April 8, 1897
Hilliard, Nettie J.
Dec. 18, 1897
June 8, 1898
Hilliard, Infant
Son of J. H. & Rosie Hilliard
July 4, 1899
July 10, 1899

Houston, E. R.
Wife of W. M. Houston
Aug. 26, 1876
May 20, 1906

Huffines, Eliza J.
Wife of Henry Huffines
Dec. 17, 1828
Sept. 5, 1900

Huffines, Henry
July 7, 1830
Dec. 1, 1888

Huffines, Mary E.
Wife of G. H. Huffines
Dec. 30, 1857
Sept. 28, 1887

Huffins, Mary A.
Nov. 10, 1868
May 10, 1903

Hungerford, Dora Ann
Mother
1873-1937

Hungerford, Edw. Carmack
Son
Sept. 22, 1909
Dec. 27, 1912

Hungerford, Thomas D., Father
Sept. 13, 1865
Dec. 27, 1912

Hurt, Elgin
May 5, 1877
Oct. 14, 1901

Hurt, F. E. (Ebb)
1881-1950

Hurt, George T.
Mar. 11, 1849
April 24, 1908
Hurt, Mallie B.
Nov. 4, 1848
July 19, 1917

Hurt, James M.
1830-1913

Hurt, Martha A.
Wife of J. M. Hurt
Born Dec. 12, 1832
Died May 8, 1897

Hurt, Mary
Dau. of Thos. & Mary
Hurt
July 15, 1880
Jan. 12, 1881

Hurt, Nettie
1884-1961

Hurt, Sarah
1884-1922

Hurt, Tom
1851-1919
Hurt, Mary
1850-1924

Jennings, W. A.
Died May 6, 1884
32 yrs.

Johnson, Albert S.
Son of Thomas & M. W.
Johnson
Aug. 7, 1862
June 21, 1885

Johnson, Mark
Died Feb. 18, 1904

Johnson, Thomas H.
Son of G. T. & F.
Johnson
May 27, 1881
June 6, 1882

Johnson, Thomas H.
Son of G. T. & F.
Johnson
May 27, 1881
June 6, 1882

Jones, J. A.
Born Sept. 16, 1836
Died Aug. 30, 1870

Jones, Nedom
1875-19
Jones, Mary
1861-1941

Jones, S. M.
Born Nov. 18, 1821
Died Feb. 24, 1906

Jones, S. T.
Son of J. A. & J. Jones
Aug. 23, 1863
Apr. 24, 1890

Jones, Sam
Died April 22, 1907

Kirk, Charlie E.
1877-1959
Kirk, Emma Jane
1882-1963

Kirk, Irvin A.
1908-
Kirk, Ora T.
1907-

Kirk, James
1932-1933
Kirk, Yvone
1937-1937

Kirk, Mearl A.
1928-1973

Leach, Eleonor W.
1916-1936

Lesdinger, Cephellar
Oct. 20, 1853
Mar. 18, 1855
Aged 16 mo. 28 days

Ledsinger, James A.
Oct. 7, 1849
Dec. 25, 1882

Ledsinger, Louisa J.
Daughter of C. H. & N. T.
April 2, 1847
Mar. 22, 1867

Ledsinger, Natia
Dau. of J. A. & Mary
Mar. 29, 1872
Sept. 23, 1883
Aged 11 yrs. 5 mos & 24 days

Lewellyng, J. E.
Mar. 18, 1833
Mar. 12, 1896

Lock, George W.
Feb. 4, 1889
April 23, 1961

Lock, Elijah W.
Father
April 16, 1882
Mar 5. 1961
Lock, Daisy H.
Mother
Oct. 17, 1885
Dec. 4, 1969

Lock, Eva M.
July 10, 1893
--

Lock, Sam E.
1891-1943
Lock, Fosten
1896-19

Lock, Tom Lane
Dec. 15, 1931
Aug. 24, 1932

Mamie, Neely Fooshee
1874-1926

McClanahan, Annie Neely
Aug. 25, 1867
Jan. 11, 1904
McClanahan, Genevieve
1900-1906

McKee, Edward
Father
1872-1937
McKee, Rhoda
Mother
1874-1936

McKee, Ernest C.
1907-1954

McQuarter, Mildred
1925-1973

Mills, John W.
July 15, 1873
April 11, 1910

Moore, Nancy
1850-1904

Moore, Raymond C.
Jan. 24, 1914
Aug. 16, 1975

Murphy, R. T.
1852-1933

Murray, Josh G.
1875-1953
Murray, Eulah E.
1875-19

Neely, Charles J.
July 27, 1845
Jan. 11, 1911

Neely, Gracie B.
Dau. of C. J. & Fannie
Neely
July 16, 1891
Sept. 16, 1894

Neely, Infant Son of
C. M. & Birdie Neely
Died Dec. 11, 1903
Age - 7 weeks

Neely, Jacob
1802-1882
Neely, Penelope
1806-1878

Norment, Jacobas Daniel
Dau. of Wm. S. & Mary Norment
Aug. 22, 1836
May 17, 1852

Nunley, Claude
Tennessee
Pvt. U. S. Army
World War I
July 13, 1894
Oct. 27, 1950

Owen, J. Robert
1878-1939
Owen, Dora P.
1882-1950

Ozment, Annie Bell
Wife of Clifford
Ozment
Died at 19 years

Ozment, Clifford
Tennessee
Pvt U. S. Army
Died Jan 31, 1919

Ozment, Dewitt
1889
Ozment, Bertha
1891-1940

Ozment, HessC.
1890-1943
Ozment, Dollie A.
1887-19

Ozment, Jessie A.
1892-1960
Ozment, Shellie B.
1902-1930

Ozment, Mildred
1918-1925

Ozment, S. B.
1902-1930

Parker, Dave
Father
1881-1937

Patterson, W. R.
Born Jan. 6, 1833
July 19, 1905
Patterson, C. Angie
Feb. 29, 1840
Dec. 22, 1897

Patterson, William P.
Son of W. R. & C. A.
Patterson
Dec. 7, 1868
Aug. 23, 1877

Payne, Mrs. N. J.
Wife of J. W. Payne
Oct. 27, 1818
Jan. 27, 1901

Permenter, Baby of
Mary C. Permenter

Permenter, Mary Carson
1922-1958

Peters, J. Bundy
Son of C. H. & S. J.
Peters
Apr. 25, 1877
Mar. 24, 1889

Petty, Deloris Ann
Feb. 13, 1940
July 2, 1971

Petty, Louis Franklin
1937-1964

Pierce, P. E.
Mar. 12, 1858
Mar. 12, 1894

Plunk, Sarah
1864-1911

Pounders, George F.
Oct. 12, 1933
Dec. 13, 1964

Price, John H.
June 24, 1848
July 9, 1908

Pickett, Samuel
Sept. 9, 1893
Aug. 5, 1916

Pursell, LIberty Fowlkes
Son of H. T. & E. E. Pursell
Aug. 5, 1876
Dec. 25, 1878
2 yrs. 4 mos., 20 days

Pursell, Thomas
Connell
Jan. 20, 1907
July 14, 1908

Ragain, John A.
Aug. 28, 1833
Nov. 7, 1885

Ragan, Even J.
Nov. 5, 1875
Oct. 19, 1958

Ragan, Prim
1907-1907
Ragan, Norman
1908-1908

Ragan, Robert
Son
Oct. 12, 1904
Feb. 28, 1927
Ragan, Rosa
Mother
Mar. 17, 1874
Aug. 26, 1919

Ragan, W. E.
1849-1913

Ragsdale, Dr. M. W.
Feb. 12, 1834
July 31, 1879

Rawles, Bedford Forest
1864-1927
Rawles, Elizabeth Apple
1875-1905

Robert, Will Dock
1891-1962
Roberts, Willie M.
1903-19

Roberts, W. M.
1852-1931
Roberts, S. A.
1853-1934

Segraves, Eliza Harret
1846-1922

Segraves, George W.
1846-1906
Age 59 yrs. 3 mos. & 19 days

Segraves, John
Nov. 19, 1871
July 4, 1921
Segraves, Nannie L.
June 14, 1873
July 11, 1920

Segraves, Sheron
Died: Nov. 20, 1893
Aged 85 yrs., 5 mos., 8 da.

Sipes, Ben F.
1885-1942
Sipes, Nealie B.
1890-1927

Sipes, William Arther
1891-1928

Smith, A. G.
June 3, 1829
Oct. 16, 1914

Smith, Abical N.
Wife of Jas. Smith
Jan. 26, 1821
Dec. 21, 1878

Smith, Addie M.
July 14, 1861
Sept. 13, 1935

Smith, Emma B.
Dau. of J. A. &
Pauline Smith
Sept. 23, 1869
July 13, 1882

Smith, Henrietta F.
Wife of A. G. Smith
May 14, 1834
Aug. 18, 1916

Smith, J. T.
Dec. 31, 1816
Nov. 8, 1891

Smith, James W.
Nov. 11, 1877
Oct. 18, 1884

Smith, Joe
1822-1902

Smith, John
Aug. 2, 1825
Aug. 21, 1854

Sullivan, Inf.
Son of W. O. & A. L.
Sullivan
Born & Died
Jan. 24, 1904

Summers, Sallie
Wife of L. J. Summers
Nov. 3, 1853
Apr. 19, 1880

Tarrant, John H.
Sept. 1, 1844
April 21, 1926

Tarrant, M. A.
Wife of J. H. Tarrant
April 26, 1812
Feb. 6, 1902

Tarrant, Nat B.
Sept. 3, 1848
Nov. 5, 1889
Tarrant, Virginia
Jan. 18, 1850
Mar. 10, 1922

Thetford, Sarah B.
1919-1955

Tickle, William R.
1838-1887
Tickle, Nellie
1838-1923

Tisdel, Jesse L.
1876-1918

Tisdel, Lindel L.
Mar. 2, 1904
July 26, 1906

Tisdel, Ron U.
1870-1950

Vaden, Willie A.
Tennessee
Pvt. Btry E. 115 Field
Arty
World War I
Feb. 8, 1896
Dec. 15, 1957

Van Buren, Julia Ann
Amanda
Dau. of W. S. & Mary
Norment
Oct. 15, 1841
Nov. 4, 1853

Vaughn, Joseph H., Jr.
May 22, 1922
May 19, 1923

Wagoner, Elmo
Sept. 20, 1897
Mar 28, 1911

Wagoner, Lizzie
June 10, 1855
May 29, 1895

Walker, G. W.
1864-1938
Walker, Cora
1877-19

Walker, George W.
1849
1930
Walker, Betty J.
1859
1924

Walker, Mrs. Vivian
Died April 2, 1972
69 years 8 mos., 23 days

Ward, Ollie
June 2, 1873
July 10, 1945
Ward, Martha
Dec. 25, 1881
April 19, 1933

Washman, Will H.
Died June 25, 1960
79 years 1 mo. 6 days

Watson, Sylvester W.
1882-1939

Watt, Arthur
1881-1955
Watt, Julia
1881-19

Whitson, James E.
Feb. 22, 1835
June 16, 1855
Aged 20 yrs. 3 mos. 19 days

Whitten, Lorinda
Wife of S. D. Whitten
Dec. 1, 1830
Oct. 16, 1857

Wiggins, Joe E.
1895-1966
Wiggins, Jessie M.
1893-19

Wooley, Baby
Died Aug. 30, 1938

Wooley, Daniel W.
1915-1957
Wooley, Virginia
1920-

Wooley, Ray
1887-1963
Wooley, Fannie R.
1893-1968

Wyatt, Edd R.
1879-1962
Wyatt, Benanna
1879-1963

Wyatt, Francis Remington
1853-1936
Wyatt, Maggie Rickman
1855-1939

Wyatt, James V.
1905-1964

JONES CEMETERY

In 1852, having acquired from the Col. Hardy Murfree heirs of Murfreesboro, Rutherford County, Tennessee, a land grant of some magnitude in West Tennessee, Anderson and Anna Thompson Jones, their children and their slaves left Rutherford County and settled two and one-half miles southeast of what is now Trimble, at Davenport General Store on the present Trimble to Fairview Road in the northeast corner of Dyer County, joining the Mrs. Lizzie Jones Pitts farm, which is part of her Grandfather Jones's original tract.

In their flower garden Anderson and Anna Jones set aside the Family Burial Ground. Some of their slaves buried in the corner of the plot were Lize, Kiz, Isum, and Gran Jones and others.

The Jones descendants are still using this cemetery as a burial ground.

Cawthon, Roy Emmett
Feb. 14, 1888
Oct. 17, 1967
Quartermaster Corps
World War I - Italy
(Duration)
Cawthon, Abbey Jewel House
May 25, 1901

Coffer, Ethel Pitts
May 25, 1887
May 15, 1947

Headden, David P. (Bill)
Jan. 30, 1912
--

Headden, Lucille Pitts
April 11, 1912
Jan. 8, 1968

Hollomon, Ida Jones
July 29, 1864
Jan. 17, 1925

Hollomon, Vella B.
Sept. 10, 1891
Feb. 1, 1911

Hollomon, W. L.
Feb. 5, 1854
Death Date unknown

House, Abbie Jones
May 4, 1843
July 10, 1901

House, Elizabeth Lucille
Inf. of Anderson & Letha
Feb. 1, 1899
Dec. 1, 1899

House, Josiah Stewart
Jan. 11, 1843
Dec. 17, 1915
Pvt. Co. H
Confederate Army
47th Tenn. Inf.

House, Letha Moore
Nov. 13, 1868
Jan. 16, 1938

House, Mary Jane
July 13, 1910
--

House, Will K.
Aug. 18, 1870
Aug. 15, 1938
House, Minnie Watson
Nov. 3, 1872
June 13, 1959

House, William Anderson
Oct. 27, 1876
Oct. 20, 1954

Inman, Annie Thompson
Wife of C. F. Inman
Sept 20, 1873
Oct. 18, 1904

Jones, Anderson
March 28, 1805
Dec. 18, 1872

Jones, Anna Thompson
Feb. 25, 1811
Feb. 22, 1889

Jones, Azariah Lafayette
Son of R. T. &
Elizabeth House
Sept. 28, 1884
Dec. 19, 1885

Jones, Baby Bunch
Daughter of R. T. &
Susanna Laney
Oct. 5, 1892
Sept. 3, 1895

Jones, Elizabeth House
1st wife of Robert T.
Jones
Nov. 25, 1845
Jan. 3, 1886

Jones, Emma Whitsett
April 15, 1885
Dec. 29, 1973

Jones, Enoch House
May 27, 1878
Mar. 28, 1959
Jones, Bessie Harris
June 27, 1879
Jan. 25, 1967

Jones, Ezra
May 29, 1835
Jan. 16, 1884

Jones, Infant of Mose T. &
Emma Jones
Born & Died May 17, 1918

Jones, John William
Son of R. T. & Elizabeth
House
Sept. 30, 1868
Oct. 16, 1870

Jones Joseph Ira
April 2, 1882
Dec. 8, 1898

Jones, Mose Thompson
Oct. 5, 1871
May 16, 1939

Jones, Robert Ezra (Judge)
July 18, 1874
Jan. 3, 1896

Jones, Robert L.
Son of Mose T. &
Emma Jones
July 26, 1908
June 14, 1911

Jones, Robert Thompson
Jan. 9, 1837
Mar. 10, 1920
2nd Lt. Co. H, 47th Tenn.
Inf., Confederate Army

Jones, Susannah W. Laney
2nd wife of Robert T.
Jones
Mar. 1, 1854
Oct. 29, 1922

Lee, Stella House
Dec. 27, 1907
March 29, 1967
Interred in Memorial Gardens
Memphis, Tennessee

Meadows, Elizabeth Jones
June, 1850
April 28, 1874

Meadows, William Latta
Son of Elizabeth J. & Gus
June 1, 1872
Aug. 31, 1879

McIntyre, Mary Sue Pierce
April 19, 1920
Jan. 21, 1975
McIntyre, Jesse Ralph
Nov. 14, 1924
--

Pierce, Katie Jones
Sept. 9, 1887
Jan. 3, 1954

Pitts, Anderson Edward
April 2, 1871
Nov. 22, 1928

Pitts, Andrew Hall
July 8, 1880
Oct. 16, 1954
Pitts, Ora Alphin
Aug. 13, 1882
May 24, 1964

Pitts, Andrew Lafayette
1845
Feb. 22, 1932
Pitts, Isabelah (Ibby)
Jones
Mar. 31, 1846
Oct. 9, 1934

Pitts, Annie Jones
Jan. 2, 1873
July 28, 1967

Pitts, Irving L.
Mar. 24, 1884
Mar. 25, 1952
Pitts, Elizabeth Jones
Sept. 30, 1890
--
Pitts, Margaret Elizabeth
June 4, 1875
Sept. 19, 1896

Taylor, Dora Pitts
April 20, 1869
July 13, 1943

Taylor, Mabel
Inf. Dau. of
W. O. & Dora
Sept 12, 1891
Feb. 3, 1892

Taylor, Dr. William O.
May 16, 1865
Feb. 3, 1927

Tenny, Mose Thompson
Inf. of Mr. & Mrs.
J. W. Tenny
Born & Died April 27

Thompson, Two Infants of
Joseph Thompson
Names & Dates Unknown

Thompson, Jennie F.
Mar. 12, 1877
Dec. 8, 1898

Thompson, Joseph
Brother of Anna T. Jones
April 18, 1813
March 15, 1869

Thompson, Louisa Gauldin
Jan. 29, 1839
Aug. 14, 1912

Thompson, Moses Sr.
May 7, 1820
Aug. 21, 1899

Thompson, Mosie Jr.
Nov. 28, 1882
April 23, 1899

Watson, William Henry
Oct. 15, 1836
Dec. 9, 1891
Pvt. Co. F
Confederate Army
12th Tenn. Inf.
Watson, Mary Jones
Mar. 8, 1848
Apr. 27, 1936

Whitsett, Sara E.
Mother of Emma Jones
June 22, 1852
June 22, 1911

Whitsett, R. A.
Father of Emma Jones
Born - Date Unknown
July 17, 1926

The Meacham Cemetery is four miles west of Newbern off the Lanesferry Highway. Turn left at the Maxey Community Center and stay on the road until you come to a fork in the road. Turn right and the cemetery is hardly one-half mile on the left of the road.

Abbott, Billy A.
Jan. 15, 1933
April 25, 1936

Bailey, J. B.
Feb. 27, 1826
July 10, 1904
Bailey, Mary E.
Jan. 8, 1837
May 21, 1912

Barrett, Frances D.
1950-1967

Buchanon, Edd
June 20, 1896
--
Buchanon, Addie Mae
Dec. 16, 1892
Nov. 21, 1971

Buchanon, Mat
Son of B. B. & A. M.
Buchanon
1890-1892

Burnham, Albert (Father)
1880-1943
Burnham, Willie May (Daughter)
1914-1915

Butler, Lee
1903-1938
Byars, Edward E.
1929-1968

Byars, L.
1909-1941
Byars, Clara O.
1911-1941

Collins, Mark
1908-1964
Collins, Alice
1914-19

Connell, Pollie
Jan. 24, 1904
Jan. 9, 1905
Connell, Joe E.
Aug. 3, 1897
Sept. 18, 1897

Curran, Dixie H.
1924-1954

Davis, Janice R.
1942-1943

DiPriest, Rosie Fair
1912-1956

Fair, Jim
1883-1963

Fair, Rosie Lee
1884-1972

Gleaves, J. B. (Son)
1903-1919
Gleaves, Lela (Mother)
1888-1922

Kirk, Sarah
April 15, 1843
Aug. 3, 1903
Kirk, A. H.
Died Sept. 29, 1883

Moody, Webb A.
1871-1960

Odom, Elmer
1924
Odom, Bertha
1931

Oldham, W. F.
1881-1931

Owens, Jesse W.
1888-1969
Owens, Sarah A.
1904-

Owens, Mattie Lou Doss
May 13, 1837
June 15, 1920

Shaw, Jessie D.
1906-1942

Spence, H. L.
April 3, 1830
Feb. 2, 1903

Spradley, Myrtle
Wife of W. A. Spradley
No Dates

Spradley, William A.
1877-1954

Walker, Charles C.
Feb. 5, 1932
Sept. 18, 1932

Walker, Clyde C.
Sept. 15, 1912

Warden, John F.
1865-1940

Warden, Mary Lue
June 4, 1910
June 2, 1935

Warden, Pauline
1914-1951

Warden, Thomas L.
1905-1973

Wilson, E. L.
July 4, 1870
Feb. 8, 1937

Wilson, Torbit V.
1932-1936
Wilson, Cherry Ann
Died Jan. 4, 1936

Wright, Alexander
Son of S. G. and
Grant Wright
1898-1898

Wright, Grant
1865-1937

Wright, John A.
Tennessee
Pvt. U. S. Army
World War II
June 15, 1901
Aug. 4, 1960

Wright, Sarah Gordon
Wife of Grant
Jan. 4, 1879
Feb. 16, 1919

McCORKLE CEMETERY

The McCorkle Cemetery is located about four miles east of Newbern. In Newbern at the intersection of Highway 51 North and Highway 77, turn east on Highway 77 and travel three and one-half miles. Turn to the left on the third road (a narrow gravel road) from Newbern. Follow the road .8 of a mile and it will lead to the cemetery which is on the right hand side of the road.

McCorkle Cemetery was purchased for $107.15 from H. R. A. McCorkle on October 2, 1871, with J. E. McCorkle and R. W. Lock as trustees. Well kept and neat, the cemetery is maintained by a perpetual trust fund.

Alexander, Harriett Virginia
Wife of J. D. Alexander
Dec. 24, 1852
Nov. 22, 1916

Algea, S. E. "Mother"
Oct. 16, 1829
Dec. 11, 1893
Algea, Carrie "Sister"
Dec. 30, 1859
June 27, 1921

Barkley, Allen
July 20, 1886
Jan. 2, 1959
Father
Barkley, Jenette Pope
Nov. 18, 1886
Dec. 19, 1958
Mother

Blankenship, Phillip
Son of Mr. and Mrs.
J. W. Morrow
Nov. 6, 1912
May 24, 1916

Camper, Jess
1904-1975

Chitwood, Audrain
1921-
Chitwood, Rebecca W.
1923-
Chitwood, Harold L.
Tennessee
PFC Co. A 61 Inf.
S In Div.
VietNam BSM & OLC-PH
July 31, 1949
Feb. 22, 1970

Coleman, James Thomas
Dec. 22, 1882-
July 22, 1964
Coleman, Viola
Mar. 9, 1891-
Oct. 24, 1969

Cotton, Juliet
Grandmother
1812-1896

Crowe, Loyd Lynn
Son of A. G. & P. P. A.
Crowe
April 20, 1916
April 26, 1916

Dickey, Peggy
Dec. 22, 1793
Oct. 23, 1869
Age 75 years

Fair, Clarence
1907-
Fair, Elizabeth
1907-1967

Flatt, Alice R.
Dec. 28, 1888
Jan. 9, 1899

Flatt, Alice Walker
Wife of J. J. Flatt
Dec. 4, 1856
Jan. 4, 1889

Flatt, Carl H.
July 4, 1906
Jan. 3, 1963

Flatt, Dwight, E.
July 18, 1930
Dec. 9, 1936

Flatt, Everett
Son of J. J. & M. V. Flatt
April 30, 1903
Feb. 20, 1923

Flatt, Ewell
1913-1927

Flatt, Dr. F. Alton
Died Oct. 30, 1975
Age 71 years 0 mos. 27 days

Flatt, Franklin T.
Son of F. A & Thelma Flatt
May 9, 1929
May 9, 1929

Flatt, H. M.
1844-1930

Flatt, Ida D.
Died Sept 17, 1912

Flatt, Ida May
Died Sept. 17, 1912

Flatt, J. J.
Oct. 6, 1855
Sept. 27, 1941
Flatt, Mary V.
June 1, 1869
June 17, 1937

Flatt, J. M.
No 'Dates

Flatt, James Gibbons
Jan. 30, 1913
Feb. 3, 1915

Flatt, James Mack
Aug. 31, 1959
Feb. 18, 1971

Flatt, Mamyme
June 12, 1902
Feb. 11, 1919

Flatt, R. D.
Sept. 5, 1901
Mar. 4, 1976
Flatt, Maude Thompson
July 21, 1903
      --

Flatt, William T.
1876-1958
Flatt, Cattie M.
1882-1959

Franklin, Bertha
Dau. of J. J. & E. J.
Franklin
Feb. 26, 1876
Mar. 8, 1876

Franklin, Edwin W.
Son of W. H. & M. J.
Franklin
Died July 17, 1861

Franklin, Eliza J.
Dau. of W. H. & M. J.
Franklin
Died April 20, 1863

Franklin, Manie
Dau. of D. C. & M. B.
Franklin
Oct. 5, 1880
Dec. 2, 1881

Franklin, Martha A.
Dau. of W. H. & M. J.
Franklin
Died June 10, 1845

Franklin, Robert H. A.
Son of W. H. & M. J.
Franklin
Died Oct. 13, 1846

Franklin, Sarah E.
Dau. of W. H. & M. J.
Franklin
Died Oct. 25, 1846

Franklin, W. H.
June 21, 1813
Oct. 3, 1897
Franklin, Margret J.
Wife of W. H. Franklin
Mar. 6, 1821
May 17, 1892

Franklin, William A.
Son of W. H. & M. J.
Franklin
Died Jan. 16, 1854

Frazier, Missouri Elizabeth
Nov. 26, 1839
April 30, 1915

Graham, Albert Newt
1890-1964
Graham, Mabel Estelle
1894-1963

Graham, Paula Joan
June 10, 1936
Aug. 11, 1936

Gregory, John L.
1899-1917

Gregory, John T.
1840-1922
Gregory, Latina M.
His wife
1844-1883

Gregory, Maurice J.
Nov. 23, 1894
Sept. 16, 1961
Gregory, Robyn Jones
May 18, 1886
July 14, 1961

Gregory, Ollie P.
1874-1964
Gregory, Edwin C.
1869-1942

Hall, Helen
Dau. of J. A. & Etta Hall
Mar. 1, 1891
Dec. 2, 1891

Hall, Jonathan
Mar. 1, 1821
Dec. 2, 1904
Hall, Louisa Loumira
Wife of Jonathan Hall
Nov. 26, 1822
July 21, 1896
Hall, Sarah Goodle
Sister of Jonathan Hall
Oct. 22, 1822
June 14, 1894

Harrington, J. S.
1878-1962
Harrington, Grace
His wife
1882-1928

Headden, Lula Morrow
1886-1929

Hendricks, G. M.
Apr. 4, 1840
July 22, 1921

Hendricks, Galen (Sonny)
1927-1937

Hendricks, Gladys
Dau. of W. M. & M. G.
Hendricks
July 4, 1900
Jan. 3, 1906

Hendricks, J. C.
Oct. 4, 1854
Dec. 12, 1887

Hendricks, William M.
1877-
Hendricks, Minnie G.
1877-1945

Hopson, Mary G.
Wife of Wm. Hopson
Jan. 7, 1774
Feb. 8, 1848

Huie, "Baby" Ralph
Son of H. A. &
Sophie Huie
April 1, 1914
June 14, 1916

Huie, Benjamin E.
Mar. 28, 1865
Sept 30, 1866
Huie, James A.
Aug. 11, 1860
Nov. 30, 1872
Children of J. M. &
S. E. Huie

Huie, Howard A.
Nov. 6, 1870
Jan. 3, 1935

Huie, Howard Ewing
July 6, 1907
June 15, 1971
Huie, Joyce Cope
Nov. 11, 1915
    --

Huie, J. A.
1867-1895
Huie, Ora M.
1869-1938
Father & Mother of
Maury A. Huie

Huie, Julius M.
Jan. 31, 1828
Jan. 12, 1911

Huie, Sarah E.
Wife of J. M. Huie
1839-Oct 19, 1893

Huie, Sophie King
Wife of H. A. Huie
July 31, 1882
April 30, 1915

Karnes, Ruth Dale
Dau. of T. M. & Eula
Karnes
1899-1902

Karnes, Thomas M.
1856-1937
Karnes, Eula McCorkle
1872-1922

Kirk, George W.
1871-1917

Locke, Bessie
Dau. of R. W. Locke
Sept. 18, 1880
Sept. 10, 1882

Locke, Mattie
Dau. of R. W. Locke
Sept. 21, 1861
Aug. 6, 1869

Locke, Sarah L.
Wife of R. W. Locke
April 22, 1838
Nov. 3, 1876

McCorkle, A. H.
Died Sept. 26, 1873

McCorkle, A. J.
1834-1922
McCorkle, M. E. Scott
His Wife
1836-1886

McCorkle, Addison A.
Died June 3, 1854

McCorkle, Alexander Franklin
1835-1911
McCorkle, Martha G.
1840-1888
McCorkle, Nancy Pruitt
    -1900

McCorkle, Annie E.
Jan. 17, 1877
Sept. 14, 1934

McCorkle, Annie H.
Wife of G. R. McCorkle
1876-1925

McCorkle, Edwin
Died Jan. 10, 1853

McCorkle, Errett C.
March 6, 1887
--

McCorkle, Gillom E.
Aug. 18, 1872
Feb. 21, 1894

McCorkle, Glen R.
1876-1953

McCorkle, H. C.
Son of A. F. & M. A.
McCorkle
Nov. 26, 1865
Nov. 5, 1872
Age 6 yrs. 11 mos. 9 days

McCorkle, H. R. A.
Nov. 6, 1827
July 1, 1907

McCorkle, Hubert Strawn
1899-1960

McCorkle, Irma King
1886-1956

McCorkle, J. T.
Died Feb. 4, 1899
Age 39 yrs. 3 mos. 8 days

McCorkle, James
1855-1926
McCorkle, Mary
1852-1906
McCorkle, Susie
1867-1888
McCorkle, Leona
1853-19
McCorkle, A. L.
1865-1935
McCorkle, Fannie
1860-19
McCorkle, Edna Mai
1880-19

McCorkle, Jamie
No Dates
McCorkle, Juliet
No Dates
"Our Twins"

McCorkle, Jane M.
Wife of Edwin McCorkle
Feb. 11, 1802
Jan. 30, 1855

McCorkle, Jehiel M.
Jan. 3, 1803
Dec. 7, 1849
Age 46 yrs 11 mos. 4 days

McCorkle, Jennett C. Menzies
Wife of H.R.A. McCorkle
Oct. 14, 1836
Dec. 5, 1903

McCorkle, Joe S.
1843-1924
McCorkle, Mary C.
1844-1891

McCorkle, John E.
Son of W. E. & Una
McCorkle
Sept. 15, 1903
Oct. 2, 1905

McCorkle, John E.
May 17, 1839
Jan. 19, 1924

McCorkle, John Edwin
Nov. 14, 1883
Feb. 27, 1900

McCorkle, Lulu
Dau. of H. R. & M. A.
McCorkle
Dec. 8, 1865
Nov. 16, 1885

McCorkle, Margaret
Wife of Robert
McCorkle
Died Nov. 21, 1848
Age 76 years

McCorkle, Margaret A.
(Cowan)
Wife of H.R.A. McCorkle
Jan. 3, 1833
Oct. 20, 1870

McCorkle, Margaret L.
Wife of D. P. McCorkle
July 15, 1841
Dec. 15, 1862

McCorkle, Mary E.
Aug. 11, 1847
June 9, 1927

McCorkle, Parley P.
Son of R.A.H. & T. M.
McCorkle
Aug. 28, 1845
Feb. 12, 1865

McCorkle, Robert
Oct. 29, 1764
Died 1828

McCorkle, Robert E.
Died Jan. 30, 1861

McCorkle, Mrs. Tennie A.
Oct. 31, 1850
May 27, 1879

McCorkle, Tirzah E.
Died Jan. 7, 1875
McCorkle, Nellie R.
Died Jan. 7, 1875
Daus. of J. S. & E. O.
McCorkle

McCorkle, W. L. A.
Dec. 31, 1847
Jan. 12, 1889
McCorkle, Alice J.
Aug. 18, 1864
Nov. 30, 1900

McCorkle, Welborn Scott
July, 1907
Oct., 1908

McCorkle, William Edwin
1870-1922
McCorkle, Una Pace
1877-1970

McCorkle, Wm T.
Died Nov. 18, 1832

McNail, Robert Edward
Son of R. H. & S. L.
McNail
Dec. 18, 1870
Nov. 3, 1888

McNail, Robert H.
1818-1899
McNail, Susan L.
1835-1923

Miller, John C.
1843-1919
Miller, N. J.
1848-

Miller, Melvin
Son of T. B.& Etta
Miller
1901-1924

Miller, T. B.
1867-1939
Miller, Etta
1871-1949

Miller, T. R. (Dutch)
1897-1951
Miller, Annie L.
1900-

Moore, Annie
Wife of J. L. Moore
Sept. 11, 1867
Feb. 3, 1901
Moore, Clarence A.
Son of J. L. & Annie Moore
Sept. 13, 1899
Oct. 9, 1901

Moore, E. W.
Oct. 10, 1819
Feb. 5, 1884

Moore, M. E.
His Wife
Oct. 30, 1836
Jan. 20, 1902

Moore, E. W.
Broken Stone

Moore, Elsie E.
Dau. of W. F. & S. E.
Moore
Nov. 3, 1886
Jan. 7, 1889

Moore, Fred Ross
Oct. 23, 1923
Oct. 30, 1923

Moore, Ida Parrish
1874-1953

Moore, Joe H.
Tennessee
Sgt. Army Air Forces
World War II
Jan. 18, 1911
Dec. 27, 1968
Moore, Marion F.
Born Oct. 2, 1908
Died --

Moore, Joe L.
Feb. 20, 1864
Jan. 30, 1943

Moore, Josie
Nov. 23, 1854
June 1, 1909
Age 54 yrs. 5 mo. 30 days

Moore, Sallie Belle **Harris**
Wife of J. L. Moore
June 24, 1879
Oct. 14, 1917

Moore, Sally K.
Dec. 18, 1947
July 9, 1972

Moore, William F.
1862-1927
Moore, Bettie
1867-1943

Morrow, Cora
Feb. 6, 1858
Sept. 10, 1931

Morrow, Eley Marion
Dau. of G. M. & C. A.
Morrow
Feb. 28, 1902
Feb. 18, 1904

Morrow, G. M.
Dec. 21, 1851
Apr. 9, 1916

Oliver, Wm. T.
1859-1888

Peevyhouse, Henry
1861-1912
Peevyhouse, Betty
1864-1942

Pope, A. L. McCorkle
Wife of E. P. Pope
1854-1924

Pope, B. Haywood
Oct. 30, 1924
Jan. 26, 1971
Pope, Billie F.
May 14, 1932
    --
Pope. E. P.
1850-1934

Pope, E. P. Jr.
Tennessee
Pvt. Co. B 137 Infantry
World War I PH
June 13, 1895
Oct. 20, 1966
Pope, Myrtle
1896-

Pope, Eugene A.
Mar. 10, 1882
Oct. 27, 1944

Pope, Mary Ann
Sept. 26, 1930
Aug. 4, 1968

Ritter, Micheal Lynn
Dec. 28, 1960
June 22, 1973

Roache, H. H.
Apr. 10, 1862

Roache, Howard
Died April 10, 1862

Roberson, Eudora McCorkle
1883-1905

Scobey, "Capt." Joseph
Dec. 1, 1775
Oct. 3, 1849
Scobey, Elizabeth
Jan. 26, 1782
May 11, 1851

Scott, Clarence
1875-1876

Scott, David E.
Sept. 1, 1853

Scott, Edwin
Died June 13, 1842

Scott, Ella Viola
1880

Scott, Emma Iola
1880

Scott, Ernest, R.
1884-1934
Scott, Sallie O.
1850-1937
Scott, Allen (Tobe)
1844-1897

Scott, Etta Iona
1880

Scott, Infant Dau.
1884

Scott, Infant Son
1882

Scott, J. J.
March 19, 1840
Dec. 2, 1862

Scott, John A.
Died July 12, 1854
20 years 8 mos 9 days

Scott, John H.
Died Oct. 25, 1857
Age 19 yrs 10 mos. 29 days

Scott, Lemuel
Sept. 2, 1804
Sept. 17, 1866

Scott, Maratha
May 28, 1842
April 6, 1870

Scott, Margaret
Wife of Lemuel Scott
Died Nov. 19, 1853

Scott, Thomas Elihue
1845-1904
Scott, Artie Hall
1851-1924

Shelby, E. K.
1845-1919
Shelby, Nancy C.
1848-1904

Speight, Lela Pope
July 29, 1875
July 12, 1953

Speight, Wm. O.
Jan. 6, 1875
Mar. 29, 1939

Sullivan, Infant Son of
W. O. & A. L. Sullivan
Born & Died
Jan. 22, 1911

Taylor, Frank
1865-1955

Taylor, Mattie Lou Troutt
His Wife
1871-1927

Taylor, "Infant"
Born & Died
Sept. 29, 1899
Taylor, Shellie V.
Jan. 19, 1893
Sept 30, 1893
Children of J. F. & M. L.
Taylor

Taylor, John W.
Nov. 25, 1841
Jan. 23, 1905

Taylor, Lawrence K.
Jan. 31, 1908
Apr. 3, 1921

Taylor, Wesley Moore
Son of J. A. & M. W.
Taylor
Dec. 19, 1895
Oct. 24, 1900

Thompson, Jack D.
1879-1957
Thompson, Nettie
1885-1961

Thompson, Thomas
Oct. 9, 1909
  --
Thompson, Mittye Brashear
Aug. 10, 1911
  --

Trimble, Jame L.
Dec. 3, 1831
April 29, 1909
Trimble, Tirzah Clementine
Scott
April 22, 1849
April 14, 1877

Van Eaton, B. L.
Aug. 30, 1834
Mar. 19, 1903
Van Eaton, Lemira
His Wife
Jan. 28, 1838
Aug. 22, 1913

Waddy, E. W.
1835-July 25, 1871
Waddy, G. N.
Dau. of E. W. Waddy
Jan. 6, 1863
Aug. 22, 1871

Wharey, Mrs. L. C.
July 22, 1829
July 1, 1896

Wharey, Legrand
Oct. 31, 1824
June 21, 1862
37 years 7 mos 21 days

Wharey, William D.
June 28, 1849
Feb. 17, 1869

White, Gilbert J.
2nd Lt. 6 Inf. Reple. Regt.
World War I
Oct. 13, 1893
Feb. 8, 1968

Williams, Jane M.
April 14, 1814
Aug. 26, 1850

Willis, Gertrude Pope
Wife of M. V. Willis
1890-1920

Worley, James W.
1857-1931
Worley, Amanda Bechtel
1862-1929

Worley, Joseph L.
1890-1973
Worley, Ludie R.
1902-1964

McCULLOCH PLOT

Travel on Highway 51 South from Dyersburg to Upper Finley
Road. Turn left and go one and one-half miles to the J. W. Anderson
homestead. A relative sent the stone to have refinished and established the authenticity of the inscription. Major McCulloch had a
land grant and settled in the locality in 1826.

McCulloch, Major Alexander
1786-1846

Mount Carmel Cemetery and Church are located five miles east of Newbern. Travel north on Washington Street to the intersection of Highway 77. Turn east on Highway 77 for four and one-half miles and turn left at Lemalsamac Church and travel one and one-half miles; Mount Carmel Church and cemetery are on the left side of the highway.

Mount Carmel was named from the 18th Chapter of First Kings in the Bible. The church is 84 years old. Mount Carmel was organized by Reverend G. W. Evans, in November, 1890. The land was sold on October 14, 1891, by a A. C. Hendricks and wife, Georgia Ann, to the following trustees for the Methodist Episcopal Church South: G. H. Holder, A. C. Hendricks, A. J. Grills, W. W. Haynes, and J. S. Haynes.

The first building was a wooden structure. This building was used as a place of worship until 1923. During the pastorate of Reverend S. B. Morrison, the present brick building was erected over the same spot of ground as the former church.

From the original 2 acres, one and one-half acres of land was laid off on the west side of the church for a cemetery.

Banks, James
Aug. 19, 1849
Dec. 10, 1917
Banks, Elmine
Sept. 2, 1855
Jan. 25, 1904

Baker, Lizzie E.
1901-1957

Banks, Marian Fred Sr.
1892-1956
Banks, Nettie Stephens
1893-1951

Banks, Walter J.
1882-1964
Banks, Bessie G.
1882-1963

Bradford, J. L.
1870-1951

Bradford, John W.
1893-1973
Bradford, Emma P.
1897-

Bradford, Mary F.
1871-1935

Bradford, Ollie Omega
Dau. of
J. L. & M. I. Bradford
Aug. 31, 1911
May 23, 1912

Bradford, Sylvaia Fay
Dau. of
J. W. & EMMA Bradford
1935-1937

Burkeen, Minnie Lue
1870- 1951

Burkett, John M.
May 25, 1844
July 3, 1917

Burkett, Mary A.
July 7, 1854
Jan. 2, 1937

Clifton, Gail Lynn
Nov. 18, 1945
June 8, 1946

Cope, Ira Mitchell
Nov. 10, 1879
Aug. 18, 1949
Cope, Notie Headden
June 1, 1886

Crowder, Anna Lee
G. G. & Fannie Crowder
Aug. 14, 1914
Sept. 25, 1914

Crowder, Floyd
Jan. 17, 1904
Jan. 12, 1919

Crowder P. G.
1856-1942
Crowder, Mary A.
1864-1942

Edward
1942-
Edwin
1939-

Elam, Cleo
1897-1950

Elam, Mant
1863-1946

Forcum, Narcissus Cope
Mar. 22, 1844
April 11, 1931

Glidewell, J. T.
June 6, 1838
Aug. 17, 1904

Glidewell, Mary E.
Dec. 7, 1837
June 2, 1916

Gregory, Pavin
1873-1954
Gregory, Lucille C.
1880-1948

Grills, Andrew J.
July 13, 1847
Feb. 10, 1905
Grills, Luella E.
May 16, 1854
June 2, 1920

Grills, Carl F.
1894-1963
Grills, Mary M.
1892-19

Grills, J. T.
Son of J. D. & M. R.
Grills
Aug. 19, 1901
June 18, 1903

Grills, Leon M.
1915-1916

Grills, Raymond
1902-1918

Grills, Riley M.
1875-1948
Grills, Delia C.
1876-1962

Grills, Sue E. Bright
Dec. 7, 1890
April 3, 1913

Grills, Vivian
1901-

Grills, W. D.
1872-1930
Grills, Minnie
1871-1947

Grills, Niles P.
1877-1952
Grills, Elizabeth Glasgow
1881-1975

Haire, Edd
1868-1935
Haire, Ella
1872-1960

Henderson, Alton
Henderson, Kathleen E.

Hendricks, Albert C.
1846-1930
Hendricks, Georgia A.
1848-1911

Hendricks, Irl
1888-1951
Hendricks, Lillie
1887-1972

Henley, Clarice
Mar. 14, 1915
Aug. 21, 1917

Henley, William N.
1873-1952
Henley, Daisy Cope
1878-1958

Henley, William S.
Feb. 8, 1908
Aug. 24, 1908

Henley, William T.
1850-1932
Henley, Nannie F.
1851-1931

Holder, George H.
May 12, 1839
Feb. 21, 1901
Holder, Mary V.
Nov. 4, 1841
May 28, 1919

Howell, Carolton
Son of
J. S. & G. A. Howell
Sept. 21, 1893
April 16, 1898

Jackson, J. A.
May 20, 1847
April 14, 1926
Jackson Julia
Dec. 12, 1844
Dec. 6, 1917

Jackson, John R.
1869-1932
Jackson, Laura L.
1869-1937

Jackson, Johnny S.
PFC U. S. Army
Dec. 4, 1933
Jan. 12, 1975

Jackson, Manson V.
Kentucky
PUR COL 45 Inf.
World War II
Nov. 29, 1891
Oct. 24, 1964

Jackson, Mary Bell
Dau. of
W. A. & S. J. Jackson
March 14, 1904
Jan. 25, 1905

Jackson, Thomas Wyatt
Sept. 6, 1902
Jan. 25, 1904

Jackson, W. Andy
1867-19
Jackson, Sara Jane
1872-1933

Kilpatrick, Dovie
Dau. of J. H. & Luna
Kilpatrick
Oct. 14, 1898
Feb. 4, 1904

Ladd, W. Thomas
1879-1916

Marcum, Mrs. Ruthie
July 13, 1967
51 yrs. 5 mos. 3 days

May
Infant Son of W. J. & S. E.
May
Born & Died
Feb. 21, 1907

Mayes, Landon
April 16, 1921
Nov. 2, 1938

McNabb, Nickson
1882-1958
McNabb, Vicie
1886-19

Michael, Tim
1863-1928
Michael, Lina Micheal Tuten
1880-1946

Mitchell, Maxine
Dau. of
A. D. & A. B. Mitchell
Nov. 16, 1933
Jan. 27, 1934

Morgan, Clara
1896-1931

Morgan, Ruth Kay
1928-1948

Mullins, Ernestine
Wife of Joe A. Mullins
1921-1942

Neely, F. A.
1871-1946
Neely, Menetia D.
1872-1934

Newsom, C. B.
Jan. 5, 1842
Feb. 17, 1923

Newsom, Daniel
Dec. 1, 1870
April 17, 1962
Newsom, Sallie
July 11, 1873
Feb. 4, 1963

Pardon, Sallie M.
Jan. 14, 1861
Jan. 27, 1940

Redding, A. E.
1865-1928
Redding, Mary C.
1868-1934

Simons, J. B.
April 22, 1826
Jan. 10, 1912

Simmons, J. B.
Jan. 15, 1899
Simmons, Velma
Nov. 5, 1899
Nov. 7, 1948

Simons, Lue A.
No Dates

Smith, Dorris
Dau. of Q. K. & L. R.
Smith
July 3, 1913
Mar. 5, 1920

Smith, George M.
1882-1955
Smith, Gladys Headden
1891-1933

Smith, George W.
1846-1920
Smith, Cornellia D.
1856-1941

Smith, Leland S.
Mar. 27, 1895
Mar. 6, 1962

Spain, J. R.
1872-1906
Spain, Hollice P.
1900-1900
Spain, Wiley L.
1901-1902
Spain, Hubert E.
1904-1904

Spence, George W.
1859-1900
Spence, Allie
1863-1952

Stephens, Morris Ray
Feb. 28, 1932
July 16, 1935

Stephens, R. M.
Nov. 11, 1869
Dec. 7, 1949
Stephens, Alice
Oct. 16, 1871
April 24, 1966

Stephens, Wm. F.
June 1, 1837
June 19, 1911

Symons, Elias Hicks
1861-1939

Symons, Mary P.
1872-1943

Townes, Robert T.
Dec. 23, 1867
Mar. 16, 1955
Townes, Era Grills
Mar. 16, 1875
June 19, 1947

Troutt, Gorah J.
1879-1924

Troutt, H. Thomas
1873-1934
Troutt, Lucy M.
1879-1927
Troutt, Iva Lee
Infant Son

Tucker, Leathy Maud
Dau. of
M. C. & M. J. Tucker
Dec. 27, 1898
Oct. 20, 1901

Tucker, Shirley Ann
Mar. 18, 1957
Mar. 18, 1957

Tucker, William T.
1894-1960
Williams, Edith E.
1891-1963

Tyson, Billy Murph
Tennessee
A2C U. S. Air Force
Korea
July 23, 1933
April 22, 1973
Tyson, Nancy
Jan. 5, 1931

Williams, A.
Jan. 11, 1854
May 20, 1898
44 yrs. 4 mos 18 days

Wilson, Jim
1874-1958
Wilson, Florence
1888-1964

Winters, Ambus Monroe
Died Sept. 20, 1974
64 yrs. 8 mos. 14 days

Winters, Emma A.
1874-1943

Winters, J. W.
1880-1952
Winters, Garland
1904-19

Winters, Millard F. "Red"
Brother
Tennessee
TECS U. S. Army
World War II
April 13, 1907
Jan. 8, 1973

Yates, A. L.
Dec. 23, 1866
Aug. 1, 1904

Yates, Ellen
Wife of J. M. Yates
Dec. 25, 1840
Dec. 30, 1905

Mt. Pisgah Cemetery is located **about fourteen miles from** Dyersburg. Travel Highway 20 for about 10 miles. Then turn right at a sign inscribed "Bonicord". Travel this black-top road three miles until you come to a cemetery on the right marked Mt. Pisgah.

Churchman, Eva Jane
1842-1908

Duncan, Luelle
Aug. 27, 1887
Feb. 17, 1908

Gentry, Kate Churchman
1877-1908

Grogan, George L.
1853-1930
Grogan, Hettie H.
1855-1924

Grogan, Paul
1894-1911

Grogan, Baby
1917

Leggett, Clyde W.
1881-1962
Leggett, Josie G.
1889-1931

Martin, Eva
Consort of W. F. Martin
Aug. 29, 1836
April 21, 1907

Martin, W. T.
Feb. 11, 1836
Nov. 26, 1923

Morgan, R. W.
Nov. 20, 1839
June 20, 1898

Redding, W. V.
May 11, 1813
Dec. 1, 1892

Taylor, E. A.
Sept. 11, 1860
Oct. 25, 1914

Taylor, Nannie
Wife of E. A. Taylor
June 2, 1865
Jan. 21, 1903

Taylor, Susie
No Dates

Webster, J. M.
March 16, 1851
Dec. 18, 1901

The Murray Cemetery is located on the W. P. Murray farm about ten miles from Dyersburg, in the Bonicord territory. Travel on Highway 20 about 7 miles then turn to the right at the Bobby Bell farm and continue on three miles. Located on a hill on the left-hand side of the road, the family burial plot is directly back of the farm house.

Nunn, Issac Bunkner
1900-1931

Nunn, Lucille Easen
1902-1923

Murray, Clyde Walker
Mar. 22, 1899
Aug. 14, 1901

Murray, Johnnie Ernest
Nov. 1, 1897
Nov. 23, 1902

Murray, Will P.
1861-1937
Murray, Lila Parrish
1875-19

Parrish, Cora
Dau. of W. N. & V.
Parrish
April 9, 1863
Sept. 10, 1865

Parrish, W. N.
Aug. 19, 1839
Aug. 28, 1903

Reason, George W.
Nov. 3, 1879
May 25, 1903

Reason, J. S.
Son of G. W. & K. S.
Reason
March 22, 1903
June 1, 1904

NEELY CEMETERY

Neely Cemetery is northwest of Dyersburg. Travel Highway 78 to
second black-top road. The road is known as the Nauvoo-Lennox Road.
Turn left and travel about two miles. The cemetery is on the left
side of a curve.

Akers, Franklin
Dec. 10, 1937
Nov. 26, 1962

Asbridge, Charlie C.
1903-1970
Asbridge, Ora J.
1905-19

Asbridge, Joe
1877-1963
Asbridge, Callie
1879-19

Asbridge, J. D.
1855-1934
Asbridge, Lue Sendy
1870-1932

Asbridge, J. M.
1880-1969
Asbridge, Lee
1884-1950

Asbridge, James Marvin
Died July 21, 1958
Son of George & Wilma
Asbridge

Asbridge, Jimmie B.
T Sgt. U. S. Army
Nov. 19, 1912
May 8, 1971

Asbridge, Robert L.
1888-1945

Asbridge, Thomas Henry
1878-1971

Asbridge, William M.
1878-1961
Asbridge, Etta M.
1887-1957

Banks, Billy Wayne
1952-1975

Barker, Donald Ray
Oct. 11, 1946
Oct. 12, 1946

Barker, Doris June
Dec. 29, 1940
Feb. 8, 1941

Becklehimer, Arthur Moody
May 18, 1927
July 27, 1931

Becklehimer, Otto
Sept. 20, 1880
Jan. 24, 1965
Becklehimer, Dora A.
Feb. 14, 1894

Bennett, Ben H.
1902-1974
Bennett, Mary E.
1899

Brim, Ruby Lucille
Died Dec. 24, 1940
15 yrs. 10 mos. 22 days

Brimm, Claudie E.
July 1, 1911
July 10, 1957

Brimm, Deborah D.
Sept. 12, 1957
Jan. 1, 1966

Brimm, Jerry Odell
June 3, 1907
Dec. 6, 1965
Brimm, Mary V.
Aug. 3, 1911
--

Brimm, Raymond Lynn
Died May 3, 1975
Age 39 yrs. 11 mos. 23 days

Burk, Charles Thomas
PVT U. S. Army
1941-1975

Clemen, Mrs. Mandy S.
Died Mar. 11, 1968
60 yrs. 9 mos. 17 days

Climer, Jimmie
Died Mar. 24, 1968
20 yrs. 10 mos. 23 days

Clopton, James P.
1872-1944

Cooper, Amanda E.
May 16, 1882
Mar. 27, 1959

Cooper, George L.
Jan. 9, 1880
Feb. 2, 1943

Cooper, John N.
1882-1937

Cooper, Lester A.
Dec. 11, 1905
Oct. 12, 1943

Cooper, L. R.
Tennessee
PVT CO D 803 Repl. Bn.
World War II
Oct. 11, 1917
Dec. 13, 1964

Criswell, Albert W.
Died May 3, 1965
Age 47 yrs. 0 mos. 29 days

Criswell, William T.
1865-1939
Criswell, Elizabeth A.
1874-

Davis, James A.
May 7, 1961
May 8, 1961

Davis, John L.
May 7, 1896
April 26, 1963

Dudley, W. D.
Nov. 5, 1861
April 25, 1929
Dudley, Mattie B.
Aug. 20, 1859
Oct. 22, 1921

Dycus, Jesse C.
Tennessee
PVT U. S. Army
World War II
Dec. 9, 1911
April 11, 1965

Eaton, T. T.
Oct. 22, 1876
Eaton, Bell
Mar. 21, 1881
Feb. 25, 1936

Fletcher, Mabel
Mother
1912-1972

Green, Jevain
May 13, 1932
Aug. 11, 1932

Green, Porter
June 9, 1927
May 17, 1934

Hall, Donnie R.
1936-
Hall, Freda T.
1939-

Hall, John A.
1960-

Harber, William James
1882-1956

Harris, Charlie Mucclain
Feb. 3, 1911
Dec. 2, 1964

Harris, D. C.
Feb. 9, 1886
--

Harris, Bertha F.
Jan 31, 1892
Mar. 18, 1970

Harris, Kathleen S.
Sept. 5, 1924
Nov. 12, 1963

Haycraft, Charles
Feb. 19, 1904
Dec. 9, 1967

Hollis, Nathan W.
"Grandson"
1896-1907
Hollis, Ann
"Grandmother"
1840-1913

Holt, Effie Thedford
1888-1932

Hudson, Charley
July 18, 1891
April 24, 1914

Huffine, Marion Wesley
No Dates

Johnson, Doss
Dec. 10, 1883
Mar. 18, 1970
Johnson, Nellie
July 29, 1893
Sept. 1, 1936

Johnson, Herbert Vernon
Son of J. A. & L. B.
Johnson
Oct. 26, 1916
Mar. 20, 1917

Kinc, Buddy Joe
1930-1963

Kirk, Leroy
Jan. 2, 1902
Jan. 1, 1966
Kirk, Birdie
Jan. 31, 1904
--

Kolwyck, Floyd
Sept. 10, 1920
Kolwyck, Laverne
Jan. 12, 1926
April 25, 1970

Long, Lafe
1877-1961
Long, Mary
1890-

Lowery, Sam Earl
1938-1940
Pruitt, Sam Edward
1930-1931

Mabry, Alvis Henderson
Died July 4, 1969
Age 72 yrs. 0 mos. 7 days

Mabry, Cecil
Tennessee
PFC Co. C 331 Inf.
World War I
Sept. 29, 1919
June 20, 1967

Manley, Hulon E.
1917-1920

Marry, M. W.
May 11, 1861
June 9, 1904

McDaniel, Julia W.
Mother
1896-1967

McGuire, Jane
1861-1935

McGuire, T. G.
1851-1934

Miller, Chesley
1894-1919

Mince, M. C.
June 29, 1868
Aug. 23, 1911

Monroe, E. D.
1882-1962

Monroe, Roger D.
Tennessee
SGT. 3 D Bde
101st Airborne Div.
Vietnam
1966-1968
1947-

Morgan, Everett
Nov. 9, 1914
Dec. 11, 1969

Morgan, Henry
Died 1925

Morgan, Ida
Mar. 30, 1911
Aug. 31, 1968

Morgan, Nellie
1889-1933

Nelms, Nancie B.
1917-1919

Palmer, Alvin
1923-1932

Palmer, David C.
1897-19
Palmer, Virgie M.
1902-1963

Palmer, Freano
1925-1928

Palmer, John W.
Nov. 17, 1884
Oct. 24, 1919

Palmer, Stanley
Son
Feb. 9, 1915
Sept. 24, 1926
Palmer, Fanny
Mother
Mar. 4, 1882
April 30, 1920

Peckenpaugh, Jim
Dec. 5, 1896
Jan. 8, 1939
Peckenpaugh, Lessie J.
Sept. 23, 1901
Oct. 15, 1941

Pike, Emmett
1885-1936

Pike, Vicey
1901-1925

Pilkenton, Sidney Wall
Died Jan. 19, 1971
Age 71 yrs 1 mo 29 days

Roberts, James P.
Jan. 21, 1972
Jan. 25, 1972
Roberts, Kevin Lynn
Dec. 10, 1966
May 13, 1972
Roberts, Mary Alice
Oct. 19, 1945
May 13, 1972

Stone, Albert
1917-1965

Stone, Wm. David
1889-1960
Stone, Queen V.
1890-1964
Sykes, C. P.
Father
1905-
Sykes, Hattie L.
Mother
1903-1970

Thedford, John T.
1900-19
Thedford, Lottie May
1903-1969

Thurman, James
Son of J. H. &
Mormie Thurman
Mar. 8, 1921
Feb. 22, 1931

Thurmond, Evelyn C.
1938-1964

Walker, Anita Rose
Died Mar. 11, 1968
Walker, Norvella Ann
Died Mar. 1, 1968

Walker, Mrs. Rosie C.
Died Mar. 11, 1968
62 years. 0 mos. 7 days

Webb, James Millard
Tennessee
Bglr. 118 Inf.
Died Nov. 12, 1932

Whitlaw, "Baby Boy"
Died April 7, 1971
2 days old

NEWBERN CEMETERY (NEGRO)

The Newbern Cemetery (Negro) is located approximately one-fourth of a mile from the intersection of Highway 51 and the Roellen Highway in the City limits. Located on the right of the highway, it contains approximately three acres. The cemetery is divided into three parts. The Methodists are buried on the south of the cemetery and the Presbyterians in the middle. So few of the older graves are marked that it would be difficult to ascertain the year the cemetery was established.

Anderson, Deal
Tennessee
PFC U. S. Army
World War I
June 26, 1888
Aug. 22, 1970

Anderson, Louise
Dec. 29, 1884
Mar. 11, 1971

Atkins, C. P.
Tennessee
PFC Co. A 414 Service BN QMC
World War I
Mar. 24, 1893
Nov. 7, 1953

Atkins, Fostena
Dec. 9, 1884
Nov. 9, 1969

Bailey, Dennis
1871-1936

Bailey, Jame P.
Jan. 5, 1897
Dec. 17, 1967

Bailey, John
1850-1932
Bailey, Sidney
1953-1920

Bailey, Linnie
1886-1902

Bailey, Miller
1849-1913
Bailey, Mollie Tucker
1871-1942

Bailey, Pearlie
Dau. of B. B. &
Tennessee Bailey
Nov. 16, 1897
Jan. 17, 1914

Benson, Ben A.
Died Mar. 12, 1918

Benson, Royce L.
1907-1927

Benson, Sarah A.
1878-1964

Bostic, Annie
1886-1956

Bransford, James
Died Jan. 8, 1924

Britt, Annis Grintee
1906-1938

Britt, Tom
1888-1942

Caldwell, Lou
Mother
1879-1919
Caldwell, Nona Oliver
Daughter
1897-1919

Campbell, Robert
1845-
Campbell, Louiza
1856-1918

Crook, Sylvester
1892-1947

Depriest, Ervin
Died Aug. 19, 1975
82 years

Drane, Bob Joe
Tennessee
PVT U. S. Army
Jan. 18, 1896
Sept. 22, 1969

Draper, Allie
1879-1939

Ellis, Joe Hammie
Dec. 25, 1877
June 1, 1966

Ferguson, Mrs. Aruthur
Died Oct. 21, 1974
86 years

Ferguson, Octavous
Tennessee
CPL Army Air Forces
World War II
Dec. 24, 1919
Mar. 5, 1973

Ferguson, Preston
Died July 29, 1974

Flowers, Laura
Jan. 1, 1856
Feb. 1, 1952

Fowlkes, Odis C.
Tennessee
PVT Co. C 445 Labor BN
QMC
World War I
June 11, 1896
Oct. 31, 1970

Frith, Bill
Sept. 13, 1874
Sept. 13, 1974
100 years old

Fuller, Vennie
1891-1921

Gant, Elnora V.
July 24, 1888
June 23, 1959

Gauldin, Linnie Bell
1932-1936

Goward, Leroy
1876-1961

Graham, Dock
Tennessee
Pvt. 813 Pioneer Inf.
Died Nov. 17, 1941

Hale, Hardee
1898-1934

Hale, Steve B.
Jan. 19, 1906
Mar. 23, 1931
Hale, Katy B.
Born & Died
Oct. 19, 1931

Hamilton, Issac
Feb. 15, 1892
Feb. 5, 1971

Hampton, Hattie M.
1188-1974

Harris, Eula Mae
1917-1964

Harris, Robert
April 19, 1900
Jan. 27, 1970
Harris, Alice
Mar. 20, 1915
--

Haskins, A. L.
1884-1936

Haskins, Bob
1870-1914
Haskins, Jennie
1880-1941

Haskins, Solomon
Tennessee
PVT U. S. Army
World War I
Mar. 15, 1885
Oct. 9, 1963

Herron, Smith
1867-1952

Hill, Rev. R. B.
Mar. 25, 1900
April 23, 1969

Horton, Cornelia
Nov. 29, 1897
Oct. 19, 1935

Jennings, Mrs. Mary
Died Sept 20, 1975
56 years

Jones, Collie
Jan. 27, 1894
Nov. 30, 1963

Jones, Walter
Tennessee
Pvt 802 Pioneer
Div.
Died Nov. 20, 1920

Kelly, Bessie Bailey
No Dates

Kimmins, Johnnie C.
Tennessee
PVT 1447 Station Com
Unit
World War II
Aug. 8, 1925
Oct. 5, 1952

Knight, Minnie
Oct. 11, 1900
Dec. 31, 1969

Lomax Bland
Died March 11, 1934

Mayberry, Robert
1889-19
Mayberry, Miranda
1893-1942

McNeil, Jessie M.
1906-19
McNeil, Marie
1910-1966

Oliver, Eugene
1927-1969

Parks, Alonzo
1867-1936

Pinson, Ben
1861-1948

Pritchard, Green
1869-1934

Pritchard, Hardee
1894-1970

Pritchard, Ola
1891-1939

Rawls, Cherry
April 26, 1927
April 2, 1947

Reed, Elick
Died June 17, 1974
72 years

Rucker, Issac
1888-1963

Saunders, Elizabeth
1885-1937

Scott, Beverly Joyce
Born & Died 1945

Scott, Eddie B.
1870-1951

Scott, Jesse Laura
1906-1934

Scott, Johnnie Melvin
Dec. 17, 1902
Feb. 5, 1967

Sharp, L. D.
Tennessee
PVT U. S. Army
Died Dec. 16, 1931

Shorter, Joe
January 18, 1976
66 years

Singleton, Amelia
1871-1933

Taylor, Jap
1890-1951
Taylor, Lucille Gary
1905-

Tyter, George
Kentucky
PVT
Died July 26, 1910

Walker, Larry
1875-1943

Walker, Ruth
Died June 23, 1974
57 years

Welch, Charles Bernard
Tennessee
S Sgt. U. S. Air Force
Korea
Jan. 4, 1931
June 28, 1969

Wiggins, Alvin
Husband
April 23, 1890
Sept 27, 1973

Wiggins, Wesley Lee
Pvt. U. S. Army
April 19, 1888
Feb. 14, 1975

Williams, Elizabeth
1918-1936

Williams, Joe C.
Tennessee
CPL U. S. Army
Korea
March 12, 1931
Oct. 19, 1972

Wilson, Etta Lomax
Nov. 26, 1880
Dec. 26, 1970
Sister

Wood, Alice
Wife of Wink Wood
1879-1931

Woods, Archie
Born 1899
Died July 11, 1970

Woods, Price
1869-19
Woods, Annie
1885-1944

Wright, Henretta
1866-1947

Wyatt, Flossie
Wife
July 12, 1915
Mar 6, 1969

Oak Grove is four miles north of Dyersburg on Highway 78. Turn right at Oak Grove Church of Christ; cemetery is adjoining church grounds.

Asbridge, Maud
Wife of T. H. Asbridge
1897-1957

Atchinson, Sallie Brown
1920-1924

Babb, Thomas Louis
1931-1968

Baker, Ella
1879-1937

Baker, Richard
1880-1950

Bennett, Benjamin
Dec. 25, 1829
Jan. 23, 1913
Bennett, Mary C.
July 2, 1841
April 11, 1913

Bennett, C. B.
1869-1943

Bennett, C. C.
1875-1902

Bennett, Eliza D.
April 15, 1884
Aug. 10, 1967

Bennett, M. E.
1916-1937

Bennett, Swannie C.
1884-1919

Bennett, W. H.
1891-1937

Blackley, Emmaline
1877-1940

Boals, Virginia
1928-1964

Bursey, J. T.
1860-1940

Canada, Luther E.
1887-1950

Carroll, Josie Lee
1884-1929

Carroll, Lorene
1920-1959

Clark, Ocie F.
1906-1968

Davidson, T. J.
1899-1917

Davis, Louise
1915-1937

Dunaway, Pamela J.
Born & Died July 11, 1957

Epley, Charlie V.
1898-1958
Epley, Anna R.
1902

Epley, Josephine Virginia
Aug. 21, 1916
Nov. 14, 1917

Fisher, J. S.
Son of J. S. & M. A.
Fisher
Aug. 28, 1876
Jan. 13, 1899

Fisher, J. F.
1815-1918

Floyd, Lester W.
Son of A. & Lonie Floyd
Dec. 3, 1907
Jan. 10, 1910

Floyd, Lonie
Died June 27, 1919
Age 87

Fisher, Tommie F.
1927-1936

French, Hugh R.
1887-1937
French, Leata V.
1903-1936

French, Lela Pitts
1895-1932

Garner, Cynthia D.
Died Sept. 6, 1969

Garrison, Albert D.
1892-1955
Garrison, Mary Bessie
1890-19

Garrison, B. D.
1860-1939
Garrison, Lou
1869-

Garrison, Jimmie
1854-1938

Garrison, L. R.
Sept. 8, 1889
Feb. 13, 1969

Gentry, James L.
Oct. 3, 1861
Nov. 16, 1910

Gregory, James W.
Sept. 2, 1877
June 7, 1907

Gurien, Lockey Riggins
1917-1937

Horner, Cora
1879-1964

Horner, Emmie
1920-1923

Horner, Jack
1883-1942

Horner, Jere May
May 3, 1936
Aug. 7, 1936

Horner, Joe
No Dates

Horner, Suely
No Dates

Hummer, William H.
1866-1925

Inman, Eddie Webb
1930-1933

Kennedy, M. L.
1888-1937

King, Lucy Lorene
1919-1932

Knight, Mannie G.
1900-1947

Knox, Eddie L.
Mother
1891-1924

Knox, James H.
1874-1955

Lewis, Elsie
1880-1947

Manley, Lidie B.
1902-1926

Maynor, Antia
1906-1936

Palmer, John Harner
Died Feb. 14, 1964
82 yrs. 3 mos 12 days

Palmer, W. G.
Nov. 10, 1887
April 29, 1923

Parker, Maggie B.
May 10, 1907
June 27, 1943

Parker, Rose E.
1885-1970

Parker, William
1877-1934

Phebus, W. W.
1862-1924

Pleasant, Billie
1923-1929

Pleasant, Cora Louis
Aug. 3, 1916
March 16, 1917

Pleasant, Herman
1894-1955
Pleasant, Nettie
1904-1965

Powell, Thomas Edward
Sept. 29, 1921
Sept. 29, 1921

Pruitt, Asilee
1870-1947

Reynolds, Arthur L.
1904-1942

Roak, Dallan Odell
Died April 5, 1974
65 yrs. 9 mos. 17 days

Rook, W. W.
1889-
Rook Nora
1890-1937

Seaton, Ben S.
Tennessee
PVT Co. F 118 Inf.
World War I
Feb. 13, 1898
April 14, 1963

Seaton, Edgar A.
1889-1966
Father
Seaton L.
1901-19
Mother

Short, Florence
June 27, 1900
June 10, 1929

Simms, J. R.
Feb. 23, 1888
Mar. 27, 1937

Sparks, Maibell
Died July 31, 1975
70 yrs. 6 mos. 25 days

Sparks, W. B.
July 10, 1875
Nov. 15, 1949

Stewart, James D.
Tennessee
PFC 92 Field Art
World War II
Aug. 27, 1917
Feb. 28, 1945

Strawn
Infant Twins
Son and Dau. of
J. P. and Bertha Strawn

Thurmond, Peter M.
Jan. 5, 1862
April 3, 1918

Townsend, Brown Benjamin
Tennessee
PVT 327 Inf.
32 Div.
Feb. 22, 1932

Warren, John
1865-1939
Warren, Sallie A.
1873-1958

Webb, Gracie
1886-1920

Welch, Myra Janice
1933-1935

Whitaker, Sarah F.
Mother
1869-1945

Whitaker, See
Father
1870-1950

Williams, Charley
1868-1931

Wilmatt, Bird
1884-1943

Wilson, J. F.
Sept. 8, 1851
March 24, 1923

Winberry, Robert
1901-1974

PARKER CEMETERY

The Parker Cemetery is located two and one-half miles south of a farm owned by Green Smitheal. He inherited the farm from his mother, Mrs. Annie Laurie Parker Smitheal, who was the daughter of John Parker. John Parker was the son of Daniel E. Parker, Jr., and the grandson of Daniel E. Parker, Sr.

Hart, John M.
Oct. 23, 1821
Sept. 16, 1872

Hart, Nancy
Wife of Gilbert Hart
Oct. 18, 1794
March. 18, 1873

Parker, Daniel E.
June 9, 1789
Dec. 6, 1856

Parker, Mary Wood
Our Great Grandmother
No Dates

Parker, William
Feb.   , 1793
June 21, 1859
About 66 yrs of age
Brother of Daniel E. Parker

Patterson, Lycurgus
No Dates
Confederate Soldier

Smith, Tabitha Caroline
Born in Halifax Co, Va.
July 8, 1876
Sept. 16, 1876

Wood, Elizabeth
Wife of George A. Wood
No Dates
(Note: Sister of Daniel E.
Parker

Wood, George A.
Feb. 2, 1779
April 24, 1852

PETTUS FAMILY PLOT

In 1822, Samuel Knox and Elizabeth Marable Pettus purchased a North Carolina land grant of 708 acres for $1470. from George Doherty on the N. E. Dyer and Gibson County line. They moved their family and 127 slaves from Charlotte, North Carolina. Near their house they set aside a 2 acre plot for the Family Graveyard.

After leaving the Jones Cemetery on the Fairview Road to Rutherford, take first right-hand gravel road to Cool Springs Church. About one-half mile to the south, a grove of virgin oaks keep watch over this unkept resting place of these brave pioneers and descendants.

Bone, Elizabeth
Born 1855
Inf. Dau. of
Emily Pettus and
Dr. Samuel James Bone

Bone, Emily Pettus
April 11, 1827
Nov. 1, 1859

Bone, James Samuel
Oct. 25, 1859
Apr. 26, 1926

House, Azariah Coburn
Dec. 14, 1834
Jan. 27, 1911

House, Mary Ann Pettus
Jan. 17, 1818
Sept. 22, 1899

House, Moses A.
Oct. 9, 1804
Mar. 22, 1873

House, Samuel Knox Pettus
In Memory of
May 5, 1837
Jan. 12, 1876
Capt. ot Co. F
Confederate Army
12th Tenn. Inf.
Interred in Berry
Family Graveyard
1 mile north of Trenton,
Tennessee

House, Tom Knox
Jan. 3, 1873
Jan. 19, 1943

House, William Wadkins
Feb. 14, 1840
Feb. 3, 1862
Pvt. Co. F, 12th Tenn. Inf.
Russell's Command
Wounded and Died in 1st
battle of Civil War,
Belmont, Ky.
Nov. 7, 1861

Marable,, Jamima Glover
About 1764
Oct. 14, 1844

Marable, Matthew
About 1760
Dec. 4, 1830

Pettus, Elizabeth Marable
May 19, 1798
Nov. 6, 1865

Pettus, Samuel Knox
Mar. 8, 1793
Jan. 6, 1866

PIERCE CEMETERY

Pierce Cemetery, Trimble, was donated by Jesse Pierce in 1891. He was the son of John Pierce, pioneer, circa 1825. The cemetery was deeded to J. H. Pierce, R. N. Mitchel, M. R. Hendricks, J. F. Thompson, W. F. Pierce, N. A. Pennington and their successors in office; the fifth generation now being P. B. Moore, V. G. Emge, Hamilton Parks, E. P. Thompson, and W. H. Parks, Superintendent. They deeded it to the Town of Trimble, Tennessee.

There are about 600 graves, 536 markers, 308 recorded to date, and others are unmarked. The oldest marked grave is dated 1845.

Pierce Cemetery is a non-profit organization, maintained by a Parks Trust Fund of $7,000.00 and other donations. The cemetery is located on a hill, with a large cross, on the left side of the road off of Highway 51 N. just before the turn to go to Trimble. The cemetery can be seen from Highway 51.

Allen, Annie H.
Mar. 14, 1893
Nov. 2, 1973

Allen, Thomas B.
Feb. 23, 1871
Dec. 15, 1939

Alphin, Georgie
Wife of B. Alphin
June 12, 1882
Oct. 13, 1914

Anderson, Oberia
April 29, 1920
--

Armstrong, Roisa Lee
1893-1941

Arnn, Billie
1876-1949

Arnn, C. P.
1919-1971

Arnn, George Richard
Son of G. R. & Willie
Arnn
Oct. 5, 1903
Oct. 4, 1915

Arnn, Harry Calvin
Son of G. R. & Willie
Arnn
Jan. 4, 1902
Oct. 19, 1918

Arnn, T. C.
No Dates

Arnn, Willard
Son of G. R. & Willie
Arnn
Mar. 28, 1917
July 24, 1917

Autry, Mrs. Beulah Cornelia
Died Dec. 13, 1973
83 years 8 mos 16 days

Artry, William P.
1878-1947

Bailey, F. M.
1882-1940

Bailey, J. M.
Tennessee
12 Regt. Tenn. Vols.
Confederate States Army
No Dates

Bailey, Minnie Lee
1872-1970

Baker, Ada Wesson
1879-1923

Baker, Clara B.
Dau. of P. M. & L. J. Baker
July 23, 1886
Dec. 23, 1887

Baker, F. M.
No Dates

Baker, Floyce Leland
Feb. 5, 1888
Jan. 11, 1920

Baker, Francis Marion
June 7, 1843
May 7, 1903

Baker, Freddie
Son of P. M. & L. J.
Baker
April 18, 1898
June 17, 1898

Baker, Glenda R..
Dec. 9, 1901
Nov. 17, 1971

Baker, James Leland
Nov. 21, 1912
Nov. 9, 1913

Baker, Juanita
Oct. 24, 1923
Jan. 4, 1938

Baker, Jesse May
Dau. of P. M. &
L. J. Baker
May 19, 1892
Aug. 10, 1893
1 year 3 mos.

Baker, Jo W.
Aug. 15, 1903
May 2, 1971

Baker, Laura
Died Mar. 2, 1903
40 yrs.

Baker, Lottie Wesson
Nov. 14, 1913
Nov. 27, 1914

Baker, M. J.
Wife of R. P. Baker
Died Apr. 14, 1892

Baker, Matilda
Wife of F. M. Baker
June 15, 1847
July 13, 1884

Baker, Perry F.
1893-1957
Baker, Alma E.
1899-19

Baker, Pinkney P.
Mar. 11, 1821
Jan. 14, 1898

Baker, William H.
Dec. 7, 1865
Nov. 14, 1914
Baker, Laura
July 15, 1865
April 2, 1906

Baldridge, Mills, H
1868-1953
Baldridge, Dooly W.
1880-1941

Bandy, J. M.
1860-1937
Bandy, Rebecca
His Wife
1861-19

Barker, Mandy M.
Aug. 29, 1879
Mar. 11, 1968

Barker, Willis H.
Dec. 17, 1872
Dec. 28, 1935

Bingham, Ira
PFC U. S. Army
World War I
Nov. 16, 1894
Aug. 28, 1975

Bingham, Laura
Dec. 25, 1889
Nov. 24, 1963

Bingham, Tennessee
1872-1911

Bishop, Ivory C.
1903-
Bishop, Clara M.
1905-1972

Blair, J. R.
Nov. 19, 1836
Dec. 30, 1891

Boyd, Delbert N.
1897-1923

Boyd, F. M.
1865-1929
Boyd, Annie L.
His wife
1868-1949

Boyd, William H.
Oct. 14, 1887
Oct. 17, 1918
Co. M 46 Inf.

Brown, James
Illinois
PVT ICL
323 Serv. BN OMC
February 1896
July 29, 1935

Brown, Jessie
Dec. 24, 1881
May 9, 1956
Brown, Burie
Aug. 8, 1892
Feb. 19, 1960

Brown, Katie
1888-1955
Brown, John
1885-1956

Brown, Mrs. Nettie
Died April 2, 1976
57 yrs.

Bunn, Thomas J.
Sept. 28, 1890
Feb. 12, 1971
Bunn, Florence A.
Sept. 8, 1891
Jan. 19, 1965

Butler, Johnnie B.
Son of E. D. &
O. M. Butler
June 26, 1910
Aug. 20, 1911

Butler, W. M.
July 8, 1836
Aug. 24, 1924

Butter, T. B.
1838-1876
Butter, Susan E.
His wife
1850-1876

Calvin, Young C.
Father
Dec. 17, 1850
Dec. 11, 19o7
Calvin, Mary Frances
Mother
Feb. 22, 1858
Feb. 16, 1904
Calvin, Elvaretta
Sister
DEc. 29, 1885
Nov. 24, 1906

Cantlon, Jacob
June 25, 1844
May 12, 1909

Chambers, Frelon C.
1898-1974

Chandler, Richard T.
1865-1944

Cole, Columbus P.
July 23, 1895
Jan. 26, 1950

Cole, Kate
Oct. 10, 1838
June 10, 1919

Coleman, Abbie M.
1895-1969
Coleman, Marion
1890-1962

Collins, George
Tennessee
SGT Field Artillery
World War II
Dec. 3, 1918
July 20, 1949

Collins, R. H.
1858-1933

Cox, Minnie Pierce
1886-1953

Cryer, Pauline
June 6, 1925
Sept. 11, 1925

Cummings, Paul
1912-1924

Daniel, Dorthie
Dau. of John Daniel & Wife
Dec. 4, 1922
July 13, 1923

Davis, Mattie Elizabeth
Wife of V. Davis
Sept. 12, 1883
Oct. 30, 1914

DeVasier, Nancy May
Jan. 3, 1901
Feb. 20, 1916

DeVasier, Polly Ann
1888-1968

Dew, Flora L.
Wife of P. E. Dew
Aug. 10, 1910
Sept. 11, 1940

Edwards, Allen
Mar. 2, 1902
Mar. 4, 1904
Edwards Mary
Aug. 19, 1900
June 28, 1904

Edwards, Moses A.
Mar. 12, 1862
Apr. 28, 1906
EDwards, Hellen L.
Aug. 12, 1871
May 16, 1904

Emge, Annette
Baby
1931-1932

Epperson, T. J.
1864-1933
Epperson, Azzie
1869-1952

Faulkner, Cora Bell
Wife of L. F. Faulkner
May 15, 1876
Jan. 22, 1923

Faulkner, Dora
Wife of D. Faulkner
Oct. 15, 1863
Nov. 10, 1883

Faulkner, L. F.
Nov. 14, 1873
Jan. 6, 1952

Faulkner, Louisa Bell
June 19, 1891
July 16, 1956

Ferguson, Peaner B.
Aug. 20, 1916
June 13, 1917

Fielder, Johney J.
Son of R. J. & S. E. Fielder
May 16, 1878
May 29, 1892

Fielder, Lillie O.
Dau. of R. J. &
S. E. Fielder
Dec. 28, 1876
Feb. 18, 1888

Fields, D. R.
Sept. 18, 1838
June 30, 1911

Fields, Ellen
1876-1905

Fields, Susan G.
Wife of
Daniel R. Fields
April 1, 1843
Jan. 15, 1888

Fisher, Lee Orion
Son of R. O. & E. I.
Fisher
Died Sept. 17, 1903
5 mos. 25 days

Fisher, Robert Lynn
July 20, 1907
Aug. 29, 1921

Fisher, Robert Orgen
1876-1947
Fisher, Effie Irene
1880-1962

Fortner, Mrs. Georgia
Mar. 3, 1886
Aug. 15, 1931
Age 44

Freeman, Obie Bowl
July 23, 1901
Dec. 17, 1904

Gaines, Fred
Arkansas
PVT ICL 356 Inf.
39 Divison
Died June 8, 1930

Gaines, James K
1848-1923
Gaines, Lydes G.
1858-1916

Gamble, Rev. Henry C.
Dec. 7, 1847
Sept. 2, 1908

Gamble, Sarah C. Morefield
Wife of Rev. H. C. Gamble
July 27, 1861
Dec. 4, 1915

Gammon, J. G.
No Dates

Gammon, J.R.C.
No Dates

Gammon, Joanna
Born Sept. 12, 1871
Died June 13, 1889

Gammon, Susan E.
Dau. of J. R. & L. Gammon
Died July, 1881

Gatlin, C. S.
1881-1970
Gatlin, China
1884-1954

Gatlin, Carl
Son of
J. A. Gatlin and Wife
Mar. 1, 1920
Mar. 8, 1920

Gatlin, Fate
1888-1957
Gatlin, Pavie
1892-19

Gatlin, Jodie A.
1884-1938
Gatlin, Nettie E.
1895-

Garrett, Oscar A.
Feb. 26, 1867
May 8, 1911
Garrett, Rebecca Henry
His Wife
April 7, 1858
Mar. 2, 1914

Gauldin, M. A.
Oct. 20, 1856
Feb. 26, 1927
Gauldin, Luna D. Pierce
His Wife
April 6, 1863
Jan. 25, 1936

Gauldin, Stella E.
Wife of J. H. Gauldin
Mar. 4, 1887
April 23,1908

Glasgow, Alburn
1873-1959
Glasgow, Zona
1879-1949

Glasgow. George W.
Feb. 24, 1870
Nov. 26, 1948
Glasgow, Cassie A.
Sept. 9, 1875
June 26, 1947

Glasgow, Thelbert
June 13, 1905
June 20, 1906

Glasgow, Uriel
April 13, 1910
Jan. 28, 1913

Godwin, Tobie William
Son of D. & E. B. Godwin
Aug. 25, 1915
Aug. 7, 1917

Goodwin, George W.
Dec. 11, 1852
Mar. 18, 1883

Green, Sallie
Wife of Mertie Green
Sept. 1, 1878
Sept. 8, 1913

Griffin Eunice
1884-1963

Griffin, George
1880-1967

Griffin, Leslie L.
Apr. 21, 1899
Feb. 27, 1920

Gunnells, Addie Bell
Dec. 22, 1898
Gunnells, Campbell, S.
Aug. 22, 1891
Feb. 22, 1963

Gunnells, Edward
March 28, 1921
April 26, 1933

Gunnells, Wm. Thomas
Nov. 28, 1915
Gunnells, Hattie Lean
Aug. 22, 1913
Sept. 30, 1954

Halford, J. G.
Feb. 27, 1924
Oct. 15, 1948

Halford, William
1881-1961

Hargett, Alfred L.
Tennessee
CPL 117 Inf.
World War I
Mar. 16, 1898
Nov. 5, 1966

Harper, Angie
1887-1934

Harper, Nancy J.
Wife of A. Harper
July 14, 1852
April 12, 1884
Reece, Mary M.
Wife of C. M. Reece
Feb. 15, 1824
Mar. 22, 1884

Harris, J. H. "Sut"
1881-1969

Harris, Lucille
1890-1957

Harrison, Clarence
1888-1949
Harrison, Zonie
1889-

Henderson, Fred
1880-1954

Hendricks, M. R.
Sept. 12, 1836
Sept. 6, 1909

Hendricks, Sallie Luetta
Dau. of M. R. &
Sallie E. Hendricks
Apr. 13, 1875
Oct. 2, 1886

Hinson, Ima Baldridge
1915-1969

Hinson, Kerry Eugene
Son
1961-1961

Hodge, Ola May Mitchell
Wife of C. H. Hodge
May 14, 1878
Dec. 2, 1912
34 yrs. 6 mos. 18 days

Hollomon, Paul F.
1899-1965

Hollomon, Wm. A. "Billy"
1930-1965

Hooper, Dan
Aug. 25, 1897
Feb. 15, 1909

House, Don William
Died Feb. 22, 1972
31 years 6 mos. 25 days

Hubbs
Son of
J. M. & E. Hubbs
Born Oct. 4, 1869
Sept. 26, 1880

Hubbs, James M.
Jan. 7, 1842
May 16, 1881

Hunter, Bennie
Son of C. D. & S. J.
Hunter
May 2, 1903
Sept. 31, 1904

Jacobs, John L.
Oct. 12, 1841
Sept. 13, 1905

Jacobs, Johnnie
Dau. of J. L. & S. J.
Jacobs
Sept. 7, 1876
Aug. 24, 1910

Jacobs, Mabel Terry
1887-1949

Jacobs, Sarah J.
June 9, 1845
Sept. 22, 1906

Jacobs, William Joe
June 10, 1885
July 9, 1918

Jacobs, William T.
Oct. 28, 1868
Feb. 5, 1949
Jacobs, Belle B.
July 18, 1870
Mar. 19, 1949

Jetton, L. B.
Wife of
R. L. Jetton
Oct. 22, 1863
Mar. 6, 1892
Jetton, Robert L.
July 1, 1858
May 9, 1900

Kee, John J.
Tennessee
PVT Co H 14 Regt
Tenn CAU
Confederate States Army
1845-1919

Kenndy, Cheatum
June 15, 1866
   --
Kenndy, Tennie
Dec. 1869
Dec. 26, 1915

Kirk James F.
1857-19
Kirk, Mary J.
1860-1936

Ladd, Lela D.
Dau. of
F. P. & M. C. Ladd
June 25, 1881
July 7, 1886
Ladd, Infant
Dau. of
F. P. & M. C. Ladd

Lankford, Tom
1887-
Lankford, Hattie
1888-1963

Lewis, Aline
Dec. 24, 1930
June 27, 1970

Mathenia, A. J.
May 10, 1848
Mar. 20, 1913

Matheny, Bell
1878-1956

Matheny, Buster
Son of A. J. and Z. B.
Oct. 11, 1905
Oct. 29, 1905

Matheny, Homer L.
June 4, 1901
Apr. 26, 1974
Matheny, Fannie
Feb. 9, 1898
   --

Matheny, Maggie Kee
Dau. of Earl and Monnie
July 15, 1914
Aug. 29, 1914

Mathis, William A.
1881-1958

McCorkle, Burlah
1898-1969

McCorkle, Caroline
1853-1925

McCorkle, Fraseanna
Wife of Doc McCorkley
April 10, 1843
June 1, 1913

McCorkle, George
1890-1944

McCorkle, James
1876 1898

McCorkle, John
Tennessee Pfc.
U. S. Army
World War I
April 17, 1887
Dec. 23, 1961

McCorkle, Jordon
1843-1916

McCorkle, Maggie Maxwell
Aug. 25, 1883
June 25, 1952

McCutchen, Leah
May 15, 1828
Mar. 9, 1909

McKee, Abner
1865-1911

McKinnon, Alene
April 25, 1904
May 5, 1972

McKinnon, L. A.
1871-1955
McKinnon, J. M.
1882-1932

McKinnon
Our babies
1894-1898
Children of
J. M. & L. A. McKinnon

McManis, Ella
Wife of
L. W. McManis
Feb. 3, 1888
July 31, 1916

McManis, Eugene
Nov. 11, 1915
Jan. 15, 1916
McManis, Howard
Feb. 14, 1914
Feb. 17, 1914
Sons of A. & Sudie
McManis

McManis, Evie
1905-1952

McManis, Ivy
Son of
A. & Cora McManis
June 19, 1898
Apr. 17, 1916

McManis, Jas. Leonard
Feb. 17, 1936
May 27, 1938

McManis, Jas. Otis
1910-1936

McManis, Joe S.
1876-1928
McManis, Martha F.
1876-1929

McManis, Lemuel Wilmington
Died Sept. 10, 1975
93 yrs 8 mos 29 days
(Johnson Funeral Home marker

McManis, Luther
1893-1948

McManis, Nathan
April 13, 1839
Jan. 17, 1910
McManis, Frances
His wife
Mar. 4, 1846
Feb. 15, 1910

McManis, Paul
1905-1959

McManis, Rovean Henderson
Dec. 18, 1928
Jan. 10, 1952

McManis, Toney
1910-1971
McManis, Lura
1915-

McManis, Will J.
1870-19
McManis, Ida L.
1880-1947

McMillon, E. M.
June 14, 1834
May 9, 1899

McTurnan, Julious
May 12, 1863
Oct. 19, 1929

Meadows, Legreta Jane
Mar. 17, 1949
April 2, 1949

Meeler, Myrtle Guin
Dau. of P. E. &
E. L. Meeler
Oct. 22, 1915
Nov. 19, 1918

Millrany, J. D.
Sept. 11, 1849
Milraney, Lou C.
His wife
July 18, 1917

Millrany, Martha G.
Feb. 27, 1855
Dec. 16, 1910

Mitchell, L. C.
July 3, 1825
May 4, 1902

Mitchell, Mary A.
Wife of L. C. Mitchell
Nov. 23, 1825
Aug. 6, 1891
Reed, Amanda
Mar. 20, 1821
May 21, 1890

Moore, Ella W.
1867-1958

Moore, Forrist
Dau. of L. W. &
Maud Moore
Mar. 18, 1905
Nov. 22, 1905

Moore, Howard
1887-1956

Moore, James Gordon
1907-1961

Moore, Sgt. James Hamilton
1921-1944

Moore, James Hamilton, Sr.
1885-1946

Moore, Jess R.
1890-1966

Moore, Joel H.
1861-1948
Moore, Nettie
1867-1932

Moore, W. D.
1858-1939

Morefield, Elizabeth
Wife of John Morefield
Mar. 5, 1823
Mar. 25, 1906

Morris, George P.
Feb. 6, 1917
Feb. 14, 1917

Morris, Lee
1896-1959

Morris, Otis B.
Dec. 5, 1914
July 9, 1916

Morris, Ray O.
April 6, 1906
July 9, 1973
Father
Morris, Sadie C.
Mar. 30, 1909
    --
Mother
Morris, Emmett
Jan. 20, 1927
Jan. 31, 1929
Son

Morris, Willice
Son of T. S. & M. B.
Morris
May 9, 1903
Mar. 14, 1913

Moss, James Davison
Tennessee
S2 USNR
World War II
Aug. 9, 1916
Sept. 20, 1964

Moss, Solon P.
Feb. 19, 1855
Oct. 25, 1907
Moss, Sarah F.
Mar. 10, 1855
April 17, 1941

Moss, Walter
Son of S. P. &
S. F. Moss
Oct. 4, 1884
Nov. 9, 1921

Nichols, Gertrude Elizabeth
Dau. of
R. H. & W. M. Nichols
Nov. 9, 1902
Feb. 10, 1905

Nichols, Grace Audry, Dau. of
R. H. & W. M. Nichols
Jan. 19, 1906
Nov. 6, 1906

Nichols, Lorene
Dau. of R. H. & M. C. Nichols
Jan. 19, 1906
Nov. 6, 1906

Nichols, Mamie, Dau. of
R. H. & W. M. Nichols
Nov. 16, 1903
Jan. 31, 1905

Nichols, Oscar Henry
Son of
R. H. & W. M. Nichols
Dec. 3, 1904
Feb. 14, 1908

Nichols, R. H.
1859-1918
Nichols, Maude, His Wife
1871-1941

Nool, Amanda M.
Mar. 2, 1849
June 23, 1898

Page, C. F., Father
1869-
Page, Katie
1906-1968

Pannell, Samuel
Nov. 20, 1839
Mar. 22, 1922
Pannell, Mollie, His Wife
May 10, 1850

Parker, J. A., Father
No Dates
Parker, Anna
Mother
No Dates

Parker, Julia
Wife of M. Parker
Aug. 1, 1865
July 21, 1917

Parks, Carolyn Smythe
1894-1974

Parks, Dora
Mother of Jessie,
William and Eva Parks
Mar. 21, 1853
Mar. 22, 1917

Parks, Emerson Etheridge
1857-1942

Parks, Jessie
Son of
Emmerson & Dora Parks
Born, Sept. 10, 1883
Died, Feb. 16, 1892

Parks, Rachel Bird
Nov. 21, 1867
Dec. 8, 1933

Patrick, Emmie
1897-1942

Pennington, Newton A.
Co. G, 27 Tenn Inf.
C.S.A.
June 12, 1840
Mar. 10, 1919

Petty, Elbert Sr.
1901-1950

Pierce, Ann Eliza
Wife of J. H. Pierce
Aug. 22, 1846
July 22, 1909

Pierce, "Infants"
Children of J. H. &
Anliza E. Pierce
No Dates

Pierce, Claude H.
1888-1950
Pierce, Ethel Daniels
1893-1927

Pierce, Essex
1847-1919
Loyal Slave & Servant of the
Pierce Family

Pierce, Felix
Aug. 20, 1821
June 26, 1900

Pierce, Gasander
Wife of J. T. Pierce
July 1, 1819
Nov. 18, 1860
41 yrs. 14 mos. 17 days

Pierce, J. B.
1916-1953

Pierce, J. H.
Died Oct. 25, 1903
67 years 2 mos. 2 days

Pierce, Jana A.
Wife of S. H. Pierce
Jan. 20, 1867
April 29, 1899

Pierce, Jesse
Feb. 17, 1826
Aug. 9,1896

Pierce, Jesse
Feb. 17, 1826
Aug. 9, 1896
Pierce, Susan
Wife of J. Pierce
May 2, 1831
June 1, 1877
Pierce, Joseph H.
Mar. 23, 1857
April 23, 1858
Pierce, Emmer T.
Aug. 6, 1870
Feb. 17, 1873
Son & Dau. of
J. & S. Pierce
Pierce, John C.
Dec. 12, 1859
Aug. 30, 1865

Pierce, Jesse Essex
1881-1906

Pierce, John
1791-1854
Father of Jessie, Jerry,
Morris, Felix, Tom, Susan
Pierce

Pierce, John A.
April 17, 1864
Aug. 12, 1919

Pierce, John H.
Son of T. J. &
Catherine Pierce
Born Aug. 1850
Died Oct. 1879
29 yrs. 2 mos.

Pierce, Lou W.
1881-1969

Pierce, Mary A.
Dau. of J. H. &
Anliza Pierce
Oct. 28, 1864
Mar. 8, 1884

Pierce, Martha
Born May 25, 1838
Died Aug. 25, 1845

Pierce, Mattie Franklin
Dau. of
Ollie & Mattie Pierce
June 7, 1905
June 15, 1905

Pierce, Mollie J.
Wife of W. F. Pierce
May 2, 1840
Mar. 2, 1904
Pierce, W. F.
Apr. 11, 1840
Oct. 18, 1917

Pierce, Neal
Tennessee
PVT 48 Co 158
Depot Brid.
World War I
June 1, 1895
Dec. 28, 1964

Pierce, Ollie
1868-1935

Pierce, Rosaline P.
Dau. of J. H. &
Anliza Pierce
Dec. 14, 1874
July 19, 1879

Pierce, Ray
1889-1968

Pierce, Sally Park
1889-1959

Pierce, Samuel H.
Feb. 6, 1869
April 18, 1912

Pierce, Thomas A.
1869-1934
Pierce, Bertha T.
1881-1969

Pierce, Thomas J.
Apr. 18, 1818
Jan. 23, 1853
34 yrs. 9 mos. 5 days

Pierce, W. Walter
1877-1950

Pierce, William Franklin
Feb. 10, 1907
June 15, 1972

Pierce, Willis
Dec. 10, 1896
Feb. 5, 1972

Poiner, Hiram C.
1867-1953

Pollock, J. H.
Mar. 2, 1831
May 16, 1900

Pollack, Sarah E.
Wife of J. H. Pollock
Apr. 16, 1830
July 18, 1896

Powell, Benjamin F.
May 30, 1884
Apr. 9, 1959
Powell, Matilda
Nov. 23, 1885
Nov. 23, 1965

Powell, Betty P.
Dec. 4, 1872
Nov. 12, 1971

Powell, Delores
Jan. 9, 1923
May 22, 1971

Powell, James Robert
Feb. 23, 1916
Feb. 27, 1970

Pruett, Bertha Boyd
1889-1919

Renfro, Eddie A.
Oct. 27, 1905
--

Renfro , Odie S.
Dec. 14, 1904
May 24, 1960

Riley, James F.
1916-1933

Rogers, Rollie E.
1901-1955

Rutherford, John W.
Tennessee
PFC 3S Pioneer Inf.
World War I
Jan. 29, 1895
June 5, 1969

Sharp, Clara May
Aug. 22, 1940
Mar. 20, 1941

Sharp, John S.
Nov. 5, 1966
76 yrs. 4 mos. 16 days

Sharp, Pearl
1894-1968

Sharp, Tom
1891-1986

Simmons, Bettie E.
1869-1952

Simmons, Ira T.
1885-1965
Simmons, Della M.
1887-1971

Simmons, Ralph H.
1918-1936

South, Evie
1912-1966

Spain, Aubry
1884-1966

Spain, Mitchell
Died Jan. 17, 1971

Stewart, Charlie
1916-1958

Stewart, George
1885-
Stewart, Cora
1894-1957

Stewart, Jimmie
1946-1966

Sturdivant, B. F.
1924-1969

Sturdivant, James E.
Sept. 22, 1896
Aug. 8, 1972
Sturdivant, Ora C.
July 19, 1894
    --

Sullivan, Flavius J.
Tennessee
Sgt. Co. F 4 Rgt.
Tenn. Inf.
Spanish American War
Jan. 22, 1876
June 16, 1961

Sullivan, Willie Pierce
Oct. 30, 1882

Swift, Annie Lee
1944-1970

Swift, Edward
1900-1956

Swink, Ora
Dau. of T. J. &
S. L. Swink
Aug. 7, 1879
Feb. 3, 1906

Swink, T. J.
Aug. 27, 1849
Nov. 14, 1900
Swink, S. L.
Dec. 25, 1848
A½ril 30, 1904

Tate, Bennie G.
Died Jan. 7, 1974
73 years 6 mos. 5 days

Tate, Early B.
Better known as "Curly"
1900-1916

Tate, Verna Rogers
Sept. 11, 1887
Jan. 30, 1970

Terry, Joseph I.
1857-1915
Terry, Clementine
1857-1919

Thomas, Elizabeth
Died 1910

Thomas, R. V.
1875-1923

Thomason, Floyd D.
1903-
Thomason, Earlie May
1903-1960

Thompson, Flora M.
Dau. of S. F. &
M. L. Thompson
March 30, 1882
March 30, 1884

Thompson, Infant Dau. of
S. F. & B. B.
No Dates

Thompson, Leland William
May 13, 1898
July 21, 1952

Thompson, Lizzie May
Dau. of
S. F. & M. L. Thompson
Aug. 31, 1876
Oct. 17, 1891
15 yrs. 1 mo. 17 days

Thompson, Mary Lou
Wife of S. F. Thompson
Oct. 18, 1857
June 4, 1897

Thompson, S. F
May 5, 1852
Dec. 22, 1900
48 yrs. 7 mos. 7 days

Thompson, Virginia Lou
Dau. of W. C. &
Bertie Thompson
Feb. 2, 1915
Dec. 17, 1919

Thompson, William C.
1884-1964
Thompson, Bertie L.
1884-1960

Tillman, Bert
April 22, 1894
Sept. 25, 1895

Tillman, Lela
July 18, 1881
Oct. 10, 1895

Tillman, M. I.
Wife of W. J. Tillman
Oct. 19, 1856
Aug. 28, 1908

Tillman, W. J.
Mar. 31, 1858
Nov. 11, 1917

Trout, Roy A.
1901-1960
Trout, Lula F.
1904-

Trout, Stella
1888-1936

Tulley, B. Altas
Nov. 22, 1900
Oct. 14, 1924

Tulley, L.
1903-1932

Tulley, Reggie
Aug. 4, 1909
Feb. 14, 1930

Tummins, Caroline
April 11, 1858
April 24, 1931

Vawter, Herbert H.
Son of Louis and Nina
Feb. 24, 1906
June 24, 1906

Via, Ethel May
Mar. 2, 1878
May 10, 1888

Via, Mary Jane
Mar. 23, 1867
Mar. 24, 1894

Via, S. H.
Feb. 17, 1843
June 3, 1903

Vinson, James D. B.
Mar. 23, 1868
July 22, 1916
49 years 3 mos. 29 days

Wagner, Elizabeth
1843-1929

Wagner, M. H.
Jan. 8, 1830
Feb. 2, 1904

Walker, A. E.
Wife of W. P. Walker
Dec. 2, 1846
Mar. 6, 1884

Walker, Mose
1903-1958

Walker, W. P.
Nov. 21, 1835
Feb. 27, 1888

Wallace, J. T.
1873-1926

Wallace, James
Dec. 1, 1874
May 11, 1914
40 years 50 mos 10 days

Wallace, Joe
Son of I. & M. A.
Wallace
Oct. 3, 1883
July 27, 1904

Wallace, L. D.
Mar. 7, 1884
July 16, 1912

Warren, C. Franklin Jr.
Aug. 18, 1957
Oct. 2, 1957

Warren, J. W.
Feb. 19, 1904
Mar. 22, 1928
Warren, Duffie
His Wife
Jan. 16, 1904
Feb. 19, 1925

Watkins, Nettie Lou
Feb. 22, 1886
Dec. 15, 1918

Webb, Lular Ireen
Dau. of Mr. & Mrs.
George Webb
Dec. 29, 1913
July 28, 1916

Wesson, Allen B.
1882-1972
Wesson, Mary Z.
1878-1971

Wesson, Mancel E.
1889-1944
Wesson, Gladys E.
1894-1929

Wesson, William J.
Dec. 17, 1833
Mar. 25, 1918
Wesson, Livonia L.
Mar. 17, 1847
Mar. 6, 1921

White, Gleen, Jr.
July 11, 1930
Sept 1, 1971
White, Dorris
--

White, Vance Oneal
Dec. 26, 1900
April 17, 1901

Whitsitt, Bettie Lou
Dau. of Richard &
Bertha Whitsitt
Born & Died
Dec. 21, 1917

Whittle, Wm. H.
1905-1948

Wilson, Lora V.
1864-1957

Witherington, Minnie J.
Wife of Dr. R. L.
Witherington
1878-1912

Wright, James Richardson
January 17, 1976
67 yrs. 5 mos 2 days

Wright, Kenneth Owen
Nov. 1, 1955
June 3, 1975

Wright, Reuben Carlos
June 22, 1928
Oct. 5, 1958

Wright, Weather
1898-1960

Yates, James M.
Nov. 9, 1892
June 5, 1916

Woodmen of World
Memorial

Young, George E.
Tennessee
TECS TRP B 16 CAU
Recon SQ
World War II PH
Jan. 21, 1919
May 17, 1960

PLEASANT HILL CEMETERY

Pleasant Hill Cemetery is located six miles west of Dyersburg off of Highway 20. Turn north at the Methodist Church in Finley. Travel north one-hlaf mile to the Ellis Pritchett Home. Then travel east about 300 yards on a gravel road. Turn left on first gravel road until you reach top of a hill to a dead-end fence. Walk one-fourth mile to the cemetery which is grown up in vines, briars, and trees.

Anderson, Henry
Born 1874
Died April 7, 1916

Andersen, S. A.
1843-1914

Austin, Mittie
Dec. 31, 1869
Nov. 17, 1937

Berkley, James
Son of J. W. & P. E.
Berkley
Mar. 9, 1910
Oct. 2, 1912

Biggers, A. W.
Jan. 3, 1893
Oct. 22, 1918

Biggers, May Ona
Feb. 16, 1896
June 4, 1920

Bush, Walter
1881-1898

Butler, W. E.
Nov. 7, 1879
June 17, 1912

Cook, J. D.
Dec. 18, 1868
June 11, 1909

Daniel, G. W.
May 15, 1840
Oct. 4, 1906
Daniel, N. E.
His wife
May 18, 1843
--

Dickinson, A. B.
July 11, 1868
Dec. 30, 1940

Hardwick, E. S.
Dec. 16, 1826
Dec. 10, 1901

Hardwick, Katie
Dau. of J. M. & Rosa
Hardwick
Dec. 12, 1906
June 8, 1907

Hatcher, Luther
1892-1899
Hatcher, Sterling
1889-1899
Children of L. D. &
J. A. Hatcher

Jackson, Callie
Wife of Jim Jackson
Mar. 22, 1868
April 28, 1913

Jackson, Ethel
Dau. of J. M. & A. C.
Jackson
Oct. 28, 1895
Sept. 29, 1903
Jackson, Infant Son
Born and Died
April 22, 1906

James, G. W.
1865-1905

Jones, John Algenan
Mar. 6, 1878
May 11, 1903

Joslin, G. W.
May 26, 1859
Jan. 10, 1911

Joslin, Nora
Oct. 20, 1872
Jan. 16, 1904

Joslin, Octer V.
1874-1932

Joslin, R. W.
April 1, 1872
June 12, 1917

Joslin, W. H.
Jan. 28, 1862
Aug. 8, 1924

Ledbetter, Clarendon
Father
Feb. 18, 1893
June 20, 1922

Ledbetter, J. W.
Father
Jan. 12, 1846
May 21, 1916

Ledbetter, Sue L.
Mother
Sept. 23, 1824
July 19, 1922

Little, Albert
Oct. 29, 1891
Mar. 15, 1917
Age 26 years

Little, Daisy
Wife of George Little
1895-1936

McClain, C. A.
1852-1908
McClain, Elisbeth
1855-1946

Murley, Dora
Died May 10, 1903
Murley, Carona
Died May 13, 1903

Murley, J. M.
1861-1918

Peek, Frances Viola
Mother
Wife of J. L. Peek
June 5, 1879
Aug. 5, 1912

Permenter, Sarah
Born Aug. 6, 1867
Died 1935

Permenter, William Homer
Dec. 11, 1899
Mar. 12, 1924

Jerry, Jimmie P.
Son of J. R. & Linnie Perry
Jan. 12, 1902
Aug. 10, 1902

Puritt, J. W.
Feb. 4, 1883
Dec. 7, 1910

Rawles, Harriet
Mother
1830-1915

Stephens, William
Tennessee
PVT U. S. Army
30 Div.
Died Dec. 6, 1929

Taylor, James William
1881-1896

Walker, A. B.
1865-1925
Walker, M. L.
His Wife
1881

Walker, David
April 18, 1838
Dec. 20, 1915

Walker, Joe
May 2, 1863
Aug. 18, 1913

Walters, Ed Carmack
Son of G. W. & B. J.
Walters
Born June 5, 1893
Died (stone broken here)

Walters, George
Oct. 28, 1861
Feb. 12, 1910

Warren, Baby
Infant son of
Mr. & Mrs. Z. P. Warren
Died Dec. 21, 1938

POPLAR GROVE

Poplar Grove Cemetery is located on the Yorkville Highway northeast of Newbern. Turn right at the intersection of Highway 51 N. and Yorkville Highway in Newbern. Cross the Illinois Central Railroad, and the cemetery is in view on the right.

At first a large wooden shed, covered with cypress, was built under the guidance of Reverend Hamilton Parks in about 1840, but with the establishment of other places of worship there was no continuing need for the meeting shed; therefore it seemed expedient to sell the land for a cemetery. In March, 1852, for the sum of $30.00, Thomas Pace sold George Dickey, E. Haskins, W. H. Harris, H. P Strawn, D. W. Scobey and Thomas Pace, Trustees of the Cumberland Presbyterian Church at Poplar Grove, "three acres to be more or less" for a burial ground.

For many years interested families gathered the first Monday in August to clean the plot. Over the years, with no leaders to push the matter, the cemetery grew into a dismal thicket of briars and bushes. Then through efforts of A. O. Cochran, and other interested people, a Poplar Grove Cemetery Association was formed, and the Association asked for contributions to be used for mowing and maintenance of the cemetery. This extended for twelve to fourteen years. Later the ladies of the group suggested a perpetual endowment fund to raise money. This required about one year. The fund will remain intact and be controlled by a group of five trustees.

Andre, Floyd Hazen
1905-
Andre, Lena Mae
1908-

Anderson, Bennie
son of F. & G.
Anderson
July 19, 1911
Dec. 17, 1911
4 mos. 28 days

Avants, Amanda
Wife of J. T. Avants
Nov. 3, 1851
Jan. 14, 1897

Avants, Arter E.
Dec. 29 1872
Dec. 2, 1888
Baird, A. G.
Aug. 24, 1865
34 yrs. 7 days

Baird, David
Jan. 14, 1862
84 yrs. 8 mo.

Baird, Robert C.
Son of Wilson B. &
Martha A. Baird
Dec. 27, 1853
Mar. 28, 1869

Baird, Wilson B.
Oct. 24, 1817
Feb. 18, 1861
Baird, Martha Ann
Dec. 21, 1827
Jan. 30, 1913

Marlow, M. T.
74 yrs.

Barlow, Mary A.
63 yrs.
Barlow, Elizabeth
4 yrs.
Barlow, Ella
21 yrs
Barlow, Lafayette
29 yrs.
Barlow, Robert & Wife
30 - 28 yrs.
Barlow, Columbus
42 yrs

Barlow, T. E. J.
Dau. of M. T. &
M. A. Barlow
Oct. 18, 1853
Sept. 23, 1854

Beckett, Dora
Wife of J. W. Beckett
May 24, 1884
19 yrs. 10 mos. 23 days

Binkley, Fred M.
Son of Fred M. & S. O.
Dec. 14, 1890
June 18, 1903

Blankenship, (Illegible)
Aug. 3, 1885
30 years

Blankenship, George W.
Nov. 15, 1815
Jan. 4, 1912

Blankenship, Martha Ann
Wife of C. W. Blankenship
Dec. 15, 1830
Nov. 26, 1899

Bleadsoe, Emily
Wife of A. B. Bleadsoe
Feb. 20, 1847
June 7, 1881

Bleadsoe, (illegible)
Dau. of A. B. & Emily
Bleadsoe
Dec. 15, 1880
Aug. 29, 1889

Boyd, J. Ella
Dau. of W. M. &
M. D. Boyd
May 9, 1874
Sept. 22, 1894

Boyd, John W.
1876-1940
Boyd, Dollie W.
1880-1959

Boyd, Margaret J. Parnell
Nov. 10, 1842
March 4, 1929
Boyd, W. M.
Oct. 19, 1840
Jan. 18, 1897

Bradford, Zane Lucille
1917-1940

Brightwell, Annie Alford
1877-1965

Brightwell, Robert Sidney
1899-1971
Brightwell, Grace Meadows
1900-19
Married April 8, 1922

Brown, Clifford
Son of T. R. &
M. P. Brown
June 5, 1878
July 21, 1878

Bryant, Gracie B.
Nov. 24, 1888
Aug. 15, 1965

Bryant, Henry V.
1887-1968
Bryant, Vester Cross
1886-1948

Bryant, Lavenia E.
Dau. of Leroy & Alice Bryant
Oct. 26, 1894
Nov. 1, 1895

Bryant, L. N.
1855-1928
Bryant, Mary Alice
1858-1907

Bryant, Robert Thea
March 21, 1885
Sept. 7, 1955

Buchanan, Jasper P.
1873-1935
Buchanan, Dora
1876-1939

Burkeen, Ruth A.
1873-1938
Burkeen, Columbus
1865-1932

Burkeen, Vera
1910-1916

Burkett, Burney B.
Jan. 17, 1885
May 18, 1964

Burkett, Elizabeth
Sept. 20, 1848
March 12, 1905

Burkett, Elizabeth
Sept. 20, 1848
March 12, 1905

Burkett, Ollie Mae
Dau. of Walter & Bessie
Pace
March 1, 1918
April 25, 1924

Burney, Bettie Waller
Wife of J. W. Burney
May 27, 1853
Sept. 13, 1876

Burney, James
March 28, 1821
Oct. 1, 1851

Burney, John F.
Jan. 1, 1824
Dec. 12, 1851
26 yrs. 11 mos. 12 days

Burnside, Beulah M.
Dau. of H. S. &
C. J. Burnside
Aug. 22, 1880
Aug. 8, 1881

Caldwell, A. E.
Oct. 31, 1906
Feb. 28, 1973
Caldwell, Mozelle
No Dates

Campbell, James Abner
Brother
Sept. 16, 1848
Aug. 29, 1872
Campbell, Sarah Ann
Sister
June 27, 1859
Sept. 25, 1862

Campbell, Robert
Father
Apr. 1, 1818
Mar. 9, 1899

Campbell, Sarah Ann
Born July 25, 1826

Campbell, Willie I.
Aug. 17, 1854
Feb. 1, 1883

Carlin, Hattie W.
Dau. of Dr. J. and
Annie Richardson
Feb. 5, 1824
(Illegible) 1901

Cavit, Uno W.
Feb. 9, 1863
May 12, 1912

Cawthon, Emmet W.
Jan. 17, 1863
Mar. 8, 1904

Cawthon, James H. Sr.
April 13, 1788
Oct. 9, 1879
Cawthon, Sarah
Dec. 4, 1794
Oct. 21, 1879

Cawthon, J. H.
Sept. 16, 1813
April 6, 1885

Cawthon, Mrs. M. A.
Wife of
Dr. J. H. Cawthon
July 16, 1819
April 9, 1886
60 yrs. 8 mos. 28 days

Cawthon, Z. H.
Born in Wilson Co. Tn.
Nov. 20, 1829
Died in Gibson Co. Tn.
Sept. 26, 1859
29 yrs. 10 mos. 6 days

Chapman, Virginia L
Wife of J. S. Chapman
Oct 16, 1872
Dec. 7, 1890

Chisman, Geo. W.
No Date

Churchman, Eliza
Daughter of
T. G. & Ruth Churchman
Born July 27, 1855

Churchman, Robert J.
Son of T. G. & Sarah H
Dec. 21, 1858
Aug. 17, 1859

Clark, E. M.
May 19, 1899
Nov. 3, 1944

Clark, S. B.
Oct. 1, 1869
Dec. 8, 1943
Clark, Oda
July 12, 1872
May 26, 1927

Clark, Tabmage
Aug. 6, 1895
Aug. 10, 1931

Clement, Laura A.
Jan. 25, 1859
May 25, 1899
Father
Clement, Rhodie N.
Dec. 14, 1850

Cochran, Albert
Nov. 5, 1836
Sept. 20, 1910
73 yrs. 10 mos. 15 days

Cochran, Albert Hobson
Son of
A. & S. M. Cochran
Sept. 26, 1879
Aug. 27, 1899
19 yrs. 11 mos. 1 day

Cochran, Frank Burney
Son of
J. M. & L. E. Cochran
Jan. 15, 1897
Oct. 23, 1897

Cochran, James M.
Oct. 26, 1861
June 28, 1935

Cochran, John Alison
Son of J. M. & L. E.
Cochran
Jan. 27, 1888
Apr. 18, 1902
14 yrs. 2 mos. 21 days

Cochran, John C
Son of A. & S. M.
Cochran
Died Sept. 9, 1877
14 yrs. 7 mos. 2 days

Cochran, Jonnie
1879-1949
Cochran, Ira
1877-1966

Cochran, Infant Son of
J. M. & L. E. Cochran
Born & Died
Mar. 3, 1888

Cochran, Mrs. L. E.
Wife of
J. M. Cochran
June 16, 1864
Sept. 29, 1909
45 yrs. 3 mos. 13 days

Cochran, L. W.
Sept. 8, 1838
Jan. 24, 1920

Cochran, Martha Ann
wife of
L. W. Cochran
Aug. 27, 1838
Aug. 3, 1901

Cochran, Masel
1896-
Cochran, George S.
1894-1971

Cochran, Mauda E.
Dau. of
A. & S. M. Cochran
Died Aug. 7, 1877
1 yr. 10 mos. 20 days

Cochran, Ollie B.
Wife of
C. R. Greene
Died July 24, 1929

Cochran, Paul
Son of
J. W. & L. E. Cochran
July 27, 1899
July 16, 1900

Cochran, Rachel
Dau. of
L. W. & M. A. Cochran
Mar. 22, 1864
Sept. 16, 1908

Cochran, Robert C.
Sept. 18, 1884
May 14, 1936
Erected by Hallie

Cochran, Robert L.
Son of
A. & S. M. Cochran
Feb. 4, 1883
Sept. 8, 1883

Cochran, Susan Miley
Wife of
A. Cochran
Feb. 4, 1840
Oct. 21, 1914
74 yrs. 8 mos. 17 days

Cochran, T. M.
Sept. 8, 1888
Nov. 8, 1894
26 yrs. 2 mos

Cochran, William E.
Mar. 18, 1832
May 29, 1889
Cochran, Elizabeth L.
Wife of
W. E. Cochran
Sept. 10, 1838
Sept. 10, 1868

Cochran, W. T.
Oct. 10, 1859
Mar. 11, 1915
Cochran, Laura
Mar. 24, 1869
Feb. 4, 1952

Cole, Geneva Vesta
Dau. of
J. A. & N. T. Cole
Aug. 13, 1890
July 11, 1891
Cole, Aggie Alfred
Son of
J. A. & N. T. Cole
Dec. 9, 1887
Feb. 23, 1888

Cole, Idella J.
Mar. 3, 1881
Nov. 12, 1882

Cole, Mrs. Irma E.
Nov. 13, 1962
62 yrs.

Cole, Jas. Cleveland
Sept. 26, 1888
Aug. 24, 1889

Cole, John A.
May 29, 1861
May 24, 1940
Cole, Nancy T.
Dec. 6, 1867
Oct. 14, 1946

Cole, J. R.
Oct. 3, 1858
Aug. 31, 1928

Cole, Ludie
July 12, 1885
July 1, 1909

Cole, Pearl P.
Mar. 31, 1888
Nov. 13, 1968

Cole, Samuel A.
Nov. 13, 1829
May 1, 1912
Cole, Eliza Jane
Nov. 25, 1837
Nov. 17, 1900

Cole, Sudie L.
Wife
Mar. 6, 1861
May 17, 1897

Cole, Thelma C.
Dau. of
W. S. & I. E. Cole
Nov. 11, 1903
Nov. 27, 1903

Cole, Thomas Henry
1856-1942
Cole, Mary Jane
1856-1942

Cole, Willie Lee
Sept. 27, 1898
Feb. 11, 1920
Cole, Jessie Gordan
May 10, 1883
Oct. 13, 1897

Cole, Infant
Born and Died
Mar. 20, 1883

Cook, Cornelia M.
Wife of
W. H. Cook
Feb. 19, 1859
July 2, 1906

Cook, Dora Nesbitt
Our daughter
Jan. 9, 1917
Sept. 17, 1920

Cook, G. W.
1854-1931
Cook, H. S.
His Wife
1861-19

Cook, Mother of
G. W. Cook
No Dates

Cook, Herbert B.
1882-1931

Cook, Wesley Newton
Son of
W. H. & C. M. Cook
Oct. 22, 1894
Mar. 24, 1913

Cook, William Jere
Our baby
Apr. 9, 1923
Oct. 9, 1928

Crawford, J. A.
March 24, 1857
Feb. 19, 1911

Crow, Amanda C.
Daughter of J. B. &
Elizabeth Crow
Aug. 6, 1857
2 yrs. 10 mos.

Crow, Elizabeth
Nov. 21, 1821
March 15, 1896

Crow, John D.
Jan. 30, 1819
Mar. 8, 1835

Crow, W. R. D.
Jan. 20, 1815
Feb. 8, 1868

Crowe, John G.
1869-1957
Crow, Arah J.
1872-1961

Cunningham, Jas. B.
Aug. 14, 1835
May 18, 1871

Cunningham, Mary Jane
Wife of
Jas. B. Cunningham
Dau. of Rev. H. & M. Parks
May 31, 1838
Jan. 26, 1865

Curtis, Brewer
Sept. 12, 1907
May 20, 1964
Curtis, Annie B.
Nov. 16, 1907
April 7, 1967

Curtis, David A.
Tennessee
PVT U. S. Army
World War II
Sept. 25, 1919
Oct. 12, 1973

Curtis, George M.
Aug. 9, 1870
June 30, 1947
Curtis, Nancy E.
April 25, 1882
Sept. 1, 1943

Curtis, James Michael
Tennessee
PVT U. S. Army
Vietnam
July 26, 1952
June 5, 1972

Curtis, Sarah F.
Wife of G. N. Curtis
April 27, 1830
Feb. 23, 1875

Davis, W. P.
No Dates
Davis, Aunt Betty
Davis, Grandmother
No Dates

Dew, Arthur L
1886-19

Dew, Mattie L.
1886-1964

Dew, Henry L.
1873-1903

Dew, Thomas J.
Feb. 14, 1847
Dec. 17, 1927
Dew, Nancy
Oct. 13, 1854
Sept. 7, 1934

Dickerson, Pearl C.
Dau. of A & L. M.
Dickerson
Mar. 16, 1900
July 2, 1900

Dickey, C. D.
Feb. 17, 1842
Sept. 29, 1929

Dickey, Clyde
1904-1936

Dickey, J. H. Son of
S. A. Dickey
Mar. 10, 1882
Oct. 18, 1911

Dickey, Mary
Nov. 19, 1839
Aug. 11, 1880

Dickey, Matie J.
Wife of S. A. Dickey
Aug. 22, 1849
May 8, 1884

Dickey, M. L.
Wife of S. A. Dickey
June 1, 1865
June 22, 1886

Dickey, Polly Ann
Sept. 27, 1850
April 5, 1926

Dickey, Ruth A.
Wife of S. A. Dickey
Sept. 25, 1850
June 2, 1921

Dickey, S. A.
Born June 18, 1850

Dickey, R. W.
Father
Dec. 1, 1847
Oct. 19, 1919

Dillon, Daniel
Husband of Polly Dillon
March 2, 1789
Oct. 5, 1872
83 yrs. 7 mos. 2 days

Dillon, Mary
Wife of D. Dillon
May 4, 1909
82 yrs. old

Doss, James M.
Co 33 Tenn Inf.
C. S. A.
No Dates

Dowland, Timothy Houston
Aug. 31, 1875
Oct. 11, 1960
Dowland, Bessie Page
Jan. 24, 1879
Nov. 24, 1959

Dozier, J. A.
1858-1907

Dozier, Mildred
Mar. 23, 1867
Dec. 2, 1937

Dozier, R. F.
1883-1900
Dozier, Infant
1891-

Drane, J. F.
Son of J. M. & L. P. Drane
Nov. 1, 1861
15 yrs. 25 days

Dunahoo, Boyd G.
1908-1932

Dunahoo, Gilbert
1867-1933
Dunahoo, Mary Ada
1871-1945

Dunahoo, Ida
March 1, 1893
July 24, 1906

Dunahoo, Jennie
Mother
Dec. 21, 1866
July 8, 1906

Dyer, Lurline
Mother
1908-1938
Dyer, Jessie Glen
Son
1931-1955

Eatherly, Ross Irvin
Oct. 16, 1894
Sept. 30, 1896

Elles, L. N.
Dec. 20, 1844
Oct. 21, 1900
55 yrs. 10 mos. 9 days

Ellis, A. J.
May 17, 1855

Ellis, Rebecca
His Wife
July 4, 1887

Ellis, Frankie M.
July 6, 1881
Dec. 17, 1962

Ellis, James R.
Aug. 13, 1877
July 1, 1958

Ellis, J. T.
Oct. 27, 1838
Nov. 24, 1907

Ellis, John W.
April 16, 1832
Nov. 9, 1895

Ellis, Johnnie T.
Son of J. W. &
M. J. Ellis
June 30, 1876
Oct. 3, 1881
5 yrs. 3 mos. 3 days

Ellis, Infant Son of
J. W. & M. J. Ellis
April 7, 1873

Ellis, Infant Son of
J. W. & M. J. Ellis
Born July 26, 1874

Ellis, Julia Mai
Inf. Dau. of Lloyd
and Ola Mai Ellis
March 3, 1932

Ellis, Leona P.
Dau. of J. W. & M. J.
Ellis
Aug. 28, 1879
Sept. 11, 1881
2 yrs. 11 days

Ellis, Lloyd M.
1902-1974
Ellis, Ola Mai D.
1902-

Ellis, Lloyd Mallard
Jan. 14, 1975
72 yrs. 5 mo 5 days

Ellis, Manerva J.
Nov. 19, 1838
Mar. 10, 1905

Ellis, Margret L.
Wife of Michael Ellis
Sept. 6, 1815
Sept. 8, 1857
and infant son

Ellis, Martha L.
Oct. 24, 1850
Dec. 28, 1923

Ellis, Michael
Sept. 19, 1798
Mar. 24, 1861

Ellis, Rebecca A.
Wife of J. N. Ellis
May 16, 1844
Feb. 10, 1888

Ellis, Samuel Watkins
1877-1969
Ellis, Mittie Kelso
1877-1969

Ethridge, David Solomon
Oct. 6, 1865
Jan. 15, 1938
Ethridge, Nancy Ann Moran
Mar. 13, 1861
Aug. 22, 1947

Evans, Vera M.
Mar. 19, 1901
Feb. 26, 1848

Faris, Elizabeth
April 10, 1839
Sept. 30, 1891

Faris, William Walter
June 20, 1870
April 16, 1909

Farris, Edith Hall
Oct. 29, 1920
Aug. 29, 1928

Farris, William A.
Tenn. PVT
248 Station Hospital
World War II
Sept. 9, 1898
Oct. 18, 1965

Featherston, Emma
Mother
1876-1943

Fields, Allie J.
July 31, 1857
Oct. 23, 1899

Fields, Darsie Fain
Son of S. H. & Viola
Fields
Dec. 20, 1903
Aug. 19, 1905
(Note: In Jackson plot)

Fields, Infant Son of
T. F. Fields
No Dates

Fields, Uriah J.
Son of T. F. Fields
July 1, 1853
11 yrs. 5 mo.

Flack, J. P.
1872-19
Flack, Davie
1883-19
Flack, Hattie
1915-

Flack, W. P.
July 3, 1867
Mar. 29, 1920

Flatt, Bernard D.
1895-1965
Flatt, Ruth B.
1901-19

Flatt, Charlie Earl
Son of Will & Minnie
Flatt
Sept. 25, 1904
Dec. 1, 1915

Flatt, Marion D.
Son of Bernard &
Ruth Flatt
Mar. 30, 1923
July 3, 1924

Flatt, H. D.
Feb. 23, 1875
Oct. 4, 1892
27 yrs. 7 mos. 11 days

Flatt, Roy E.
Oct. 3, 1901
Aug. 6, 1965

Flatt, William T.
1873-1961
Flatt, Minnie L.
1878-1965

Fones, Cora Moffitt
1887-19

Forester, Laura M.
Wife of H. C. Forester
Nov. 11, 1867
July 30, 1891

Freeman, Frank Mrs.
1847-1925

Frost, Arry
Son of B. L. &
L. Z. Frost
Born & Died 1899

Fry, No First Name
Mar. 11, 1904
Mar. 28, 1904
Fry, Maggie
Oct. 3, 1898
Mar. 16, 1903

Fuller, Emma G.
Wife of C. R. Fuller
Aug. 16, 1853
Sept. 18, 1877

Gambill, Anna
1874-1934

Gambill, Asa
Nov. 17, 1903
Dec. 23, 1903

Gibbons, Amma
1916-19
Gibbons, William R.
1913-1958

Gibbons, Doris Ann
July 14, 1947
June 26, 1966

Gibbs, Finis R. Jr.
June 13, 1943
June 17, 1943

Gibson, James H.
1913-1969
Gibson, Eva M.
Married May 25, 1935

Gibson, Joe B.
Son of
W. E. & L. M. Gibson
March 9, 1930
July 12, 1931

Gibson, Lessie L.
1882-1952
Mother

Gibson, Luther H.
Aug. 12, 1883
June 20, 1943
Father

Goodwin, James
No Dates

Gordon, Milford
1915-1931
Son of
Mrs. Myrtle Kelso Gordon
Gordon, Myrtle Kelso
Dec. 24, 1895
July 8, 1970

Green, Infant Son of
D. L. & E. M. Green
No Dates

Green, Infant Son of
J. R. & M. A. Green
No Date

Green, Finis
1875

Green, James T.
May 7, 1849
Mar. 10, 1912
Green, Elizabeth S.
Wife of James T. Green
Sept. 21, 1838
July 13, 1906

Green, Jasper R. D.
1870-1948
Green, Laura Flowers
1875-1921

Green, Martin
1851-1874

Green, Mary A.
Mother
Jan. 22, 1831
Nov. 22, 1874
Bourland, Elizabeth
Dau.
Mar. 7, 1862
June 28, 1941

Green, William
1876

Green, William H. H.
Son of C. & Jane Green
Sept. 17, 1840
Dec. 22, 1858

Gregory, Lucinda P.
Wife of William C.
Gregory
Oct. 20, 1820
Aug. 16, 1861
Gregory, Lucinda
Inf. Dau. of
W. C. & L. P. Gregory
April 13, 1861
Sept. 1, 1861

Gregory, Mary Alice
Dau. of M. C. & Lucinda
P. Gregory
Oct. 12, 1846
Dec. 3, 1864
17 yrs. 11 mos. 21 days

Gregory, William C.
Tenn.
PVT. CO, K 47 Rgt. TN. INF.
Confederate States Army
Nov. 22, 1818
Aug. 23, 1870
51 yrs. 9 mos. 1 day

Grier, Martha E.
Feb. 5, 1839
Mar. 18, 1862

Griffey, Bertha Lee
Dau. of
C. J. & r. A. Griffey
Mar. 15, 1901
Mar. 21, 1904
3 yrs. 6 days

Grisham, Nancy Ann
1857-1945
Grisham, Ephriam J.
1847-1906

Grogan, Owen Ross
1891-1966

Grogan, Beatrice L.

Guess, Andrew F.
1886-1940
Guess, Hattie J.
1891-19

Guess, Ellis A.
Son
1909-1928

Guess, Millie Z. Lee
Mother
Mar. 7, 1885
May 9, 1928

Hale, Amanda C.
Wife of Robt. Hale
Nov. 24, 1836
Nov. 9, 1874

Hale, Robert Gentry
Son of Robt. & Amanda Hale
Dec. 14, 1868
July 31, 1869

Hall, Fannie
April 10, 1875
Dec. 1, 1939

Hall, S. C.
June 20, 1844
Hall, J. M.
Aug. 30, 1838
Jan. 10, 1916

Hallum, Addie
1872-1872
Hallum, Infant
Oct. 21, 1896

Hallum, A. G.
Sept. 18, 1815
May 3, 1890

Hallum, David M.
Dec. 23, 1848
May 19, 1872

Hallum, Herbert
April 2, 1902
Feb. 9, 1963

Hallum, James B.
1857-1930
Hallum, Robell C.
1874-1944

Hallum, Lauraney
Dec. 14, 1819
Feb. 8, 1904

Hallum, Opelia
Wife of A. G. Hallum
Dec. 21, 1867
April 7, 1911

Hallum, Sona
Nov. 4, 1900
Nov. 17, 1918

Hamilton, Adaline
July 7, 1849
Died 1866

Hamilton, Addie L.
Son of W. S. &
N. A. Hamilton
Died Oct. 8, 1882

Hamilton, Annie Clay
Feb. 15, 1872
Oct. 20, 1872

Hamilton, Callie D.
June 3, 1836
Dec. 17, 1882
Mother

Hamilton, Ira G.
Dec. 22, 1872
Sept. 25, 1875

Hamilton, James H.
Mar. 14, 1822
Mar. 26, 1899
Father

Hamilton, Mallie
Dau. of J. J. & V. A.
Hamilton
Nov. 29, 1881
Sept. 12, 1895

Hamilton, Martha A.
Mar. 6, 1847
Sept. 24, 1875

Hamilton, Virgie B.
Dau. of W. S. &
N. A. Hamilton
June 9, 1821
Sept. 27, 1831

Hamilton, W. R.
Oct. 4, 1865
Apr. 10, 1888

Hamilton, William S.
Sept. 12, 1840
Sept. 16, 1891
Hamilton, Sannie A.
Aug. 9, 1844
Nov. 23, 1902

Harbison, Nancy C.
1862-
Harbison, Robert J.
1860-1891
Harbison, George W.
1856-1896
Harbison, Mary L.
1852-1941

Hargrove, Osie E.
Father
Nov. 6, 1897
Feb. 7, 1924

Haskins, Creed
July 30, 1844
Jan. 5, 1924

Haskins, Douglass
Son of J. C. & A. E. Haskins
Nov. 20, 1869
Sept. 14, 1876

Haskins, Edward
April 3, 1804
Sept. 5, 1870
69 years

Haskins, Edward J.
Nov. 13, 1823
July 6, 1874
50 yrs. 8 mos. 21 days

Haskins, Edward T.
Son of Edward & Harriet
Haskins
Aug 30, 1840
Aug. 28, 1863
22 yrs. 11 mos. 28 days

Haskins, Ellen
Feb. 20, 1864
Mar. 30, 1941

Haskins, Harriet J.
July 22, 1856
Jan. 17, 1873

Haskins, James F.
Son of Edward &
Harriet Haskins
Nov. 20, 1842
Jan. 25, 1862

Haskins, Neddie
Son of J. C. &
A. E. Haskins
July 14, 1887
Aug. 20, 1888

Haskins, Pattie
Wife of A. B. Haskins
Feb. 2, 1854
April 26, 1881

Headden, Oliver
Son of D. C. & N. M.
Headden
Aug. 27, 1881
Aug. 12, 1884

Headden, Scott
1848-1928
Headeen, Mary Ada
1851-1912

Heath, Leslie
Tennessee
Pvt. 56 Det. of Brig.
June 1, 1932

Hendricks, Newt.
1883-19
Hendricks, Ethel M.
1883-1948

Herrin, Ellender
Wife of U. M. Herrin
Dec. 9, 1810
Oct. 20, 1881

Herrin, J. B.
Nov. 3, 1829
Mar. 1, 1879

Herrin, James R.
Son of R. & M. C.
Herrin
Sept. 27, 1883
Sept. 11, 1884

Herrin, Jeanette
Dau. of R. & M. C.
Herrin
Oct. 3, 1873
Oct. 14, 1873

Herrin, Martha C.
Wife of Richmond Herrin
1852-1929

Herrin, Richmond
Husband of M. C. Herrin
1852-1929

Herrin,
Dau. of T. M. & L. M.
Herrin
Born & Died Sept. 23, 1908

Herrin, Uriahm
Father
Feb. 17, 1801
Sept. 1, 1870

Hill, Mary A.
Feb. 28, 1848
Sept. 4, 1898

Hinson, Lucille Summers
1915-1938

Holder, Julion
Infant Son
Oct. 3, 1924

Hollister, Joanne Dianne
Feb. 27, 1947

Holman, Allie May
1892-19
Holman, Arthur Clay
1892-1925

Holt, Bertha
March 7, 1894
Holt, Jennings
Jan. 2, 1887
July 20, 1953

Holt, James Andrew
Jan. 4, 1930
May 26, 1941

Hood, John Marshall
Son of W. H. &
M. S. Hood
May 31, 1861
Oct. 11, 1868
6 yrs. 1 mo. 13 days

Hood, Martha S.
Oct. 6, 1841
July 9, 1888

Howell, P. B.
Father
Mar. 27, 1882
Jan. 31, 1917
Howell, A. A.
His Wife
June 26, 1863
Mother

Howell, Tice A.
Son of R. B. & A. A. Howell
Mar. 8, 1886
Oct. 15, 1887

Hugheley, Edker Cherrey
Son of L. R. &
A. L. Hugueley
Dec. 3, 1902
Feb. 15, 1907

Hugueley, Eliza A.
July 27, 1813
Nov. 30, 1884

Hugueley, James Robert
Son
Jan. 8, 1906
Feb. 3, 1966

Hugueley, John H.
Dec. 8, 1850
Oct. 25, 1872
Hugueley, Sarah J.
Sept. 23, 1848
Oct. 10, 1856

Hugueley, John Wesley
Son of S. E. &.
L. E. Hugueley
Nov. 2, 1865
(illegible), 1869

Hugueley, L. R.
Nov. 19, 1869
Aug. 9, 1933
Hugueley, Allie
Oct. 2, 1873
Jan. 25, 1931

Hugueley, Lilly Viola
Wife of W. H. Hugueley
Mar. 10, 1881
Jan. 27, 1968

Hugueley, Samuel E.
1836-1881
Hugueley, Lucy E.
(His Wife)
1844-1925

Hugueley, Tebitha
Dau. of S. E. &
L. E. Hugueley
Nov. 16, 1871
July 10, (broken stone)

Hugueley, William Henry
May 6, 1877
Dec. 27, 1959
Father

Ingram, Pinkney A.
Dec. 24, 1848
June 17, 1917

Isbell, Joseph Newton
1867-1940
Isbell, Mary Emma
1877-1963

Jackson, A. G.
Aug. 19, 1844
Dec. 2, 1914

Jackson, Benjamin D.
Feb. 17, 1878
Oct. 5, 1969

Jackson, Elen C.
Dau. of S. W. &
M. I. Jackson
Sept. 28, 1868
Nov. 7, 1868

Jackson, Elizabeth A.
Wife of
Hugh Jackson
May 11, 1816
July 17, 1861

Jackson, Ethel B.
1887-1963
Jackson, Lonnie O.
1888-1954

Jackson, Evelyn
Oct. 17, 1909
Dec. 31, 1939

Jackson, Hattie Timbs
June 22, 1880
April 8, 1933

Jackson, Hugh
May 13, 1810
Nov. 21, 1861

Jackson, James
Dec. 19, 1823
Feb. 6, 1901
Jackson, Fannie
Aug. 29, 1829

Jackson, John Ira
1889-1937

Jackson, Lue. H.
Dec. 23, 1857
July 15, 1945
Jackson, Tom M.
Nov. 10, 1847
Nov. 14, 1929

Jackson, Maggie
Dau of
Wm & M. G. Jackson
Feb. 22, 1876
Nov. 28, 1897

Jackson, Malisey M.
Wife of Wm. M. Jackson
Mar. 5, 1838
June 3, 1863
Jackson, Susan Ann
Dau. of Wm & Malisa M.
Jan. 24, 1859
July 27, 1859

Jackson, Margaret
Wife of R. S. Jackson
Died Dec. 22, 1878

Jackson, Margaret A.
1863-
Jackson, Robert C.
1866-1935

Jackson, Margaret Melvinie
Wife of A. G. Jackson
Feb. 7, 1858
Nov. 28, 1905
47 yrs. 9 mos. 21 days

Jackson, Mary Nellie
Jan. 28, 1890
Mar. 12, 1958
Jackson, Fuller F.
Brother
Jan. 19, 1892
Nov. 16, 1956

Jackson, Richard K.
1896-1939

Jackson, Robert E.
Son of I. W. & M. I. Jackson
Feb. 23, 1889
June 23, 1898

Jackson, R. E.
Son of J. F. & Matilda
July 9, 1862
May 3, 1897
34 yrs. 10 mos. 6 days

Jackson, R. S.
Dec. 5, 1812
Jan. 17, 1897
84 yrs. 1 mos. 7 days

Jackson, Ruby B.
1891-19
Jackson, George W.
1883-1966

Jackson, Tealie A.
1898-1971

Jackson, William
June 8, 1834
Mar. 31, 1913
Jackson, Martha G. Fuller
His Wife
Dec. 28, 1845
Jan. 2, 1910
Married Jan. 17, 1864

Jackson, W. R.
Son of T. M & L. H. L.
Sept. 25, 1876
Aug. 27, 1896
19 yrs. 11 mos. 2 days

Jackson, Son
Sept. 10, 1884
Son of Wm. Jackson

Johnson, Elizabeth
Wife of J. A. Johnson
Feb. 27, 1836
Sept. 8, 1877

Johnson, John W.
Nov. 26, 1883
June 28, 1968

Johnson, Lucian H.
Son of J. A. &
E. T. Johnson
July 17, 1865
Dec. 21, 1870

Johnson, Mary Martin
1903-1972
Johnson, M. Daniel
1903-
Johnson, Genie J.
1871-1958
Johnson, A. Henderson
1874-1946

Johnson, Son of
J. A. & E. T.
Johnson
Aug. 4, 1856
Feb. 19, 1880

Jones, Blanche B.
Aug. 14, 1890
July 18, 1970

Jones, Dollie
1854-1939

Jones, Wiley H.
1852-1889

Jones, Eddie B.
1885

Jones, Elbert N.
Tn.
PVT. 157 Depot Brig.
Nov. 6, 1935

Jones Henry Bryant
June 7, 1922
May 13, 1934
Son of
Elbert & Blanche
Brother of
Mary and Ruth

Jones, J. K. (Vard)
(Father)
1904-1948
Jones, Ollie Bell
Mother
1910-1953

Jones, Minnie Campbell
Aug. 7, 1881
Sept. 28, 1900

Jones, Newton Bryant
Feb. 18, 1919
Feb. 18, 1919
Baby

Jones, W. L.
Nov. 15, 1813
Dec. 31, 1899
Jones, T. L.
Wife of W. L. Jones
Oct. 8, 1849
April 30, 1902

Jordan, Effie
Wife of C. F. Jordan
April 5, 1878
Mar. 28, 1900
22 yrs. 11 mos. 23 days

Jordan, Elizabeth
Wife of
G. W. Jordan
Oct. 15, 1815
Jan. 25, 1895
29 yrs. 3 mos. 10 days

Justice, Allen Brantley
Son of A. A. & N. A. Justice
July 7, 1856
Aug. 4, 1876

Justice, Rev. Allen A.
Dec. 20, 1815
May 30, 1861

Justice, Mary Elizabeth
Infant Dau. Rev. A. A. & N. A.
Justice
July 12, 1855-July 28, 1855

Justis, Nancy Ann
Consort of
Rev. A. A. Justis
Dec. 2, 1831
Feb. 14, 1868
36 yrs. 2 mos. 12 days

Kelso, James P.
June 25, 1876
May 17, 1913

Kelso , Mary Alice
Wife of M. F. B. Kelso
Feb. 19, 1857
April 28, 1913

Kepley, J. A.
No Dates

Kirkpatrick, James S.
Mar. 15, 1844
May 1, 1905

Kirkpatrick, Minerva
Wife of
J. S. Kirkpatrick
June 9, 1847
Sept 4, 1893

Knight, A. D.
Aug. 8, 1820
Dec. 21, 1905
85 yrs. 8 mos. 8 days

LaBoe, Clara J.
Dec. 13, 1882
Nov. 10, 1970

Lambert, Callie Wilson
Born & Died 1884

Lambert, Cyrus Hill
May 16, 1889
Oct. 8, 1918

Lambert, Irene Lucille
Dau of
Ross & Madge Lambert
Died 1940

Lambert, J. Hal
1856-1936
Lambert, Lavina A.
1861-1936

Lambert, Mattie Cochran
Wife of Jessie P. Lambert
1867-1899

Lambert. T. C.
Aug. 21, 1866
Aug. 10, 1884

Lambert, Winfield
Born Aug. 2, 1889
Lambert, Nina Hallum
June 27, 1889
Nov. 26, 1965

Lancaster, Jno. H.
July 18, 1867
Nov. 4, 1903

Lawhorn, Emma
Dau. of W. R. and
L. E. Lawhorn
Born & Died
1861

Lawhorn, Nora M.
Dau. of W. R. and
L. E. Lawhorn
Oct. 13, 1859
July 28, 1860

Lawhorn, W. R.
Dec. 1, 1833
Mar. 1, 1861

Lunsford, Tishie
Wife of
Steve H. Lunsford
Nov. 8, 1883
Nov. 25, 1906
23 yrs. 17 days

Martin, Leman
Son of Frank &
Eva Martin
Jan. 8, 1912
Oct. 1, 1912

May, Andrew J.
1861-19
May, Nancy A.
1874-19

May, Ann
Daughter of D. &
N. M. May
Sept. 28, 1867
July 29, 1878

May, Dempsey
Dec. 25, 1823
June 29, 1890

May, M. J.
Wife of W. J. May
Oct. 23, 1867
March 11, 1892

May, W. J.
1864-1950
May, Sarah E.
1871-19

McCormack, Carel
Son of M. C. & B. Z. McCormack
May 6, 1897
Feb. 18, 1899
McCormack, Jennie
Dau. of M. C. & B. Z. McCormack
Aug. 25, 1894
Sept. 21, 1900

McCormack, Chas C.
1885-1930

McCormack, Marshall
1858-1932
McCormack, Belle
1860-1944

McCormack, Mrs. Myrtle
Maggie
Nov. 22, 1974
82 yrs. old 10 mo. 2 days

McCormack, W. A.
Oct. 8, 1884
Nov. 17, 1947

McCullough, Sallie May
Sept. 11, 1882
Mar. 25, 1883
Dau. of W. L. & G.
McCullough
McCullough, Luna Jane
Dec. 22, 1876
Aug. 14, 1895

McCullough, W. L.
Father
Jan. 18, 1846
April 30, 1936
McCullough, G. T.
Wife
Sept. 12, 1847
May 12, 1920

McDonald, Frank
Inf. Son of H. T.
& Rhoda McDonald
Feb. 11, 1909
Oct. 3, 1909

McElray, Rhonda
April 30, 1852
Dec. 12, 1925

Michael, Joe T.
1902-1942

Michael, W. A.
Mar. 5, 1840
Oct. 20, 1895
Michael, Adline
His Wife
Nov. 12, 1841
Aug. 12, 1919

Meadows, Elizabeth
Wife of
W. L. Meadows
Oct. 9, 1817
Mar. 10, 1889

Meadows, W. L.
Apr. 8, 1819
Jan. 22, 1880
6- yrs. 9 mos.

Milam, Luther B.
1878-1953
Milam, Ida M.
1887-

Miller, Jesse Jr.
Feb. 14, 1848
Mar. 9, 1904

Moffit, Henry
1861-1929

Moffitt, Mary Campbell
1862-1936
Mother
Moffit, Charles C.
1856-1944

Moffitt, P. M.
Jan. 29, 1858
Nov. 21, 1899

Moore, Agnes
No Dates

Moore, Caroline C. Fuller
Wife of
Samuel Moore
Aug. 1819
July 1894

Moore, Catherine Harris
Jan. 30, 1827
May 15, 1901

Moore, Douglas
No Dates

Moore, Howard
1871-19
Moore, Charles W.
1869-1942

Moore, Inf. Son of
C. W. & M. H. Moore
Born & Died
Mar. 5, 1895

Moore, James S.
1899-1948

Moore, James T.
Mar. 27, 1832
April 27, 1876
44 yrs. 1 mos.

Moore, Lula Elnora
Dau. of
S. H. & M. J. Moore
Oct. 2, 1866
Aug. 30, 1888
22 yrs. 10 mos. 28 days

Moore, Mary Jane
Wife of
James T. Moore
Sept 5, 1835
69 yrs. 3 mos. 27 days

Moore, Nan Hugueley
April 26, 1917
Oct. 18, 1970

Moore, Robert E.
1871-1956

Moore, Samuel
Husband of
Caroline C. Moore
Dec. 4, 1809
Dec. 15, 1881
72 yrs. 1 day

Moore, Samuel Alston
Oct. 1, 1820
Feb. 15, 1861

Moore, Sara Ann
Dau. of
Samuel and Sarah Moore
Sept 15, 1843
June 25, 185
9 yrs. 9 mos. 15 days

Moore, S. H.
1846-1939
Moore, Martha J. Scobey
His wife
1847-1928
Our Father and Mother

Moore, S. L.
Feb. 6, 1857
Feb. 18, 1901

Moore, Thomas Scott
Son of
C. W. & M. H. Moore
Born Aug. 7, 1892

More, Martha A.
Wife of J. T. Algea
Jan. 12, 1833
Aug. 31, (Illegible)
20 yrs. 7 mos. 19 days

Mulherin, A. B.
1859-1927
Mulherin, Rosie A.
1863-1927
Father and Mother

Mulherin, Frost
1888-1927

Mulherin, John F.
Aug. 7, 1874
Aug. 5, 1939

Murray, G. R.
Aug. 19, 1866
Dec. 21, 1898

Norsworthy, Maggie E.
1883-1969

Norsworthy, William D.
Died Mar. 7, 1973

Norsworthy, Willie A.
Wife of C. W. Norsworthy
Born Sept. 20, 1882
Died Dec. 3, 1918

Oliver, Ben P.
1894-1953
Oliver, Burl W.
1850-1917
Oliver, Julia E.
1853-1928

Oliver, Katie M.
No Dates

Pace, Albert L.
Husband of E. Pace
Died May 20, 1873

Pace, Amanda S.
1851-1941

Pace, Annie P.
Wife of J. A. Pace
Apr. 4, 1873
Jan. 22, 1891
17 yrs. 5 mos. 23 days

Pace, Benjamin Franklin
Jan. 24, 1860
Feb. 12, 1929
Pace, Sarah Sophronia
His wife
Oct. 22, 1861
Father and Mother

Pace, Eddie
Son of W. T. and
M. A. Pace
Died Feb. 24, 1877
1 yr. 3 mos. 20 days

Pace, Eliza
Wife of W. C. Pace
Oct. 1, 1824
March 18, 1863

Pace Elizabeth
June 1, 1802
Died March 11, 1863

Pace, Infant Dau. of
Eliza and W. C. Pace
Born and Died
March 6, 1863

Pace, Inf. of
J. D. and Amanda Pace
Aug. 18, 1889
Sept. 2, 1889

Pace, Inf. son of
J. T. and
L. E. Pace
Aug. 1, 1874
Aug. 1, 1874

Pace, Ellen
Wife of M. R. Pace
May 5, 1859
Feb. 17, 1921
Pace, M. R.
Aug. 26, 1858

Pace, Fannie Wright
1874-1947

Pace, Fanny F.
Wife of J. D. Pace
Aug. 3, 1850
Jan. 3, 1869

Pace, George Ewing
Son of J. W. and
M. E. Pace
Nov. 19, 1902
Oct. 8, 1903

Pace, Helen
Dau. of
W. C. and H. P. Scott
1904-1908

Pace, Henrietta
Wife of J. D. Pace
July 1, 1845
March 16, 1916

Pace, Jackson
Sept. 6, 1806
July 1, 1873

Pace, James Carroll
Son of M. E. &
J. P. Pace
March 23, 1842
July 12, 1900

Pace, James Luther
1869-1941

Pace, Jo D.
June 7, 1845
Dec. 2, 1916

Pace, Julia Ann
Dau. of
Martha C. and Thos. Pace
June 25, 1837
Oct. 5, 1854

Pace, Lena B.
Dau. of
L. and F. M. Pace
June 5, 1894
Nov. 4, 1897

Pace, Louise
1854-
Pace, J. T.
1854-1883

Pace, Margrette, Dau. of
Thos. & M. C. Pace
Jan. 24, 1851
Aug. 22, 1925

Pace, Martha C.
Wife of Thomas Pace
May 1, 1812
July 1, 1893
76 yrs. 2 mos.

Pace, Mary E.
Dau. of
W. T. and M. A. Pace
Sept. 15, 1867
Mar. 7, 1876

Pace, Matilda
Wife of R. W. Pace
April 14, 1838
Aug. 18, 1901

Pace, Maud
Daughter of B. F. and
S. S. Pace
Apr. 30, 1885
May 30, 1899

Pace, M. E. J.
Wife of J. G. Pace
Born Jan. 8, 1849

Pace, Norman
Died Oct. 24, 1975
60 yrs. 8 mos. 20 days

Pace, Una B.
Daughter of
B. F. and S. S. Pace
Mar. 7, 1899
Sept. 13, 1902

Pace, R. T.
Dau. of P. D. and
M. T. Pace
Feb. 17, 1892
April 7, 1905

Pace, Robert U.
Son of J. T. and
L. E. Pace
Born Aug. 2, 1876
July 31, (broken stone)

Pace, R. W.
Aug. 11, 1828
April 1, 1887

Pace, Thomas
Husband of M. C. Pace
July 1, 1813
May 20, 1875
61 yrs. 10 mos. 19 days

Pace, Thomas Wilma
June 10, 1882
May 14, 1904

Pace, William M.
Son of W. T. and M. A. Pace
Feb. 23, 1877
April 13, 1888

Pace, W. T. Jo
1844-1911
Pace, M. A. Hallum
His wife
1847-1940

Pace, William Thomas
Mar. 26, 1841
Apr. 22, 1902
Pace, Stacy Sobella
Wife of W. T. Pace
Born May 1, 1845
Pace, Joe Walter
Son of W. F. and S. S.
Pace
Feb. 22, 1869
Mar. 20, 1874
Pace, Pattie Pauline
Dau. of W. F. & S. S. Pace
Aug. 1, 1879
Oct. 31, 1902

Parish, Mary L
Wife of W. A. Parish
Nov. 30, 1863
Oct. 18, 1894

Parker, Banana P.
1900-1963

Parker, Zanie E.
1898-1901
Parker, Zeffie E.
1900-1901

Parkington, John G.
Mar. 6, 1844
June 14, 1865

Parks, Adaline
Wife of Dr. W. M.
Parks
Feb. 11, 1812
Oct. 4, 1873

Parks, Alice
Wife of B. R. Parks
Dau. of G. & M. H.
Douglass
May 9, 1854
Nov. 24, 1876

Parks, Andrew Stewart
July 28, 1841
July 18, 1879
38 yrs. lacking 15 days

Parks, Benj. R.
1850-1935

Parks, Bettie
Dau. of Rev. H. & R. Parks
Nov. 25, 1847
Oct. 13, 1861

Parks, Clarence, Son of M. E. &
H. Parks, Jr.
July 21, 1881
Aug. 12, 1882

Parks, Clyde
Son of B. R. &
M. A. Parks
1883-1885

Parks, Cora Lee
Dau. of B. R. & M. A. Parks
1899-1901

Parks, Dorris Marie
Dau. of W. H. &
F. G. Parks
Sept. 12, 1921
Mar. 21, 1923

Parks, Ed. C.
1906-1942

Parks, Edward Winfield
Son of Smith &
Adline Parks
Dec. 28, 1857
July 12, 1876

Parks, Elizabeth
Wife of William Parks
June 22, 1812
Aug. 13, 1858
46 yrs. 1 mo. 21 days

Parks, Faustina
Wife of H. Parks, Jr.
June 4, 1850
Feb. 1, 1875

Parks, Faustina
Inf.
Dau. of H. Jr. & Faustina Parks
Died Dec. 16, 1871

Parks, Fleata G.
1882-19
Parks, Will H.
1878-1926

Parks, Guy D.
1873-1940

Parks, Guy D. Jr.
1903-1943

Parks, H.
Dec. 25, 1849
April 5, 1931

Parks, Harriet J.
Dau. of R. H. & J. Parks
April 19, 1839
Oct. 6, 1868

Parks, Jermima
Wife of R. H. Parks
Oct. 22, 1816
Oct. 8, 1883

Parks, John Jacob
Son of Rev. H. & R. Parks
Feb. 29, 1860
April 27, 1879

Parks, Jacob
Died Oct. 1, 1811
64 yrs.

Parks, John Robert
Oct. 25, 1862
Sept. 22, 1864
Parks, Algoman
Sept. 23, 1859
Sept. 23, 1864
Sons of W. M. C. &
L. C. Parks

Parks, Leonard
Son of M. E. &
H. Parks Jr.
Jan. 15, 1884
Sept. 26, 1884

Parks, Mallie E.
Wife of George N. Parks
1854-1888

Parks, Martha Beasley
Wife of H. Parks
Died Aug. 21, 1839
Parks, Rev. Hamilton
June 8, 1809
Sept. 13, 1888
Parks, Rebecca Stewart
Wife of Rev. H. Parks
May 24, 1814
Sept. 15, 1883

Parks, Mary Allene
Dau. of B. R. & M. A.
Parks
1897-1940

Parks, Millie A.
Wife of B. R. Parks
1860-1939

Parks, Mollie
Wife of H. Parks, Jr.
Feb. 18, 1855
Aug. 15, 1899

Parks, Robert H.
Son of Rev. H. &
Martha Parks
1833-1910

Parks, R. H.
Jan. 21, 1804
July 23, 1877

Parks, Smith
Mar. 5, 1815
Jan. 2, 1894
Parks, Adeline
July 9, 1921
June 13, 1876

Parks, Smith, son of Smith &
Adeline Parks
June 21, 1855-Feb. 19 1871
15 yrs. 7 mos. 28 days

Parks, Dr. William
Dec. 30, 1800
Sept. 29, 1873

Parks, William G.
Son of Rev. H. & M. Parks
Oct. 14, 1832
Sept. 19, 1864
Parks, W. G.
Pvt. Co. H. 7 Regt.
Tenn. Cav.
C. S. A.
Oct. 14, 1832
Sept. 19, 1864

Parks, William H.
Son of W. M. O. & L. C. Parks
Nov. 15, 1861
Dec. 18, 1861

Parks, W. H.
Son of W. C. & L. C. Parks
Feb. 10, 1865
Nov. 21, 1883
Age: 18 yrs. 9 mos. 11 da.

Parnell, A. C.
Wife of R. E. Parnell
1849-1882
Parnell, T. J.
Son: 1869
Parnell, A. A.
Dau.

Parnell, Alma
1902-1937

Parnell, Charles E.
Nov. 20, 1876
Feb. 23, 1904

Parnell, Donald Wayne
1923-1943

Parnell, Eddie Jerald
Son
June 22, 1937
June 8, 1959

Parnell, Edward Lonzo
1879-1940
Parnell, Laurie Bill
1879-1917

Parnell, Franklin Lenard
Tennessee
PVT Trans. Corp
Oct. 9, 1937
April 4, 1968

Parnell, Ivey C. "Popeye"
1911-1966
Parnell, Bonnie S.
1916-

Parnell, Infant Son of
Mr. & Mrs. Eddie Parnell

Parnell, Leonard L.
1913-1970
Parnell, Lurlie O.
1908-

Parnell, Lora
April 13, 1879
July 22, 1944
Parnell, Bennetta
April 11, 1885
Nov. 29, 1947
Sisters

Parnell, M. A.
Wife of R. E. Parnell
1852-1920

Parnell, Maggie Elizabeth
May 11, 1885
Jan. 1, 1952
Parnell, Bobby Winfield
Mar. 30, 1877
June 16, 1953

Parnell, Margaret
1898-1964

Parnell, Rosalene
Wife of T. F. Parnell
July 29, 1851
May 10, 1920

Parnell, Thomas F.
Brother
1848-1934
Parnell, Mary
Sister
1830-1928

Parnell, Will
March 7, 1818
April 22, 1887

Parnell, Rev. W. H.
Son of G. & M. C.
Parnell
Sept. 4, 1866
Sept. 27, 1895
29 yrs. 23 days

Parnell, William T.
Feb. 25, 1908
Feb. 15, 1968
Parnell, Lea Ila
Oct. 14, 1917

Patterson, Cannie Cole
1893-19
Patterson, Robert Edward
1879-1945

Pitt, B. B.
Oct. 31, 1844
Dec. 1, 1919
Pitt, M. A.
His Wife
Born: Oct. 11, 1844

Pitt, Herbert H.
1888-1956
Pitt, Lillian Kelso
1889-1957

Pitt, Lula
Dau. of B. B. &
M. A. Pitt
Mar. 12, 1864
Jan. 18, 1873

Pursell, W. H.
1881-19
Pursell, Lula E.
1881-1930

Rasberry, Bryan
Inf. Son of Gaylon
& Gdean Rasberry
July 29, 1971

Rasberry, David Alan
Died: Nov. 25, 1974
10 yrs. 1 mo. 25 days

Rasberry, Jessie T.
July 14, 1876
Sept. 8, 1938
Rasberry, Fannie E.
Feb. 22, 1879
March 3, 1947

Rasberry, Thomas Ivie
Sept. 3, 1902
Oct. 14, 1970
Rasberry, Lillye B.
March 3, 1905
--

Rasberry, Wm. Ruby
Feb. 16, 1905
July 28, 1957
Rasberry, Thelma Bethel
Jan. 14, 1911
Raspberry, John R.
Father
July 1884
Dec. 1932
Raspberry, Eliza A.
Aug. 1888
Aug. 1939

Redding, J. S.
June 22, 1830
Mar. 3, 1900

Reed, Pearly A.
Dau. of J. N. & D. E. Reed
Died Sept. 21, 1888
16 yrs. 7 mos. 11 days

Reed, Willie G.
Son of H. R. & L. P. Reed
Jan. 21, 1861
May 16, 1872

Roberts, Fannie
Dau. of J. F. &
M. M. Roberts
July 26, 1882
Oct. 18, 1900

Roberts, J. F.
Feb. 15, 1859
Sept. 6, 1906

Rose, Lillie Thomas
Wife of A. R. Rose
Jan. 10, 1880
Sept. 6, 1908

Rose, Nancy J.
Wife of James Rose
Died Aug. 16, 1868

Runion, Ida L.
1881-19
Runion, Jeff H.
1870-1948

Runion, Rucia
Dau. of Issac &
Maud Runion
June 25, 1902
May 8, 1905

Runions, Walter B.
April 5, 1874
Sept. 22, 1940
Runions, T. Cash
Oct. 22, 1877
Oct. 21, 1949

Russell, Raphord Fulton
1856-1924
Russell, Mrs. Bettie Harris
1860-1937
Russell, Tommye
--
Newsom, Will B.
--
Newsom, Mrs. Annie Russell
1883-1942
Newsom, Martha Corinna
1911-1915

Sailsberry, Van
April 6, 1868
Jan. 30, 1935

Scobey, A. N.
Father
April 6, 1859
April 22, 1901
42 years 21 days
Scobey, Laura
Mother
Mar. 6, 1861
Aug. 26, 1941

Scobey, Billy Eugene
Aug. 21, 1932
May 31, 1934

Scobey, Bob
Jan. 18, 1875
Jan. 20, 1918

Scobey, Cora Lu
Wife of B. E. Scobey
Oct. 8, 1869
Mar. 21, 1909

Scobey, Derecia Faye
July 11, 1952
Oct. 25, 1963

Scobey, E. T. "Boss"
1905-1968

Scobey, Edna Parnell
1906-1954

Scobey, Elizabeth C.
Dau. of W. J. &
Nancy
Dec. 10, 1851
Jan. 9, 1852

Scobey, Elizabeth Mary
Wife of William J.
Scobey
June 10, 1836
Dec. 30, 1895

Scobey, Eunice
Dau. of J. H. & Tennie
Dec. 21, 1896
Oct. 1, 1897

Scobey, Finis E.
1859-1926
Scobey, Anna G. Smith
1856-19

Scobey, Florence Keirulff
Wife of N. L. Scobey
1880-1939

Scobey, H. L.
July 9, 1838
81 years old
Scobey, J. C.
His wife
Nov. 4, 1834
Feb. 14, 1912

Scobey, Hamilton G.
Son of W. J. & Nancy
July 1, 1850
Jan. 25, 1857
6 yrs, 21 days

Scobey, Hiram Q.
Son of Wm. J. & Nancy Scobey
April 25, 1853
March 22, 1855

Scobey, Homer Mack
Oct. 11, 1907
March 27, 1957
Scobey, Derotha Dew
Sept. 29, 1912

Scobey, Inf. Dau. of
N. L. & Mettie
Dec. 4, 1896

Scobey, J. H.
1868-1936
Scobey, Tennie
Herrin
1874-1921

Scobey, J. M.
Son of W. & E. M.
Scobey
Died at Bethel College
16 years of age

Scobey, Joe N.
No Dates

Scobey, Jonathan Herrin
Son of J. H. & T. H.
Scobey
May 19, 1892
Feb. 15, 1906

Scobey, L. A.
Wife of W. B. Scobey
June 25, 1845
Feb. 4, 1918

Scobey, Lonnie M.
Aug. 3, 1875
Jan. 31, 1950

Scobey, Malisa J.
Dau. of Wm. J. &
Nancy
April 28, 1845
Jan. 30, 1869

Scobey, Margaret M.
Wife of W. B. Scobey
June 9, 1839
Aug. 8, 1904

Scobey, Mary E.
Wife of F. E. Scobey
July 26, 1858
March 23, 1880

Scobey, Mattie Cook
May 25, 1881
Oct. 7, 1955

Scobey, Mettie Cochran
Wife of N. L. Scobey
1869-1921

Scobey, N. Dewitt
1897-1958

Scobey, N. L.
1863-1949

Scobey, Nancy
Wife of Wm. J. Scobey
Feb. 22, 1824
Aug. 3, 1855
31 yrs. 5 mos. 11 days

Scobey, Norvell
Nov. 11, 1893
71 yrs. 8 mos. 29 days
Scobey, Elizabeth
June 20, 1894
68 yrs. 2 mos. 19 days

Scobey, Oscar Quinton
Son of L. C. & P. A. Scobey
June 12, 1880
Nov. 6, 1892
12 yrs. 5 mos. 6 days

Scobey, Parthenia
1853-1919
Scobey, L. Clay
1850-1903

Scobey, Reuben H.
Nov. 30, 1877
Jan. 9, 1904

Scobey, Sarah E.
Dau. of W. B. &
M. M. Scobey
Nov. 19, 1862
May 5, 1887

Scobey, Sophia A.
1858-1936

Scobey, Ula
July 9, 1872
Jan. 1, 1937

Scobey, W. B.
March 4, 1840
Oct. 9, 1922

Scobey, W. Scott
Son of Wm. J. & Nancy
June 12, 1847
Sept. 13, 1852
5 yrs. 2 mos. 20 days

Scobey, William J.
Son of F. e. &
A. G. Scobey
Feb. 26, 1884
Sept. 27, 1884

Scobey, William J.
Aug. 29, 1821
Feb. 20, 1886

Scobey, Willie M.
Dau. of Wm. J. & C. M.
Dec. 23, 1878
Nov. 3, 1881

Scobey, Z. Taylor
Son of W. J. & Nancy
June 12, 18 (illegible)
Sept. 5, 185(illegible)

Scoby, Annie M.
Wife of D. T. Scoby
Mar. 20, 1865
Oct. 7, 1891

Scott, Henrietta Pace
1875-1949

Self, Joe R.
Tennessee
PFC HQ Det Station Com
World War II
June 17, 1897
Nov. 16, 1966

Self, Pearl Hugueley Michael
1904-

Sellers, Beatrice E.
Dau. of H. B. &
S. V. Sellers
Sept. 25, 1889
Aug. 1, 1893
Sellers, Inf. Dau. of
H. B. & S. V.
Oct. 23, 1892
Nov. 6, 1892

Shackelton, Luther
1868-1939
Shackelton, Cora
1871-19

Sherwood, W. H. H.
1843-1923

Shibley, Rebecca
Wife of Wm. A. Shibley
and only dau. of
A. B. & L. P. Tigrett
July 6, 1879
March 27, 1905

Shipp, Ben Franklin
March 6, 1886
April 23, 1961

Shofner, Ernest
1885-1917

Shofner, Willie J.
1905-1910

Short, Lillie Scobey
1878-1950
Short, Walter L.
1875-1942

Simmons, Adeline C.
Wife of L. C. Simmons
Dau. of Wm & Sally Martin
June 26, 1822-Nov. 6, 1855
32 years, 4 mos. 10 days

Simmons, Martha Ann
Wife of L. C. Simmons
Dau. of R. R. Shyers
May 29, 1822
June 29, 1853
31 yrs. 1 mo.

Sisler
Inf. Son of
J. B. & Estell Sisler
Sept. 1903

Skinner, E. A.
1856-1924
Skinner, Kate B.
1866-1929

Skinner, E. J.
Wife of G. W. Skinner
May 11, 1834
Jan. 8, 1897
62 yrs. 7 mos 27 days

Smith, Richard M.
Feb. 20, 1880
April 27, 1956

Spellings, R. S.
July 9, 1889
Dec. 4, 1924
Spellings Wava McCormack
His Wife
Sept. 4, 1899
April 16, 1925

Stephens, Charles William
Inf. of Mr. & Mrs. G. B.
Stephens
March 3, 1923
March 3, 1928

Stephens, Mary Pace
Nov. 13, 1895
June 7, 1942
Parnell, Mickey F.
April 21, 1936
June 7, 1942

Stephens, Ralph P.
Tennessee
PFC Army Medical
SVG-USAR
Korea
May 5, 1928
May 19, 1963

Stockton, Mary A.
1859-1935
Stockton, John S.
1849-1932

Stockton, R. C.
Feb. 5, 1828
Oct. 13, 1895

Stockton. Rev. R. G.
July 2, 1862
April 22, 1893

Stocton, J. R.
1858-1935
Stocton, Martha
1862-1906

Summers, Charlie
May 7, 1883
Feb. 13, 1908
22 yrs. 9 mos. 8 days

Tackett, Pennie
Wife of J. O. Tackett
April 24, 1881
Aug. 19, 1914

Tatum, J. E.
July 8, 1848
May 8, 1891

Tatum, Jessie L.
Jan. 8, 1850
Feb. 14, 1894

Tatum, Sarah G.
Wife of J. E. Tatum
Oct. 19, 1850
Nov. 25, 1891

Tatum, Thomas Lee
Son of J. E. &
Sarah Tatum
July 24, 1881
April 23, 1891

Taylor, J. R.
Dec. 18, 1843

Taylor, Martha Adaline
Nov. 17, 1861
Oct. 23, 1923

Taylor, Sallie
1881-1933
Taylor, J. B.
1874-1951

Thompson, Betty
Feb. 11, 1869-19--
Thompson, Jeff
Oct. 4, 1861
Dec. 4, 1942

Thompson, Joseph R.
Dec. 18, 1879
Dec. 11, 1880
11 mo. 23 days

Tigrett, A. B.
July 14, 1845
March 29, 1919
Tigrett, Lutie P.
April 15, 1853
Oct. 31, 1919

Tigrett, Emma Rebecca
Dau. of H. P. & S. N. Tigrett
Aug. 5, 1905
June 1, 1909

Tilford, Catherine F.
Wife of Samuel Tilford
Dec. 15, 1815
Aug. 29, 1886
70 yrs. 8 mos. 14 days

Tilford, Samuel
April 25, 1809
June 26, 1876
67 urs. 2 mos. 10 days

Tilford, Sarah L.
Dau. of Samuel & C. F. Tilford
Dec. 31, 1851
Jan. 14, 1860
9 yrs. 5 mos. 14 days

Timbs, Martha F.
Oct. 16, 1867
Oct. 23, 1953
(Sister Mrs. Hattie Timbs
Jackson)

Tinsley, Samuel P.
Son of G. B. & M. C. Tinsley
Nov. 25, 1852
(illegible) 27, 1854

Tinsley, Infant son of
G. B. & M. C. Tinsley
(Broken Stone)

Towns, Everett Samuel
Son of S. S. & F. C. Towns
July 22, 1898
April 23, 1899

Towns, Mrs. F. A.
His wife
Dec. 25, 1862
Aug 5, 1946
Towns, G. D.
Oct. 23, 1861
Dec. 1, 1917

Towns, Ira
No Dates

Towns, Isham A.
Mar. 2, 1860
June 26, 1914

Towns, Homer
No Dates

Towns, Mintie E.
Wife of I. A. Towns
Jan. 24, 1867
Mar. 25, 1907
Aged 40 yrs. 2 mos. 1 day

Townsend, Claudia
Dau. of R. w. & M. F. Townsend
Born 1874
(broken Stone)

Trout, Nancy Ann
Consort of H. D. Trout
June 9, 1822
Aug. 15, 1867
Age 45 yrs. 2 mos., 6 days

Trout, Sarah E.
Dau. of D. H. & Nancy A.
June 8, 1853
Oct. 5, 1859
Age 6 yrs. 3 mos 27 days

Turner, Lewis Clay
Feb. 2, 1910
Jan. 2, 1911
11 mos.

Walker, Egbert
Son of Wm. H. and
Victoria Ann Walker
April 7, 1875
Sept 29, 1878

Walker, Wm. H.
1884-1907
Walker, Victoria Ann
July 16, 1851
Dec. 1, 1876

Warpen, Mrs. Cynthia A.
Sept. 3, 1820
May 15, 1917

Warren, Elisha A.
Son of W. M. and
L. E. Warren
Dec. 13, 1861
July 5, 1887

Warren, Everett Lee
April 16, 1908
July 8, 1910

Warren, W. M.
June 22, 1839
Aug. 22, 1893

Webb, Alice
Dau. of Mrs. Azzie
Kelso Webb
(Information furnished by
Mrs. Lloyd Ellis)

Webb, Azzie Kelso
Sister of Mrs. Myrtle Kelso
Gordon and Mrs. Mitt Kelso
Ellis

Webb, Thea
Son of Mrs. Azzie Kelso
Webb
No Dates
Information by Mrs. Lloyd
Ellis

Wells, Martha Tigrett
Dau. of H. P. & Sadie Tigrett, Sr.
Wife of Jack Wells
1917-1971

Wells, Meredith
Wife of W. Burton Wells
April 11, 1950
April 6, 1971

White, Crawford E.
Sept. 29, 1803
June 14, 1873

White, Elizabeth W. Martin
Consort of J. E. White
Feb. 17, 1807
July 20, 1854

Whitson, Warn Carter
Son of S. T. and
Vergie Whitson
Nov. 8, 1921
Nov. 9, 1921

Whitten, Massalin Henry
Nov. 20, 1819
Dec. 1, 1891

Wilbanks, Carol
Died Feb. 7, 1974
12 years 3 months 23 days

Wilbanks. Ila Mae
Died Jan 25, 1974
42 years 8 months 29 days

Wilbanks, Lee Verne
Died Jan 25, 1974
42 yrs. 7 months 10 days

Wilbanks
Son of Lee and Uda Wilbanks
Died Jan. 25, 1974

Williams, Adaline E.
Wife of J. G. Williams
Born March 24, 1847
Broken Stone

Williams, John Gid
Dec. 3, 1836
Feb. 6, 1927

Williams, John R.
1855-1937

Williamson, Alice Maude
Dau. of F. G. & M. A. Williamson
June 9, 1891
July 19, 1891

Williamson, Bettie Sherwood
1857-1941

Williamson, Clark
1891-1949

Williamson, Henry Franklin
March 5, 1860
July 12, 1899

Williamson, Jessie F.
Feb. 22, 1823-April 24, 1890

Williamson, Mattie Elma
1874-1946

Williamson, Sarah Fleming
May 10, 1823
March 10, 1913

Williamson, Thomas Vance
Oct. 17, 1863
May 6, 1958
Williamson, Ada Gilkey
Feb. 22, 1873
Aug. 24, 1915

Willis, John W.
Nov. 12, 1846
April 4, 1927
Willis, Laura W.
Sept. 13, 1855
Feb. 20, 1931

Wood, Polk
Son of Rossa
Nov. 10, 1877
Nov. 22, 1881

Woods, Eleazer
Jan. 8, 1813
April 4, 1875

Woods, Sarah P.
Wife of E. Wood
July 22, 1804
Aug. 13, 1853

Woodyard, Luther B.
Tennessee
Co. C 57 Pioneer Inf
World War I
Nov. 4, 1896
Oct. 11, 1918
Woodyard, Taylor
Nov. 8, 1894
March 23, 1911
Brothers

Wyatt, Grace Golden
Dau. of G. W. and N. C.
Nov. 18, 1899
Sept. 24, 1900

Wyatt, Hardee
May 28, 1878
Nov. 10, 1944

Wyatt, Homer Parks
Feb. 1, 1889
July 23, 1902
Wyatt, Col. J. N.
March 23, 1928
March 22, 1903
Wyatt, Mrs. P. V.
March 8, 1843
Feb. 28, 1909
Married Dec. 14, 1864
Wyatt, Ira Walton
Oct. 14, 1869
Jan. 18, 1907

Wyatt, Ira Walton
Oct. 14, 1869
Jan. 18, 1907

Wyatt, Martha Ann
Wife of
J. N. Wyatt
March 19, 1835
Jan. 18, 1861

Wyatt, Inf. dau.
of J. H. and M. A.
March 18, 1858

Young, Georgia
Mother
May 17, 1901
Feb. 24, 1950

Young, Travis
Tennessee
Cook Co. F. 40 Inf.
World War I
Jan. 30, 1883
Jan. 10, 1957

PORTER CEMETERY

The Porter Cemetery is located on the Sharpsferry Road about three miles from Newbern. Originally Porter land, the plot is now owned by Burton Pledge. In Newbern, turn on to Sharpsferry Road from Highway 51 N. at the Dyer County Junior High School and travel approximately eight miles. Barely visible, the cemetery is on a hill on the left hand side of the road.

Inf., Son of S. W. &
M. H. Porter
Aug. 28, 1883
Oct. 3, 1883

Porter, James N.
Son of S. W. &
Mollie Porter
Oct. 11, 1877
May 8, 1879

Porter, John M.
Feb. 20, 1795
Nov. 12, 1875
Age 80 yrs. 8 mos. 22 days.

Porter, Mollie H.
Dau. of A. c. Herrin
Wife of S. W. Porter
1853-Nov. 1, 1883

Porter, N.
Sept. 7, 1816
Oct. 10, 1869
Porter, S. A.
Wife of N. Porter
July 9, 1820
Jan. 15, 1895
Porter, M. C.
Dau. of N. & S. A.
Porter
Feb. 14, 1840
Oct. 28, 1886

Porter, Robert Mitchell
Son of S. w. &
Sally Hampton
Feb. 1, 1881
May 1, 1886
Inf. Dau. of
S. W. & Sally Hampton
(Note: Born and Died 1887
Porter Family Bible)

Porter, Stephen William
Feb. 19, 1850
Sept. 26, 1921
(Note: Porter Family
Bible)

Porter, Willie C.
Son of S. w. &
M. H. Porter
July 22, 1879
Feb. 19, 1882
Porter, S. W.
Son of N. & S. A.
Porter
Feb. 19, 1850

Wood, Mary Catherine Porter
Feb. 14, 1840
Oct. 24, 1876
(Note: Porter Family Bible)

REHOBETH METHODIST CHURCH AND CEMETERY

Rehobeth United Methodist Church is located about seven miles east of Dyersburg, just north of State Highway 104, and about six or seven miles south of Newbern, Tennessee. The Methodists named the new church Rehobeth, which means "Broad Places" or "More Room". It is the name of one of the wells dug by Issac and his men in the valley of Gerar (Genesis 26: 17-22). Land was given to the Methodists by Mr. Steve Chitwood, the Smiths, and others for a church site. A building was erected during the year 1869 and was named Rehobeth Methodist Church, South. Rev. H. B. Avery, the father of Mrs. Nell (Avery) Walker, dedicated the church. Rev. Avery was then Presiding Elder, and he also had the deed recorded for the church grounds, which included a large tract for burying purposes. This ground was set aside for white and negro.

Many changes have taken place in the Rehobeth community but the same frame building erected in 1869 wtill remains strong, and a landmark in the community. After a century of worship many of the relatives of the Chitwoods, Rays, Smiths, Doaks, Pursells, Webbs, Hendersons, Hollands, Sawyers, Tatums, McHaneys, Roberts, Selfs, and others still worship in the same building that was erected in 1869, a hundred years ago. According to the records, the first person buried in the cemetery was Mary Chitwood. Her husband was John Chitwood, who is buried in Virginia.

Adams, J. K.
1827-1910
Chitwood, Bessie
1882-1939

Agnew, G. W.
Feb. 21, 1865
Aug. 6, 1955
Agnew, Bettie
Dec. 8, 1861
April 4, 1940

Agnew, Ira W.
Mar. 23, 1899
--

Agnew, Ned H.
Aug. 7, 1899
Mar. 13, 1966

Akin, R. E.
Nov. 17, 1863
July 26, 1891

27 yrs 7 mos. 9 days

Akin, Samie Lee
Dau. of R. E. &
T. B. Akin
July 1, 1885
Aug. 29, 1886

Anderson, Evie Powell
1907-1956

Anderson, Harvey
1906-1970

Baker, Eliza
Wife of R. C. Baker
Died Mar. 4, 1871
42 yrs. 2 mos. 13 days

Baker, Everett
Oct. 16, 1869
Nov. 9, 1877

Baker, G. C.
Aug. 20, 1881
Aug. 27, 1891

BAker, Melvin
Died Feb. 6, 1975
66 yrs. 7 mo. 28 days

BAker, Rome Ura
1889-1890

Baker, Samuel
Feb. 2, 1831
Sept. 3, 1888

BAne, Charlie
Tennessee
Pvt Co A
122 Inv. World War I
Dec. 16, 1896
Aug. 17, 1964

Bane, James W.
Tennessee
Pvt. 105 Engineers
World War I
July 22, 1890
Nov. 19, 1964

Banks, Sadie M.
Dec. 15, 1906
Feb. 14, 1958

Barker, Ellie Chitwood
1849-1932

Barker, Raleigh W.
1837-1901
Co. D 47th Tnn. Inf., C. S. A.

Barker, (Illegible)
Barker, R. W. and E.
May 25, 1875
Oct. 10, 1878
Broken Stone

Barker, Ulah J.
Dau. of R. W &
E. Barker
Dec. 21, 1872
Sept 9, 1876
31 yrs. 8 mos. 15 days

Bass, Ben
1897-
Bass, Edith
1903-

Bass, James J.
1856-1926

Bass, James J.
Aug. 17, 1930
July 29, 1961

Bates, Herbert L.
1912-
Bates, Jewell T.
1906-

Bell, Joseph W.
1888-1968
Bell, Beulah E.
1890-19

Black, S. P.
Oct. 19, 1868
Feb. 14, 1891
Son of Jim & Mary Black

Bloomingdale, E.
Sept. 11, 1854
Dec. 20, 1890
Bloomingdale, Dora
April 15, 1854
Dec. 24, 1904

Bloomingdale, Nancy P.
Died Sept. 15, 1854

Bloomingdale, Willie
Born & Died
Jan. 8, 1822

Boatwright, Arthur
1887-1902

Boone, Daniel Methias
May 4, 1849
Jan. 19, 1895

Boone, Howie
1902-1937
Boone, Nannie
1865-1940

Boone, Louise
Sept. 26, 1918
May 5, 1921

Boone, Mack
1896-1927

Bowen, Claude
1883-1970
Bowen, Lillie B.
1903-

Bowen, Mrs. M. J.
Aug. 25, 1858
Sept. 17, 1911

Bowen, Nannie McHaney
Aug. 1, 1884
Sept. 6, 1925

Bowen, W. A.
Aug. 2, 1857
Feb. 29, 1936

Bradshaw, Bessie Cotham Hales
Wife of Sam Bradshaw
Nov. 8, 1881
Feb. 20, 1903

Bradshaw, Eddy Polk
Nov. 12, 1868
Bradshaw, Delia Frances
Feb. 22, 1869
July 31, 1932

Bradshaw Infant
Son of E. P. &
D. F. Bradshaw
Born Aug. 24, 1900

Bradshaw, Haskins
Son of E. P. &
D. F. Bradshaw
Mar. 11, 1903
Jan. 10, 1904

Bradshaw, Jesse Thomas
1864-1916
Bradshaw, Ada Elizabeth
1868-1951

Bradshaw, Milam
Son of E. P. & D. F.
Bradshaw
Nov. 3, 1901
Nov. 3, 1903

Bradshaw, Sam B.
May 4, 1839
Jan. 30, 1875
Bradshaw, Lenora
Mar. 19, 1835
Jan. 4, 1914

Bradshaw, Sam Q.
"Bud"
1873-1956
Bradshaw, Alice Carrie
1879-19

Bradshaw, Joseph Samuel
Born & Died 1915
Infant

Brasfield, Ray Jr.
Feb. 13, 1945
April 23, 1945

Britton, Solomon Edward
1802-1872

Brown, Ben
1874-1942
Brown, Molly
Wife
1875-1967

Brown, Nellie
Sept. 17, 1902
Oct. 8, 1902

Borwn, Sam H.
1883-1969
Brown, Eula A.
1887-1950

Bucie, Jim A.
Aug. 20, 1877
June 15, 1952
Bucie, Sally
April 18, 1881
Mar. 12, 1965

Bucie, Luther Wesley
Feb. 20, 1923
Jan. 25, 1944

Burns, Robert Clyme
Born Dec. 5, 1889
Died Jan. 19, 1918
Camp Sevier

Bush, Della
1889-1959

Bush, James Calvin
Tennessee
Tec 5 432 AAA AWBN ·CAC
WW II
Aug. 27, 1916
Dec. 28, 1967

Bush, John
1891-19

Butler, Rose E.
1889-1959

Carpenter, S. M.
Wife of H. R. Carpenter
July 8, 1859
April 8, 1879

Carpenter, Infant Son of
S. M. &
H. R. Carpenter
No Dates

Carrell, A. Cooper
1861-1926
Carrell, Eliza D.
1861-1915

Carrell, James Marion
1886-1945
Carrell, Martha Elizabeth
1889-1955

Carroll, Mildred Delena
1881-1966

Carroll, Leana
1856-1945
    , William J.
1850-1935

Chitwood, Alfred Taylor
Nov. 22, 1888
Jan. 23, 1955
Chitwood, Carrie Hendrix
April 19, 1893
Feb. 29, 1952

Chitwood, Allice
Wife of L. H. Chitwood
Dec. 21, 1858
May 16, 1896

Chitwood, Angie K.
1879-1950
Chitwood, Maude
1882-19

Chitwood, Annie E.
Oct. 26, 1884
July 16, 1945

Chitwood, Audrey
1889-1964

Chitwood, Bettie
Wife of Creed Chitwood
1870-1939

Chitwood, Creed
1859-1942

Chitwood, Baby
1901-1901

Chitwood, Charley, C.
1851-1932
Chitwood, Alice M.
1858-1950
Chitwood, May
1877-1891
Chitwood, Gertrude
1884-1898
Chitwood, Roy
1890-1918
Chitwood, Infant
1887

Chitwood, Corinne
1909-1912
Infant Dau. 1915

Chitwood, E.
1844-1938
Chitwood, Rebecca
HIs Wife
1847-1927

Chitwood, Edmond
No Dates

Chitwood, Effie
1868-1897

Chitwood, Elener
Died Nov. 27, 1874

Chitwood, Eliher
1882-19
Chitwood, Ozella
1886-1960

Chitwood, Emer A.
Wife of S. H. Chitwood
Dec. 10, 1849
July 6, 1876

Chitwood, Exar
1891-1919
Daughter

Chitwood, Garry J.
Masonic
Father
1876-1952

Chitwood, Georgia
1889-1956
Chitwood, Lena
1882-1964

Chitwood, Hattie H.
Mother
1881-1954

Chitwood, Infant Son
1909-
(Creed Chitwood lot)

Chitwood, Infnat son
1910
(Creed Chitwood lot)

Chitwood, James W.
Tennessee
PFC WW II
Feb. 15, 1912
April 30, 1960

Chitwood, Lon
Mar. 5, 1829
July 15, 1880

Chitwood, L. H.
Mar. 31, 1859
Mar. 1, 1902
42 yrs. 11 mos.

Chitwood, Levin H.
Dec. 18, 1900

Chitwood, Lex
July 18, 1881
Oct. 31, 1902

Chitwood, L. J.
Feb. 28, 1819
Aug. 27, 1887
Chitwood, M. B.
Feb. 15, 1817
Jan. 1, 1879

Chitwood, Mary R.
Died 1826

Chitwood, Nell
Dau. of Mr. & Mrs.
Lex Chitwood
May 18, 1901
Aug. 16, 1904

Chitwood, Noel
1889-1972

Chitwood, Oren
1887-1888

Chitwood, Oren Ira
Sept. 9, 1911
May 13, 1912
Chitwood, Loren Ivy
Sept. 9, 1911
April 2, 1912

Chitwood, Roy
1890-1918
Chitwood, Lula Mae
1892-1965

Chitwood, R. J.
Aug. 9, 1860
Feb. 12, 1909

Chitwood, S. A. (Bud)
1845-1924
Chitwood, Matilda Ann
1850-1885
Chitwood, Martha Ann (Sis)
1847-1928

Chitwood, S. T.
Nov. 14, 1840
Aug. 25, 1918

Chitwood, S. T.
1889-1953

Chitwood, William Bostic
Mar. 8, 1883
Aug. 3, 1966
Chitwood, Bennie Stephenson
Sept. 7, 1884
Aug. 26, 1966

Clay, Alvie Lee
1896-1958

Clay, Ebbie Lee
Aug. 10, 1915
July 27, 1938

Clay, J. L.
1867-1956
Clay, Ollie May
1873-1953

Coker, Charlie C.
1877-1949
Coker, Hattie C.
1881-1925

Cole, Annie Velma
July 29, 1905
July 18, 1915

Cole, Ella
Wife
1874-1953

Cole, Lizzie
1877-1898

Cole, Stella
Wife
1880-1924

Cole, William Avery
1873-1962

Cooley, Jim C.
1886-1967

Cooley, Leonard C.
1896-1936

Cooley, Marvin
1890-1970
Cooley, Addie C.
1895-19

Copeland, George W.
1861-1942
Copeland, Mary Frances
1864-1929

Cowan, Harvey T.
1898-19
Cowan, Oma W.
1899-1966

Craig, Dwaine
Feb. 27, 1937
May 17, 1937
Craig, Euna B.
Dec. 10, 1906
Mar. 7, 1937

Crosthwait, J. Stanford
1889-1949

Cummings, Claude Reuben
Jan. 1, 1922
April 15, 1945

Cummings, Dorris G.
May 6, 1931
NOv. 8, 1932

Cummings, Earlen
Jan. 28, 1901
Oct. 14, 1940

Cummings, L. W.
Son of R. L. Cummings
& Wife
March 27, 1918
Oct. 24, 1922

Cummings, Odie
Died Sept. 10, 1975
77 years 6 mos. 29 days

Cummings, William E.
Dec. 22, 1862
Mar. 11, 1945
Cummings, Mattie E.
Oct. 9, 1869
Mar. 27, 1947

Curtis, Miss Bess I.
Dec. 14, 1970
72 yrs 2 mos 17 days

Cozart, Willie
May 22, 1914
Oct. 29, 1973
Cozart, Martha
Dec. 21, 1915

Davis, Bettie S.
1862-1891

Davis, Cora
Dau. of S. b. &
M. C. Davis
Dec. 28, 1873
Aug. 26, 1878
4 yrs. 7 mos 28 days

Davis, Linda Faye
Nov. 9, - Nov. 9, 1953

Davis, S. B.
18 - 1909
Davis, Martha
Wife of S. B.
1835-1907
Infant Dau.
Mar. 30, 1882   6 mos.
Davis, Cora
Died August 15, 1878
4 yrs. 6 mos.

Davis, W. D.
Jan. 16, 1883
Mar. 14, 1967
Davis, Ocie S.
Feb. 29, 1912

Davis, Wm W.
Died April 16, 1856
61 years 6 days

Dickey, James Monroe
1892-1957

Dickey, R. J.
1890-1949
Dickey, Ruth
1893-1957

Dillon, Tollie O.
1906-1963
Dillon, Kathleen
1922-

Dodson, Pearl Foster
Mother
1892-1975

Doyle, Luther B.
1875-1957
Doyle, Iva D.
1910-1964

Doyle, Luther, Jr.
Baby
1937

Drummond, J. M.
Born Jan. 16, 1838
Died July 7, 1910
Drummond, N. A.
Wife of J. M. Drummond
Born Dec. 6, 1850
Died Aug. 13, 1910

Drummond, Rosa Ethel
Dau. of J. M.
& N. A. Drummond
Born Dec. 25, 1881
Died Nov. 9, 1887
Age 5 yr. 10 mo. 14 days

Drummond, Thomas F.
Son of J. M. & N. A.
Drummond
Born Sept 27, 1871
Died Jan. 29, 1900
Age 28 years. 4 mo. 2 days

Dycus, Addie V.
Feb. 29, 1880
April 14, 1966

Evans, Clarence Lee
1907-1908

Evans, David L.
1886-
Evans, Manie H.
1890-

Evans, Edna E.
1903-1947

Evans, William J.
1859-1941
Evans, Nancy E.
1866-1955

Evans, Willie
Son of W. J. &
N. E. Evans
Aug. 4, 1890-Mar. 4, 1915

Ewing, Alfred T.
1856-1921
Ewing, Eugenia M.
1859-1941

Faulkner, Clyde
June 26, 1902
Aug. 2, 1974
Faulkner, Essie
May 14, 1911

Faulkner, Beverly Kay
Infant
June 1, 1962

Featherston, Clarence R.
1889-1964
Featherston, Mary F.
1891-19

Featherston, Homer G.
April 25, 1896
July 17, 1969
Featherston, Dessie L.
Born Oct. 4, 1904

Featherston, Purse
1887-1950
Featherson, Ona
1888-19

Featherston, W. S.
Feb. 6, 1857
--

Featherston, C. E.
Wife of W. S. Featherston
May 20, 1865
Nov. 18, 1920

Fisher, Allie Bell
June 13, 1888
Dec. 20, 1949

Fisher, Otis Guy, Sr.
Feb. 3, 1882
June 27, 1954

Fisher, Thomas
Infant

Fisher, Sadie B.
Infant
Maurine Fisher
No Dates

Flowers, Steve D.
1869-1939
Flowers, Pearl
1877-1962

Fooshee, G. A.
Wife of T. V. Fooshee
Mar. 20, 1851
Sept. 6, 1893

Fooshee, Inf. Dau. of
G. L. & C. F. Fooshee
Born & Died
April 13, 1875

Fooshee, Sydney
Died July 3, 1853

Fooshee, T. V.
Sept. 16, 1847
Oct. 7, 1909
Fooshee, Ollie A.
Wife of T. V. Fooshee
Mar. 20, 1854
Sept. 6, 1898

Fooshee, Willie Fern
Dau. of Harry & Cora
Fooshee
Sept. 8, 1904
Aug. 30, 1910

Forbes, D. C. "Doc"
1874-1935
Forbes, Shanan
1871-1935

Foust, Daniel
Apr. 26, 1840
Oct. 25, 1880

Foust, Emily
Wife of J. Foust
Nov. 13, 1848
Dec. 28, 1882

Foust, Hannah
Nov. 20, 1882
Jan. 10, 1919

Forsee, Dorris
1919-1921

Forsee, Earl F.
1884-1964
Forsee, Patsy, D.
1890-1967

Forsee, Edith
Dau. of E. F. & Patsy
Born Sept 20, 1908
Died April 29, 1914

Forsee, Nell Gray
1884-1971
(Marker from White-Ranson
Funeral Home, Union City),

Forshee, Manerva Holland
1853-1925

Fortner, Eli
Feb. 8, 1893
Aug. 15, 1973
Fortner, Delia
July 6, 1897
--
Fortner, Mack F.
1868-1955

Fortner, Susanna
1867-19

Foster, Andrew J.
Father
Dec. 14, 1883
Jan. 17, 1956

Foster, Daneula S.
June 4, 1878
Oct. 8, 1948

Foster, Earl D.
S2 U. S. Navy
W. W. II
March 24, 1923
Nov. 29, 1970

Freeman, Bob Reed
Tennessee
CPL U. S. Army
Korea
Mar. 23, 1933
Sept. 24, 1971

French, Infant
Son of Mr. and
Mrs. Lex C. French
Born & Died
Feb. 23, 1909

French, Jerry Lynn
Died Dec. 18, 1974
3 yrs. 1 mo. 6 days

French, Lex C.
1887-1974
French, Levisa
1885-

French, Michael A.
Died Dec. 18, 1974
4 yrs. 2 mos. 12 days

French, Otha
1916-1955
French, Geneva
1922-

Gannon, Miss Annie
1897-1970

Gannon, Howard Perry
Feb. 19, 1895
Oct. 9, 1901

Gannon, Quincy G.
1882-1958
Gannon, Ola G.
1886-1966

Gannon, W. C.
Dec. 16, 1843
Feb. 22, 1907
63 yrs. 2 mos. 16 days.

Gannon, William Alfred
Oct. 10, 1874
Dec. 6, 1948

Gannon, Nannie Bloomingdale
Dec. 22, 1879
Mar. 17, 1950

Gardner, Charles M.
1870-1965

Gardner, C. W.
Apr. 7, 1841
Nov. 30, 1919
Gardner, Mary
Wife of C. W.
Nov. 28, 1837
Jan. 14, 1906

Gardner, Dannie R.
1866-1954

Gaston, Huston F.
1904-1968
Gaston, Dola R.
1914-

Gibbons, Ben M.
1896-1953

Glissen, Betty Jane
Feb. 21, 1943
Mar. 7, 1947

Goodrum, Holland
1921-1939

Goodrum, Richard L.
1883-1966
Goodrum, Emma
1893-

Griggs, Carl Richard
Tennessee
PU8 U. S. Army
Died Sept. 22, 1922

Gwaltney, Ed
1875-1960

Gwaltney, Maude
Oct. 12, 1880
FEb. 16, 1971

Gwaltney, Nellie A.
1903-1908

Gwaltney, Nora M.
1869-1955

Gwaltney, O. W.
1872-1927

Gwaltney, Preston A.
1867-1949

Gwaltney, Sarah E.
Wife of D. M. Gwaltney
May 6, 1845
July 27, 1906
61 yrs. 2 mos 21 days

Hail, Infant of
Mr & Mrs. W. L. Hail
Born & Died
Oct. 22, 1906

Hales, Cora W. Bradshaw
Wife of Henry Hales
Oct. 8, 1870
Oct. 13, 1900

Hall, Bernanrd
1891-1970
Hall, Bernice
1898-

Hall, C. C.
Feb. 19, 1875
Jan. 19, 1948
Hall, Sibble A.
April 16, 1883
     --

Hall, Clara
1931-1931

Hall, Mrs. Ernestine
May 31, 1910
Dec. 8, 1934
Hall, Mr. Finis G.
Aug. 12, 1904
     --

Hall, Gertrude
1863-1911

Hall, Jesse E.
August 11, 1900
Oct. 12, 1958

Hall, Mary R.
1927-1937

Hall, Sarah Frances
Mar. 13, 1921
Mar. 7, 1922

Hamlett, Amariller
Wife of H. H. Hamlett
Aug. 25, 1848
(Broken Stone)

Hamlett, D. L.
Son of H. H. Hamlett
Sept. 12, 1879
Feb. 28, 1885
11 yrs. 5 mos.

Hammond, Minnie Harris
Died Mar. 27, 1975
88 years, 3 mos. 6 days

Harper, Ben
1901-19
Harper, Annie Belle
His Wife
1898-1942

Harrington, Andrew Walter
1869-1946
Harrington, Rubie Webb
1871-1962

Harrington, Herbert
1910-1955
Harrington, Laverne
1909-19

Harrington, Martha E.
1918-1928

Harrington, Mervyn
Son of A. W. & R. E.
Feb. 7, 1894
Jan. 18, 1896

Harris, Defoy Thomas
Dec. 9, 1926
Oct. 3, 1970

Harrison, Helen A.
1869-1944

Harwell, Hepsy J.
Dau. of S. T. &
M. E. Harwell
Oct. 11, 1876
May 7, 1878

Hastings, C. E. "Bud"
1884-1961
Hastings, Mary
1886-1970

Hastings, C. W.
Died Nov. 6, 1898
69 yrs. 7 mos. 7 days
Hastings, Preston
Sept. 31, 1891
17 yrs.
Hastings, Margaret E.
Wife of C. w. Hastings
Mar. 17, 1843
June 21, 1925
Hastings, Era
Died Oct. 10, 1876
7 mos.
Hastings,
Died Dec. 10, 1887
18 days

Hastings, INf.
Dau. of Mr. and M.
Luther W. Hastings
Oct. 19, 1906

Hastings, John A.
1873-1934
Hastings, Mary B.
1875-1957

Hastings, Luther W.
Sept. 8, 1877
Dec. 1, 1964
Hastings, Susan Gardner
Oct. 4, 1879
Sept. 30, 1961

Hastings, Savannah
May 7, 1911
May 10, 1911

Hathaway, D. W.
NO Dates
Hathaway, Mettie
No Dates
Hathaway, Eldridge
No Dates

Henderson, E. A.
Feb. 9, 1839
June 19, 1889

Hendrix, George T. (Dr.)
Born June 24, 1873
Died May 8, 1903
Age 29 yrs 10 mos
14 days

Hendrix, Inf. Dau. of
Mr. and Mrs.
J. W. Hendrix, Jr.

Hendrix, J. H.
Oct. 12, 1861
July 25, 1901
Hendrix, Helena M.
Wife of J. H. Hendrix
Oct. 23, 1861
Feb. 14, 1902

Hendrix, James H.
June 8, 1898
Hendrix, Zola B.
Nov. 25, 1899
Jan. 29, 1973

Hendrix, James M.
Son of T. S. &
S. e. C. Hendrix
Sept. 24, 1883
June 17, 1885

Hendrix, Mollie E.
Dau. of W. H. &
M. J. Hendrix
Born July 11, 1875
Died Feb. 7, 1893

Hendrix, Nannie Payne
1885-1958

Hendrix, Reuben T., Sr.
1891-1958
Hendrix, Ola V.
1889-1962

Hendrix, Rosie
Dau. of J. H. &
H. M. Hendrix
July 29, 1887
Oct. 15, 1893

Hendrix, Thomas S.
1851-1935
Hendrix, Cora E.
1856-1935

Hendrix, U. J.
Son of T. S. &
S. E. C. Hendrix
Died 1886

Hendrix, W. H.
Born Aug. 5, 1835
Died Mar. 12, 1932
Hendrix, Lucy H.
Born Jan. 2, 1840
Died Aug. 9, 1904
Age 64 yrs. 7 mos 7 days

Hickman, John
1887-1909

Hickman, John M.
Sept. 22, 1852
Feb. 19, 1916
63 yrs. 4 mos. 26 days
Hickman, Jarushia Ann
Born Dec. 20, 1849

Hickman, J. W.
Dec. 20, 1878
Mar. 20, 1932
Hickman, Lena
April 17, 1883
Jan. 16, 1971

Hill, Beverly Ann
Dau. of James T. &
Ramona Hill
April 25, 1949

Hill, Connie
Dec. 21, 1951
Dec. 23, 1951

Hill, James K.
1859-1953
Hill, Lela B.
1861-1897

Hill, Lota
No Dates

Hill, R. Dan
1896
Hill, Cula M.
1901

Hill, Ruth
No Dates

Hill, Tessie
No Dates

Hilliard, Eugene
1894-1969

Hilliard, Minnie Webb
1872-1967
(Second wife of
Rev. Hilliard)

Hilliard, Ruth
1899-1946 Dau. of Rev. Hilliard
by his first wife

Hilliard, John Ella
1905-1930
Dau. of Rev. Hilliard &
Minnie Webb Hilliard

Hobbs, Berry
1903-1974
Hobbs, Bessie
1907-

Hobbs, Charlie J.
1900-1975
Hobbs, Lizzie Mae
1906-1975

Hobbs, Mary Frances
June 15, 1941
Oct. 3, 1942

Hobbs, Robert L.
1924-1945

Hobday, Bettie May
Wife of T. C. Hobday
Born Aug. 2, 1865
Died Oct. 26, 1885

Hobday, Sarah Ella
Wife of T. C. Hobday
Born Oct. 27, 1867
Died Sept. 18, 1892

Hobday, Thomas C.
Dec. 19, 1858
Oct. 30, 1915
Age 56 years 10 mo. 12 days

Holland, Annie
Wife of R. E. Holland
June 23, 1866
Dec. 2, 1887

Holland, Archer P.
1873-1950
Holland, Stattie C.
1875-1926

Holland, Austin B.
Sept. 18, 1877
Oct. 9, 1939

Holland, Clifford L.
Tennessee
PFC Co. C.
327 In. 82 Div
Dec. 19, 1894
Jan. 4, 1964

Holland, Dennis
Apr. 28, 1850
Nov. 8, 1931

Holland, Edmond T.
Father
Feb. 3, 1860
July 6, 1929

Holland, Eula
Mother
May 24, 1868
July 10, 1937

Holland, Eli
Father
1862-1938
Holland, Veleda
Mother
1869-1958

Holland, Everette
1874-1951
Holland, Birttie Mae
1880-1955

Holland, Herschell
Sept. 19, 1905
Jan. 7, 1974
Holland, Avaleen
July 1, 1911

Holland, Infant
1890
Holland, Infant Son
1891
Holland, Clarence
1895
Holland, Infant Son
1896
Holland, Willard
1896-1898

Holland, James D.
Feb. 19, 1916
Aug. 14, 1938

Holland, J. Maurice
Died May 21, 1975
66 yrs. 0 mos. 23 days

Holland, James M. Sr.
Feb. 8, 1937
June 20, 1964

Holland, Johnnie D.
Oct. 10, 1884
Sept. 9, 1956
Holland, Gertie E.
May 1, 1890
Feb. 26, 1965

Holland, Lee Ray
1899-1974
Holland, Edna Mai
1899-

Holland, Mary H.
Aug. 17, 1903
Dec. 25, 1974

Holland, Mongeline
Wife of D. R. Holland
Jan. 22, 1851
Oct. 8, 1909

Holland, Norman Turney
1892-1952

Holland, Mrs. Ora Nell
Died Oct. 27, 1975
77 years 3 months 22 days

Holland, Sarah H.
Wife of Holland, P. H.
Oct. 18, 1819
Apr. 6, 1896

Holland, Wesley
1916-1969
Holland, Julie
1912-1968

Hooper, M. D.
1903-19
Hooper, Date
1903-1956

Hooper, W. Lee
1880-1943

House, Infant
Son of Mr. and Mrs.
Nathan House
Aug. 10, 1942

House, Mitchell, V.
Son of C. W. &
D. L. House
Oct. 8, 1901
June 27, 1902

House, Thomas F.
Aug. 10, 1880
Nov. 29, 1926
House, Mary H.
Sept. 28, 1887

Hudson, Grace
Dau. of J. F. &
Sally Hudson
1885-1964

Hudson, J. Frank. Sr.
1857-1936
Hudson, Sallie Phelan
1855-1936

Hudson, J. Frank
Born Mar. 13, 1892
Hudson, Lela McKain
Oct. 26, 1888
Feb. 19, 1970
Married April 29, 1911

Hudson, Jessica Elaine
Aug. 14, 1973
Aug. 24, 1973

Hudson, John H.
June 2, 1921
May 12, 1923

Hulme, Howard C.
1910-1972
Hulme, Ruth C.
1914-

Hurley, L. Pate
1891-1960
Hurley, Gertrude
1894-19-

Hurley, Moses (Pic,)
1882-1918
Hurley, Bettie M.
1875-1937

Irbine, Jerone
No Dates

Irvin, Callie D.
Feb. 2, 1884
Sept. 11, 1935

Irvin, Wilbern
June 3, 1913
Feb. 18, 1936

Jackson, Fletus Leach
Oct. 14, 1912
May 21, 1940

Johnson, Rebekah Frances
Dau. of Earl &
Cammie Johnson
Oct. 26, 1906
May 12, 1908

Jones, Jennie
Wife of S. H. Jones
July 27, 1861
Nov. 2, 1893

Jones, Jessie
Died Sept. 3, 1961
72 yrs. 10 mo.

Jones, John W.
Son of S. H. &
M. J. Jones
Nov. 23, 1857
Oct. 13, 1880
22 yrs. 10 mos. 20 days

Jones, Mollie
Nov. 4, 1863
Nov. 1, 1934

Jones, Nettie
May 12, 1899
June 26, 1939

Jones, Samuel H.
Mar. 11, 1821
Mar. 21, 1881
60 yrs. 10 days

Jones, William
Aug. 1, 1801
June 28, 1821

Jolly, Nancy J.
Jan. 19, 1872
Jan. 9, 1907

Ketchum, Jennie Ann
July 28, 1878
Mar. 3, 1942

Ketchum. R. T.
Feb. 14, 1861
Nov. 12, 1923
Ketchum, William
Father
No Dates
Ketchum, Permelia
Mother
No Dates

King, Donna M.
Oct. 22, 1957
June 28, 1974

King, Kathy A.
May 21, 1960
June 28, 1974

King, Michael A.
Sept. 29, 1961
June 28, 1974

King, Susie
Died March 3, 1974
72 years 11 mos. 1 day

Lancaster, Wm. Bryan
June 21, 1896
Dec. 18, 1971
Lancaster, Lillie M.
May 30, 1895
Oct. 17, 1968

Larkin, Jacob C.
1868-1937
Jacob, Jeanette
1874-1931

Larkin, Willo Maurine
1908-1915

LaRue, Charlotte
1914-1964

LaRue, John C.
June 21, 1886
July 15, 1968

Lawson, James Thomas
Died April 28, 1975
45 years 3 mos 20 days

Lawson, Walter
April 7, 1970
66 yrs. 2 mos 14 days

Leach, Johnnie M.
Brother
1905-1970
Jackson, Fletus Leach
Sister
1918-1940

Leach, Thomas C.
1882-1951

Leach, Mary B.
1884-1947

Leach, Wade H.
Jan. 13, 1888
July 2, 1949
Leach, Bessie D.
July 3, 1892
     --

Leach, Woodrow
Aug. 28, 1913
Jan. 23, 1967
Leach, Lorene
Sept. 15, 1914
     --

Leggett, Katie Faye
1928-1961

Lemons, Bobby Joe
Tennessee
Sgt. Co. D. 12 Cav.
1 Cav. Division Vietnam
BSM J olg - PH
May 7, 1949
May 19, 1970

Lemons, Mrs. Pansy Ann
Died Nov. 16, 1974
36 years 8 months 14 days

Lemons, Patrick Louis
1903-1971

Lemons, Timothy
1966-1968

Lester, Amanda Jane
2nd Wife of
S. H. P. Lester
May 7, 1842
Nov. 22, 1886

Lester, Ernest Glenn
1878-1954
Lester, Bura Ola
1884-1952

Lester, Herman Ross
March 12, 1876
Sept. 2, 1900

Lester, James C.
Nov. 11, 1866
April 21, 1901

Lester, Susan E.
1st wife of
S. H. P. Lester
Nov. 20, 1840
April 20, 1872

Lester, S. H. P.
June 7, 1833
November 26, 1887

Lester, Wm. Stafford
Son of S. H. P. &
S. E. Lester
Dec 21, 1861
Mar. 15, 1872

Lewellyng, John Walter
1874-1959

Light, Joe A.
1888-1952

Light, Joe E.
Oct. 7, 1850
July 31, 1892
LIght, Mary E.
Oct. 20, 1857
July 2, 1944

Light, Stephen
Oct. 11, 1879
July 1, 1957
Light, Berlie
April 6, 1878
Jan. 27, 1953

Lucas, Daniel W.
1878-1949
Lucas, Gladys
1892-1967

Magee, David A.
Born in Giles County
Mar. 3, 1839
May 12, 1920
Magee, Marthy J. nee Hewatt
Born in Maury County
Tennessee
Feb. 28, 1837
Feb. 27, 1916

Magee, David O.
Sept. 16, 1872
May 20, 1905
32 yrs. 8 mos. 4 days

Magee
Infant Daughter & Grandson of
T. R. Magee

Magee, John R.
Sept. 24, 1863
July 13, 1947
Magee, Hattie
Dec. 1, 1860
Feb. 20, 1941

Magee, Wm. F.
Sept. 30, 1870
July 15, 1931

Mallard, Adron Lee
1939-1967

Mallard, Camlee
1885-1952

Mallard, C. S.
Tennessee
PFC
HQ Btry 369 FA BN
World War II
Oct. 6, 1918
April 14, 1960

Mallard, Fred
May 8, 1891
Oct. 30, 1962

Mallard, J. L
1916-1955
Mallard, Sue H.
1919-1919

Mallard, Jack
Nov. 15, 1854
Oct. 30, 1930

Mallard, James
Tennessee
PVT Co. A-1
Prov. Div. Regt.
World War I
April 8, 1887
Nov. 16, 1960

Mallard, John T.
1878-1942
Mallard, Lillie E.
1880-1959

Mallard, Margrett D.
1935-1940

Mallard, Martie B.
1961-1961

Mallard, Martin
1908-1943
Mallard, Pearl
1912-1952

Mallard, Thomas
1900-1967
Mallard, Ida
1907-

Maness, Thomas
1873-1940
Maness, Minnie
1884-

Mathis, E. Calvin
1912-1941
Mathis, Cathleen A.
1911-

May, Jesse
1882-1944
Father
May, Minnie
1888-
Mother

McCormick, Linda Rena
Dec. 11-Dec. 11

McDowell, Joe Butler
1884-1936

McGavock, Coleman W.
1922-1923

McGee, John Emmett
1881-1963
McGee, Effie May
1887-

McGraw, Father
McGraw, Henry
1883-1921

McGraw, James R.
1879-1965
McGraw, Mary Etta
1885-1924

McHaney, J. R.
1850-1936
KcHaney, Martha
His Wife
1849-1931

McHaney, James Lafayette
Son of Guy Lafayette &
Estella Hamlett McHaney
July 25, 1909
Sept. 26, 1969
McHaney, Ethel Mae Holland
Dau. of Archer Preston
& Stattie Milam Holland
July 28, 1912

McHaney, Minnie
1882-1968
McHaney, Feek
1872-1938

McKain, Floice Bedford
Son of W. I. &
H. E. McKain
Oct. 16, 1897
Aug. 29, 1898

McKain, Houston
Mar. 15, 1823
May 8, 1895
72 yrs. 1 mo. 23 days
McKain, Sallie Ann
Born Sept. 2, 1827

McKain, J. F. "Doc"
Died 1918
McKain, Bettie
Died 1897

McKain, William I.
1871-1959
McKain, Hettie E.
1877-

McKenzie, Arnett L.
Mar. 18, 1908
June 3, 1973

McKenzie, Brown
Son of L. D. & Alma
1901-1930

McKenzie, DeFoy
Son of L. D. & Alma
1901-1930

McKenzie, Lacy D.
May 21, 1877
April 4, 1948
McKenzie, Alma B.
Dec. 13, 1881
Mar. 30, 1969

Merrill, Virdie Cloar
Jan. 13, 1897
Mar. 28, 1971

Milam, Add
No Dates

Milam, Icle Davis
No Dates

Milam, Dora F.
1860-1946
Sawyer, Ollie
1881-1898

Milam, Dr. J. A.
Dec. 4, 1887
34 yrs. 9 mos. 12 days

Milam, Dr. J. H.
1854-1926
Milam, Lula I.
1866-1962

Milam, L. J.
Oct. 18, 1823
May 8, 1900
Milam, Nancy J.
Born Sept. 15, 1829

Milam, Lex D.
1885-1955
Milam, Vera L.
1887-1969

Milam, Nancy Dona
1898-1943

Milam, S. E.
Aug. 20, 1850
May 20, 1928

Milam, Sarah E.
Wife of S. E. Milam
Died Dec. 2, 1887
36 yrs. 20 days

Milam, Sidney
Jan. 1, 1890
Oct. 20, 1895
4 yrs. 9 mos. 19 days

Milam, Walter Lee
July 4, 1876-Aug. 4, 1963

Milam, Luna May
Aug. 7, 1885
May 3, 1967

Miller, Josephine C.
Wife of John T. Miller
July 25, 1844
Mar. 11, 1885

Milraney, Frank
Tennessee, Pvt. 1st Class
34th Inf. 7th Div.
Sept. 2, 1894
April 1, 1945

Mines, Billie W.
1933-1942

Mines, Robert W.
1888-1965

Moore, Carrie
Wife of E. W. Moore
Nov. 7, 1890
Dec. 9, 1922

Moore, Ernest W.
Mar. 9, 1888
June 16, 1970

Morgan, Onnie
1894-1963
Morgan, Wynema
1902-

Morris, Belle Hendrix
1867-1938

Mulliniks, John D.
Oct. 21, 1875
Mulliniks, Cora Lee
April 20, 1878

Murphy, G. J.
Dec. 25, 1888
Nov. 4, 1912
Murphy, P. J.
Wife of G. J.
Jan. 19, 1842
Feb. 13, 1904

Murphy, Inf. Dau.
Grant & Dora Murphy
Born Oct. 7, 1901

Murphy, Mallie V.
Nov. 3, 1893
Sept. 17, 1908

Myrick, Lorene H.
Dec. 23, 1897
May 28, 1975

Nelson, O. T.
July 10, 1844
Nelson, S. J., His Wife
Aug. 25, 1846
April 19, 1921

Neese, William
Nov. 10, 1791
Feb. 29, 1872

Notgrass, Claud
1889-
Notgrass, Madge
1893-

Olive, Robert L.
1907-
Olive, Drudie W.
1906-1959

Oman, Rose
1839-1929

O'Neal, Harvey
Oct. 5, 1803
July 26, 1854

O'Neal, George W.
Died Oct. 7, 1841

Parker, David C.
1880-1957
Parker, Claudie O.
1883-1972

Parnell, John R.
1866-1944

Patterson, A. W.
Feb. 16, 1884
Sept. 27, 1968

Patterson, Burrell H.
1896-1944
Patterson, Gladys
1898-1947

Patterson, Effie E.
1887-1925

Patterson, James S.
Husband of
M. C. Patterson
Dec. 15, 1870
Aug. 25, 1911
Woodsman of the World

Patterson, Mary C.
July 23, 1875
Oct. 3, 1914
39 yrs. 2 mos 10 days

Payne, Thomas C.
1895-
Payne, Ena Mai
1898-1971

Peden, Clifford
Son of J. W. &
Donnal Peden
Aug. 1, 1893
Aug. 6, 1893

Peek, Tom
Jan. 10, 1904
June 12, 1968
Peek, Cathleen
Born Aug. 13, 1909

Peters, Dr. Richard H.
Nov. 11, 1934
June 20, 1972

Pierce, Guy H.
May 19, 1886
Oct. 10, 1967

Pierce, John F.
Feb. 18, 1849
March 18, 1907

Pierce, Kate
Sept. 25, 1882
Nov. 29, 1950

Pierce, Ozella
1857-1887

Pierce, Thomas Jefferson
Aug. 15, 1826
Aug. 15, 1896
60 yrs.
Pierce, Lucy Emma
Jan. 15, 1844
Feb. 10, 1899
55 yrs. 26 days
Pierce, Jefferson Wortham
Aug. 20, 1877
July 14, 1950
Pierce, W. F. (Bill)
May 26, 1880
Oct. 17, 1960
Pierce, Ettie Milam
Aug. 10, 1886
Mar. 2, 1965

Pinckley, Joe
1860-1927
Pinckley, Anner
1865-1935

Pinckley, Sam H.
Dec. 10, 1866
Dec. 31, 1946
Pinckley, Lillie Bessent
Jan. 17, 1880
Aug. 20, 1963

Pleasant, Emma E.
Wife of Dock Pleasant
July 22, 1866
Dec. 9, 1910

Pleasant, Oscar B.
Tennessee PFC. Co. A
Infantry 7
World War I
Dec. 12, 1890
Sept. 26, 1968

Pope, Frances
1856-1928

Pope, Stanley
1896-1939

Pope, W. H.
Father
1844-1926
Pope, H. L.
Mother
1846-

Poteet, Mark L.
Aug. 23, 1888
Oct. 1, 1918
Woodman of the World

Powell, Mrs. C. F.
May 23, 1856
Dec. 6, 1933

Powell, Doss T.
Dec. 20, 1877
Oct. 14, 1925
Powell, Lillie A.
Apr. 21, 1885
Mar. 11, 1968

Powell, Effie
Our Aunt
Quinton, Elizabeth & Peggy
No Dates

Powell, J. Z.
1874-1933

Powell, Seymour B.
1868-1945
Powell, Della S.
1867-1930
Powell, Clifford B.
1910-1918

Powell, W. Don
Tennessee
Pvt. 460 Engr. Depot Co
World War II
Dec. 14, 1905
Dec. 22, 1964

Powell, W. T.
1879-1953
Powell, Kate
1880-1935

Powell, William T.
July 20, 1831
Mar. 2, 1900
Powell, Mary J. Mahnon
Jan. 18, 1841
Oct. 9, 1929

Powell, Z. P.
1877-1939
Powell, Leila
1884-

Powers, Len
(Illegible -- Undertaker's marker)

Pursell, Everit Coker
1871-1951
Father

Pursell, Gilbert R.
1900-1933
Brother

Pursell, Harris Dillon
1896-1928
Son

Pursell, J. H. (Dr.)
Born Mar. 7, 1823
Died Dec. 16, 1898
Age 75 yrs. 9 mos. 8 days

Pursell, Joe Harris
Son of J. J. & E. S.
Mar. 8, 1899
Feb. 11, 1900

Pursell, Mattie L.
1874-1932

Price, L. Amieal
1896-1945

Prichard, Carl Cooper
1901-1949

Prichard, Ethel Forsee
Died June 9, 1975
79 yrs. 9 mos. 14 days

Prichard, Jefferson R.
1892-1950

Prichard, Lucy
Wife of A. B. Prichard
May 10, 1860
apr. 18, 1885

Prichard, Mattie H.
1893-1943

Prichard, Mary Elizabeth
Born & Died 1918

Primm, J. T.
Sept. 23, 1866
Aug. 25, 1902

Pritchard, James W.
Dec. 31, 1834
Sept. 23, 1887

Pritchard, Rosa Ann
Wife of J. W. Pritchard
July 2, 1883
NOv. 17, 1912

Proffitt, Colleen Hawkins
1923-1946

Rainey, Elizabeth
Wife of R. R. Rainey
Aug. 6, 1815
Nov. 18, 1895

Rainey, James M.
1862-1940
Rainey, Nannie S.
1872-1971

Rainey, Nannie Sawyers
Died May 13, 1971
98 yrs. 6 mos.

Rainey, William J.
4th Tenn. Calvary
Confederate States
Army
Aug. 5, 1845
June 24, 1935

Ramey
Faith-hope-Charity
Nov. 19, 1970

Ray, Alton
Nov. 4, 1903
Ray, Alta
Dec. 16, 1905

Ray, A. L.
April 24, 1838
Oct. 16, 1921
Ray, N. E.
Wife of A. L. Ray
Feb. 22, 1841
April 7, 1903
62 yrs. 1 mo. 15 days

Ray, Bill L.
July 13, 1898
Sept. 29, 1967
Ray, Beatrice
Mar. 30, 1904

Ray, Carroll
Oct. 31, 1863
Nov. 2, 1924

Ray, Charles S.
1896-1968
Ray, Rozetta
1898-1969
Married June 30, 1916

Ray, Charles Wm.
July 17, 1940
Sept. 9, 1952

Ray, Clabe
Father
1887-1956
Ray, Grace
Mother
1884-19

Ray, Claborn
Jan. 27, 1809
May 15, 1887
Ray, Susan
June 15, 1815
April 6, 1890

Ray, Dorsey B.
Nov. 24, 1876
Jan. 23, 1963
Ray, Rosa Lee
April 3, 1878
Oct. 27, 1967

Ray, E. L.
1870-1901

Ray, Edward T.
1910-1956

Ray, Ezell L.
Mar. 28, 1865
Oct. 28, 1896

Ray, H. C.
Son of J. S. &
S. A. Ray
1899-1899

Ray, Henry S.
Tennessee
Pvt. Co. H 128th Inf.
World War I
July 5, 1895
Jan. 12, 1970

Ray, Huel
1890-1966
Ray, Sye
1889-

Ray, J. S.
Jan. 8, 1850
Feb. 15, 1908
Ray, S. A.
Wife of J. S.
June 27, 1856
June 13, 1938

Ray, John W.
1871-1931
Ray, Mary M.
1873-1956

Ray, Lewis W.
1841-1898
Ray, Sarah
1853-

Ray, Martin L
Tennessee
Pvt. Co. H
128 Inf. 32 Div.
World War I
Aug. 15, 1892
Mar. 13, 1955

Ray, Milbern
Tennessee
Pvt. Bakers Cooks Sch.
O. M. C.
World War I
April 20, 1893
Sept. 18, 1950

Ray, Nannie
Dau. of J. W. &
Mary Ray
Nov. 25, 1907
Oct. 1, 1908

Ray, Pallie
Dau. of J. S. &
S. A. Ray
Dec. 28, 1880
July 21, 1900

Ray, Perse
Son of L. E.
& A. E. Ray
Nov. 24, 1891
April 17, 1899

Reed, Earl F.
Mar. 7, 1925
Nov. 15, 1926

Reed, George M.
Dec. 28, 1896
Reed, Evie H.
May 8, 1899

Reed, George Miller, Jr.
Feb. 28, 1937
Oct. 6, 1965

Reed, Jerry W.
Son of Mr. & Mrs. George
Born & Died
June 7, 1933

Reed, M. M.
1893-19
Reed, Bessie
1900-1935

Reed, Milton
1925-1928

Reed, Walker R.
1852-1953
Reed, Dixie R.
1861-1905

Rhondes, Edmon E.
1902-1963

Roark, Charles J.
Jan. 23, 1884
Dec. 21, 1967

Roark, W. H.
1841-1924

Robbins, Billie E.
Oct. 7, 1857
Feb. 7, 1922

Robbins, Clyde R.
1874-1958
Robbins, Claudie P.
1878-1950

Robbins, John P.
1895-1908

Robbins, John S.
Sept. 20, 1855
June 5, 1906

Robbins, Joseph O.
1866-1947
Robbins, Lillie B.
1872-1960

Robbins, Mollie
Dec. 23, 1873
Dec. 28, 1873

Robbins, Newton
Feb. 2, 1851
May 22, 1854
Son of O. R. & M. A.

Robbins, O. R.
Died Mar. 13, 1907
Robbins, Louise
2nd Wife
Died Oct. 23, 1899

Robbins, Zella
July 23, 1896
April 27, 1922

Roberts, Benton M.
1916
Roberts, Early B.
1912-1961

Roberts, G. W.
1868-1934
Roberts, Lissie
1882-19

Roberts, Luther
Tennessee
Pvt. 1 Inf
World War I
May 28, 1894
July 25, 1967

Robertson, Andrew Wyatt
1867-1951
Robertson, Lucy Maud
1875-1957

Robertson, Geroge Calvin
(Mason)
Nov. 22, 1855
Dec. 13, 1937
Robertson, Amanda Edna
Aug 22, 1863
July 19, 1938

Robertson, J. B.
1885-1946

Robertson, J. T.
1850-1927

Robertson, Mary J.
Jan. 16, 1849
June 25, 1892
43 yrs. 5 mos. 9 days

Robertson, Mary Tommie
1889-1955

Robertson, Mattie
Wife of J. B. Robertson
June 13, 1885
Dec. 3, 1901

Robertson, May
July 27, 1892
Nov. 15, 1971

Robertson, Nancy
Wife of J. T. Robertson
Jan. 23, 1856
Dec. 23, 1903

Rodgers, Frank P.
Jan. 9, 1850
Dec. 21, 1943
Rodgers, Dora E.
Dec. 1, 1866
Mar. 3, 1900
Rodgers, Charlie
April 6, 1895
Sept. 3, 1896
Rodgers, Dewitt
June 1, 1889
Nov. 19, 1896
Rodgers, Nannie Harriet
July 6, 1891
Dec. 6, 1896

Rogers, Oscar J.
1898-
Rogers, Dora M.
1901-1970

Roney, James E.
1868-1890

Rose, Dallas Franklin
1899-1936

Rose, Paul Dallas
1950-1950

Sawyer, Emma J.
March 1, 1863
June 18, 1936

Sawyer, Gailon Boyd
Sawyers, Issac Wesley
No Dates

Sawyer, John
October 23, 1830
July 14, 1906
(On same stone with John F.
Pierce)

Sawyer, Mary
February 8, 1905
May 30, 1956

Sawyer, Monroe
Born April 29, 1859
Married Miss M. J. Patin
Died Oct. 31, 1887
Age 37, yrs. 6 mo. 21 days

Sawyer, Thomas Wesley
1880-1942
Sawyers, Ida R.
1878-19

Sawyer, Wm.
April 20, 1837
August 26, 1912
Sawyers, Nancy E.
His wife
October 23, 1838
August 26, 1906

Sawyers, I. W.
Jan. 10, 1857
February 11, 1888

Sawyers, Orza
Dau. of I. W. & D. I Sawyers
1884-1885

Sawyers, Thomas Franklin
Died Oct. 18, 1975
72 years 0 mo. 2 days

Sawyers, William J.
June 12, 1861
April 15, 1919

Scott, A. C. "Wilson"
1913-1967
Scott, Kitty May
1919-1942

Scott, Bettie
Wife of R. D. Scott
Dec. 6, 1867
Mar. 31, 1894
Scott, H.P.
March 13, 1856
Oct. 27, 1935
Scott, Mattie H.
HIs Wife
Jan. 12, 1860
Jan. 5, 1893
House, Richard B.
April 23, 1905
April 14, 1925
Grandson

Seat, Thomas F.
1908-1969

Self, Era Berton
Son of W. H. &
L. F. Self
Oct. 11, 1884
Nov. 3, 1885

Self, Nellie Otto
Dau. of W. H. & M. A. Self
July 17, 1897
July 18, 1897

Self, W. H., Mason
July 10, 1852
March 6, 1927

Self, L. F., Wife of
W. H. Self
Aug. 19, 1857
July 12, 1891

Shelton, Howard
1938-1940
(Holman Funeral Home
Marker)

Sherrod, A. Ryoce
March 6, 1908
Dec. 16, 1972

Sherrod, Martha A.
July 16, 1947
June 18, 1958

Sherrod, Willie D.
1903-1969
Sherrod, Eva R., 1906-

Simmons, W. E.
Inf. Son of T. M. &
N. M. Simmons
July 29, 1899
Jan. 7, 1892

Shipwith, Austin
Jan. 19, 1877
Sept. 25, 1878

Shipwith, Edward
Sept. 23, 1866
Aug. 26, 1896

Simpson, Newton M.
April 8, 1881
April 2, 1954
Woodman of the World
Simpson, Eula Moore
May 30, 1888
Feb. 2, 1966

Sipes, Tylor M.
Jan. 27, 1924
Aug. 18, 1972
Sipes, Laverne W.
Sept. 9, 1926
        --

Smith, Alma
Jan. 1, 1880
Oct. 20, 1908

Smith, Beadie
Died March 28, 1906

Smith, Ben F.
Died Aug. 25, 1899
Smith, Mittie N.
Died March 2, 1906

Smith, Daniel Boyd
March 1904
Dec. 1905

Smith, Daniel T.
1874-1946
Smith, Mentie E.
1877-1962

Smith, Henry C.
Died Mar. 26, 1913
36 yrs. 2 mos. 27 days

Smith, Howard J.
June 22, 1875
Aug. 26, 1933

Smith, John M.
1850-1932
Sarah M.
1852-1895
Their Children, Gilbert, Inf. Dau.,
Horace, Norman
McGill, Nancy
1823-1904

Smith, Joseph Fletcher
Aug. 7, 1846
June 9, 1930
Smith, Rebecca Ann
Feb. 12, 1848
Nov. 26, 1947

Smith, Julia A.
Wife of B. F. Smith
May 21, 1845
June 21, 1891
Smith, B. F.
Oct. 1, 1842
Feb. 10, 1901

Smith, Luther
Died Sept. 11, 1910

Smith, Minnie B.
Wife of J. W. Smith
Born: Jan. 28, 1869
Died: June 21, 1898

Smith, Robert Lee
Apr. 9, 1871
Feb. 16, 1947
Smith, Ada Holland
Mar. 23, 1871
Nov. 24, 1938

Smith, Robert Wilson
Son of R. L. & Ada H. Smith
Oct. 1, 1905 - Oct. 1, 1916

Smith, Worth (No Dates)
Smith, Maggie (No Dates)

Smith, William B., Mason
June 27, 1833
Jan. 24, 1887
Smith, Mary E.
June 22, 1843
July 24, 1892
Smith, Mary Etta
Oct. 30, 1873
Jan. 30, 1895

Smith,, Lila May
Apr. 27, 1880
May 1, 1906
Smith, Infant
Son of W. B. & Mary E
Sept. 13, 1884
Sept. 13, 1884

Smith, Willie Gay
Feb. 1900
March 1900

Spencer, Billy Joe
July 2, 1933
June 28, 1935

Spencer, Frank
1889-1974
Spencer, Willie
1891-

Spencer, Joe
Oct. 6, 1884
Nov. 14, 1942

Spry, N. A. (Joe)
1886-1967
Spry, Ola
1908-

Stafford, Otis
Father
1896-1948
Stafford, Lena S.
Mother
1896-19

Stafford, W. O. "Bill"
February 15, 1860
June 11, 1951

Stegall, S. P.
Wife of Jessie Stegall
January 8, 1840
Oct. 15, 1898
58 yrs. 8 mos. 7 days

Stephens, Harry
Aug. 13, 1906
Stephens, Mary F.
Apr. 8, 1907
Nov. 17, 1970

Stephenson, (no first name)
1940
(In Raleigh W. Barker lot)

Stephenson, Clyde
1899-1934

Stephenson, Frank
1856-1937
Stephenson, Bena
1863-1935
Stephenson, Homer
1894-1895
Stephenson, Ola
1895-1909

Stephenson, Harry B.
Tennessee
St U. S. Navy
World War I
June 2, 1892
Sept. 28, 1970
Stephenson, Florence
1905-

Stephenson, Otho
1887-1947
Stephenson, Vay Tatum
1892-

Stephenson, Sallie Bet
Wife of
M. M. Stephenson
Sept. 11, 1860
Feb. 19, 1894

Stephenson, W. A.
Aug. 13, 1831
Oct. 6, 1910
Stephenson, Mary Ann
Sept. 5, 1833
Dec. 28, 1913

Stewart, Lee Washington
1891-1958

Stockton, Dovie Lee
1905-1906

Stover, J. C.
June 30, 1897
Jan. 18, 1940

Street, Lum
1882-19
Street, Eula
1878-1962

Stuts, Charlie
Died April 16, 1951
62 yrs. 11 mos. 8 days
(Funeral Home Marker)

Surratt, Henry B.
Tennessee
Pvt. 137 Ing 35 Div.
Dec. 3, 1894
Dec. 2, 1944

Tackett, Jerry E.
1876-1938

Tansil, Josephine
1852-1924

Tarlton, Eliza
Oct. 15, 1889
July 20, 1905

Tatem, A. B.
August 5, 1863
Mar. 12, 1896

Tatem, Arch Bedford
Aug. 5. 1863-Mar. 12, 1896

Tatem, Lucy Eudora
Sept. 16, 1870
Mar. 12, 1953

Tatem, Eunice B.
April 9, 1860
Nov. 10, 1911

Tatem, George Maurice
Mar. 3, 1857
Sept. 15, 1937

Tatem, J. S. May 8, 1861
Mar. 14, 1894

Tatem, M. J.
Wife of N. P. Tatem
Oct. 21, 1827
July 27, 1884

Tatem, Matilda Velma
July 17, 1887
Aug. 24, 1889

Tatem, N. P.
Mar. 15, 1816
Dec. 16, 1890

Tatem, Verna M.
Nov. 24, 1884
June 15, 1886

Tatum, John B.
Tennessee
Pvt. Co. 3
Chemical BM
World War I
Jan. 31, 1895
Nov. 26, 1956

Taylor, James
Jan. 1, 1887
Nov. 4, 1898

Terry, W. B.
1861-1938
Terry, Ella
1871-1944

Tinkle, Charlotte
Infant
Oct. 31, 195-
(Funeral Home Marker)

Tisdel, Scrapp
1878-1961

Tucker, Ellen H.
Aug. 18, 1917
Dec. 14, 1969

Tucker, Geroge F.
1854-1940
Tucker, Gracie L.
1851-1916

Tucker, Richard
July 24, 1862
Mar. 30, 1931

Tucker, Rebecca Gilbert
Sept 3, 1871
Oct. 22, 1966

Tucker, Riley Howard
1886-1950
Tucker, Essie
1893-19-

Tucker, Webb C.
Sept. 30, 1895
--

Tucker, Naomi H.
March 9, 1896
(Died 1-12-76)

Tuggle, Jim
Mar. 10, 1880
Dec. 29, 1971

Tully, M. A.
Wife of L. B. Tully
May 12, 1842
Mar. 12, 1911

Tyson, Alvis Gentry
Tenn.
Pvt Co M 46 Inf
World War I
Mar. 25, 1888
July 20, 1954

Underwood, Albert C.
1862-1942
Underwood, Clara J.
1869-19

Underwood, Aura M.
1898-19
Underwood, Ann E.
1905-1948

Underwood, Bert
1904-1963

Underwood, Roy
June 10, 1896
June 4, 1897

Vaughan, John Sterling
Son of
R. S. & M. E. Vaughan
Sept. 30, 1909
Oct. 5, 1910

Vaughan, Mary
Dau. of
R. S. & M. E. Vaughan
Aug. 25, 1895
Feb. 12, 1890

Vaughan, Mary A.
Wife of
Thomas H. Vaughan
May 5, 1839
July 19, 1895

Vaughan, P. H.
February 5, 1831-Jan. 21, 1915

Vaughan, Richard H.
Son of
R. S. & M. E. Vaughan
Nov. 18, 1903
Nov. 25, 1903

Vaughan, Sadie May
Daughter of
R. S. & M. E. Vaughan
Jan. 11, 1889
Jan. 12, 1893

Vaughan, Virginie Evalyne
Dau. of R. S. &
M. E. Vaughan
Sept. 5, 1907
Oct. 11, 1908

Vaughn, William H.
Sept. 23, 1878
March 28, 1909

Vickrey, Virgil Palmer
February 10, 1888
December 24, 1965

Waggoner, Cecil
1905-1973
Waggoner, Fallie
1903-1946

Waggoner, Joe
Sept. 2, 1900
Oct. 2, 1921
Waggoner, Rilla
Dec. 24, 1898
    --

Waggoner, Sam
Oct. 8, 1895
Aug. 27, 1969
Waggoner, Nancey
Oct. 23, 1893
    --

Waggoner, T. J.
1871-1942
Waggoner, Alice
1890-1949
Waggoner, Mary
1873-1900

Waldron, William Henry
1874-1956
Waldron, Mary Nancie
1874-1948

Walker, A. T.
Aug. 8, 1882
Dec. 11, 1930

Walker, Cannon
Tennessee
Pvt. Co E 102 Engineers
World War I
May 17, 1889
Jan. 2, 1967

Walker, Mrs. Eva
Died Mar. 17, 1973
77 yrs. 1 mo. 9 days
(Johnson Funeral Home Marker)

Walker, James F.
1903-1966
Walker, Dovie
1903-

Walker, Mary A.
Wife of W. A. J. Walker
Jan. 14, 1835
July 2, 1907

Walker, M. T.
Nov. 5, 1854
Sept. 23, 1910
Walker, Novella
Wife of M. T. Walker
Nov. 22, 1853
Apr. 28, 1907

Walker, Odis T.
1914-1947
Walker, Alean
1914-19

Walker, Sam
1884-1937
Walker, Virda
1881-1958

Walker, Willie C.
Nov. 5, 1897
    --
Walker, Nina May
May 15, 1900
May 27, 1972

Walker, William T.
1925-1931

Walker, Wortham
1886-1941

Wamble, Clint
1898-1966
Wamble, Erma
1897-1966

Ward, Charlie D.
1868-
Ward, Lula
1874-1933

Ward, Effie E.
1882-1952

Ward, Eura L.
1883-1946

Ward, Lettie
Dau. of R. M. &
R. A. Ward
Feb. 15, 1881
1 mo. 26 days

Ward, Luther B.
Mar. 7, 1872
July 27, 1931
Ward, Loutye Fisher
Sept. 4, 1878

Ward, Mattie D.
Wife of C. D.
1870-1900

Ward, Rachel Agnes
1851-1938

Ward, Rachael Virginia
1912-1941

Ward, Robert M.
1840-1900

Ward, S. M.
Mar. 2, 1857
May 2, 1928

Ward, William E.
1874-1940

Weaver, Dock
1890-1954
Weaver, Della
1899-19

Weaver, Elmer
1889-19
Weaver, Maggie Erwin
1894-1959

Weaver, Ethel Bass
Sept. 20, 1903
May 9, 1970
Weaver, Bryant
Nov. 17, 1896
Mar. 29, 1973

Weaver, Jasper N.
June 18, 1880
Oct. 18, 1939
Weaver, Mattie
Sept. 1, 1871
May 8, 1955

Weaver, John H.
1868-1949
Weaver, Susie
His Wife
1866-1940

Weaver, Linda Jean
Born & Died
Aug. 1942

Weaver, William Darnell
July 15, 1921
Sept. 1, 1921

Webb, Edward
Aug. 28, 1881
Sept 5, 1882
Webb, Zula
May 1, 1879
Mar. 1, 1880
Children of G. W. Webb

Webb, Fannye Mauldin
Dau. of J. E. & Ella Webb
Dec. 6, 1880
Mar. 18, 1898

Webb, G. W.
Dec. 5, 1848
Nov. 30, 1925

Webb, Jessie O.
1883-1971
Webb, Sue D.
1884-1969

Webb, John E.
1837-1914
Webb, Sarah Ella Tucker
His wife
1832-1923
Mother & Father of
Minnie Webb Hendrix

Webb, Kirby Smith
Nov. 12, 1872
Mar. 1, 1955
Webb, Susan Pitt
Aug. 9, 1874
May 13, 1949
Married Dec. 25, 1892

Webb, Lorenzo Dow
May 2, 1869
June 11, 1948
Webb, Lula Bell
Aug. 30, 1868
Dec. 30, 1943

Webb, Maurice Cranston
July 16, 1925
Mar. 6, 1941

Webb, Ms. Nina R.
Died Oct. 23, 1975
72 years 10 mos. 9 days

Webb, Paul Raymond
Aug. 17, 1908
Dec. 30, 1918
Webb, Lattie
April 1, 1901
May 19, 1901
Webb, Bruce
March 12, 1899
May 1, 1900
Children of Mr. & Mrs. Kirby
S. Webb

Wilbanks, Sidney Lee
1898-19
Wilbanks, Myrtle
1906-1943

Wilcox, Thomas Bryant
Aug. 22, 1879
Dec. 8, 1958
Wilcox, Emma Lou
Feb. 5, 1888

Wilcox, W. L.
Aug. 31, 1839
April 2, 1915
Wilcox, Susan J.
April 17, 1848
April 25, 1920

Wilcox, William L.
Tenn.
Pvt. Co B 20 Regt.
Tenn. Cav.
Confederate States Army
Aug. 31, 1839
April 2, 1915

Wilkinson, Dave
1889-1968

Wilkinson, Selma
1880-1963

Williams, Herman
September 24, 1975
64 yrs. 0 mos. 11 days

Williams, Mack C.
Died Oct. 18, 1974
85 years 9 mos. 15 days

Williams, Maggie
1892-1927

Williams, Mary Frances
Died June 1, 1976
65 years 7 mos. 12 days

Williams, Sarah C.
Aug. 10, 1860
Sept 26, 1919

Wilson, Vaughan
Feb. 27, 1900
June 18, 1901
Wilson, John
Dec. 29, 1902
June 18, 1903
Wilson, Clyde Haskell
July 24, 1908
Aug. 17, 1908

Winchester, S. J.
Nov. 15, 1874
Oct. 12, 1952

Windle, Andrew Lay
Died Jan. 26, 1975
44 years 9 mos. 13 days

Winters, Sherman
1868-1947
Winters, Rachel
1878-1952

Wirth, Albert
1870-1955
Wirth, Lillie L.
1877-1969

Wirth, Hattie M.
Wife of C. N. Wirth
Feb. 11, 1880
Dec. 24, 1921

Wirth, Henry B.
Sept. 4, 1867
June 17, 1906

Wirth, Joseph
June 30, 1830
May 22, 1905

Wirth, Rosina C.
Wife of Joseph Wirth
Mar. 4, 1837
April 4, 1889

Wirth, Rosa C
Dau. of Joseph
& R. C. Wirth
Dec. 17, 1875
Sept. 25, 1891

Wheatley, A. H.
1807-1896
Wheatley, E. N.
1832-1922

Wheatley, Alf M.
1862-1941
Wheatley, G. C.
1867-1950

Wheatley, A. J.
1848-1924

Wheatley, Rebecca
Wife of A. J. Wheatley
Feb. 7, 1850
Jan. 15, 1885

White, Emma L
Dau. of C. B. &
M. H. White
April 25, 1898
Oct. 25, 1900
2 yrs. 1 mo. 23 days

White, James
Sept. 2, 1861
Nov. 14, 1892

Wood, J. Everett
1907-1923

Wood, Homer
1912-1937

Wood, Jackie
Wife of J. R. Wood
1879-1915

Wood, John R. - 1874-1953

Wright, Andy
Jan. 1, 1888
July 12, 1970
Wright, Edna
Aug. 7, 1900
   --

Wright, Darnell
1914-1962
Wright, Lela Mai
1919-19

Wright, George
1876-19

Wright, Harold
1901-
Wright, Maggie
1902-

Wright, Lillie
1884-1958

Wright, Minnie Grigg
Mar. 7, 1971
81 yrs. 4 mos. 17 days

Wyrick, Allie Mai
Sept. 29, 1883
Sept. 10, 1958

ROELLEN CEMETERY

RoEllen Cemetery (White and Black) is located on a hillside approximately five miles south of Newbern. At the intersection of Highway 51 S. and Roellen Highway in Newbern, turn left at the red light and travel about five miles directly south. The RoEllen Cemetery is on the left-hand side of the road on a shaded hill. Only a wire fence separates the RoEllen White Cemetery from the RoEllen Negro Cemetery. The Negro Cemetery is to the north of the White. Plans are underway to mark the cemetery with a wrought iron sign.

Adkins, Lee R.
Oct. 2, 1884
Dec. 21, 1944

Adkins, McLisie Ellen
May 16, 1864
Mar. 5, 1922

Amisen, Callie
1865-1933

Anderson, Ernest
Tennessee
Sgt. Btry F.
83 Field Arty
World War I
Aug. 23, 1895
Dec. 31, 1967

Anderson, W. T.
1879-1909

Baity, Clara E.
1897-1935

Barker, Henry E.
Jan. 20, 1903
July 22, 1971
Barker, Helen
April 22, 1909

Barker, J. W.
1872-1934
Barker, J. E.
1873-1954

Barnett, Sarah
Wife of W. L. Barnett
Nov. 5, 1866
Dec. 8, 1912

Bradley, N. A.
1854-1940

Bradley, S. M.
Wife of N. A. Bradley
Oct. 5, 1852
Feb. 6, 1906

Brake, Annie C.
1908-1918
Brake, Thomas
1909-1909

Bryan, John D.
1919-1967
Bryan, Dorothy L.
1921-

Burch, Charlie Albert
Died April 13, 1966
65 years 5 mos. 3 days

Burch, Henry
1875-1956
Burch, Bell R.
1872-1938

Capps, Fannie
Oct. 7, 1875
Jan. 26, 1902

Carter, Sandra Kay
Oct. 19, 1944
Nov. 23, 1944

Caudle, Billy Glyn
Tennessee
SP4 U. S. Army
Vietnam
Jan. 10, 1941
Dec. 9, 1973

Caudle, Freddie Bee
1913-1950

Caudle, Tina
1882-1959

Caudle, W. A.
1877-1935

Caudle, William Clifford
1912-1969

Cobb, Christen
Wife of Tom Cobb
Feb. 15, 1863
Feb. 1, 1890

Cobb, Clara
Dec. 13, 1884
Apr. 12, 1885

Cobb, Elvin
May 5, 1890
July 13, 1890

Cockran, Jim
Georgia
PVF Inf.
World War I
Feb. 8, 1893
May 14, 1971

Cooper, William G.
Mar. 7, 1837
Mar. 30, 1909
Cooper, Martha Ann
July 25, 1849
Mar. 30, 1909
Cooper, James L.
Dec. 10, 1879
Feb. 17, 1889

Cribbs, Bead West
1867-1933
Cribbs, Jessie Hales
1886-1952

Cribbs, Robert W.
1912
Infant

Cribbs, Tom
1889-1961
Cribbs, Lena H.
1892-19

Crosthwait, Ida P.
1868-1939

Crosthwait, James O.
April 18, 1864
June 23, 1940

Crosthwait, Pete
1894-1958

Crosthwaite, Ann Luther
Dau. of L. & Ada
Crosthwaite, Died 1902

Epperson, Sammie Lane
Died May 4, 1952

Epperson, Wm. Junia
1927-1956

Elgin, Finis
Died Nov. 13, 1969
60 years 10 mos. 9 days.

Elgin, Jim P.
1871-1930
Elgin, Mellie
1886-19

Elgin, Infant Son
Died Dec. 1, 1906

Elliott, William C.
Oct. 30, 1822
Dec. 17, 1887

Ethridge, Mrs. Lou Etta
Pierce
Died Nov. 29, 1974
84 years 8 mos. 13 days

Evans, Dan E.
1896-1974
Evans, Katie L.
1912

Evans, Steve R.
Oct. 29, 1936
Dec. 3, 1936

Ferrell, Josiah
July 20, 1858
Mar. 26, 1928

Ferrell, Mary
Wife of Josiah Ferrell
April 6, 1866
Oct. 2, 1910

Ferrell, Mary Elizabeth
Wife of Josiah Ferrell
June 22, 1864
April 18, 1908

Fowler, Edward C.
Tennessee
Pvt. 1st Div.
Died Mar. 31, 1931

Gatlin, Bert B.
Aug. 17, 1894
July 3, 1970
Gatlin, Nannie Dee
Mar. 28, 1900
May 26, 1970

Gilliland, J. F.
June 18, 1867
Dec. 21, 1933

Grier, Nannie J.
1847-1940
Grier, Matina
1869-1939

Grier, Quincy M.
Jan. 9, 1862
Oct. 23, 1906

Grier, Samuel O.
July 14, 1848
April 18, 1888

Hanks, Jane
Died April 4, 1883
72 years 7 mos. 16 days

Hart, Miller J.
June 15, 1835
Sept. 23, 1907
Hart, Paralee A.
Wife of M. J. Hart
Mar. 25, 1833
Mar. 14, 1876
Hart, Paralee P.
Mar. 4, 1866
Mar. 24, 1876
Hart, Elbert B.
Sept. 16, 1861
Jan. 21, 1893
Elliott, Armine Hart
Aug. 29, 1866
July 18, 1940

Hawkins, John H.- 1901-1956

Hawkins, Robert M.
Aug. 2, 1926
Jan. 20, 1969
Hawkins, Elenora J.
July 27, 1930
--

Hobday, Carl S.
Aug. 8, 1875
July 16, 1901

Hobday, John
Nov. 22, 1824
Oct. 8, 1886

Hobday, John Jr.
Sept. 15, 1871
Oct. 3, 1889

Holland, Beckie
1855-1900

Holland, Warren
1838-1900

Howell, "Little" John
William
Son of J. W. &
L. E. Howell
Dec. 28, 1895
Dec. 20, 1900

Jones, Willie
Mar. 20, 1891
May 3, 1891

Joslin, Gurtha M.
1908-1963

Kizer, Erven
Dec. 31, 1901
Mar. 30, 1904

Kizer, Laura
Mar. 27, 1867
Jan. 20, 1910

Kizer, P. Samuel
Dec. 20, 1866
April 17, 1930

McDowell, D. R.
1881-1918
McDowell, Bettie Palmer
"His Wife"
1880-

Middleton, Florence
1901-1940

Miller, Howard
Son of J. C. &
F. B. Miller
April 13, 1912
Oct. 6, 1913

Moore, Algie B.
Feb. 14, 1890
Mar. 15, 1969

Moore, Jennie E.
Nov. 15, 1894
--

Moore, Demetra Motha
May 17, 1915
July 15, 1915

Moore, Ollie B.
1879-1932

Notgrass, J. R.
Died Dec. 9, 1899
Age about 52 years

Notgrass, Mary A.
1856-1944

Notgrass, Monroe M.
1873-1953
Notgrass, Mary E.
1870-1944

Notgrass, U. V.
Tennessee
CPL U. S. Air Force
World War II
Aug. 4, 1908
Oct. 31, 1958

Perry, Humphrey C.
Aug. 20, 1879
May 23, 1929

Perry, Lonnie E.
1902-1967
Perry, Lula N.
1903-19

Perry, Marvin E.
Son
1910-1962
Perry, Pearl
Mother
1877-1963

Pierce, C.P.
1846-1921
Pierce, Emma
His Wife
1850-1920

Pierce, Eugene W.
1874-1924

Pierce, Henry L.
1861-1897
Pierce, Hilliard G.
1892-1898
Pierce, Hellen
1861-1929

Pierce, P. L.
1880-1939

Pinkey, Nellie M.
Feb. 28, 1892
Jan. 27, 1970

Pinkley, William
Died July 6, 1967
61 yrs. 9 mos. 26 days

Pratt, Aran Carlton
Died Oct. 5, 1975
89 yrs. 5 mos. 19 days

Prisley, William
Sept. 24, 1858
Nov. 30, 1887

Ragan, Robert Dalton
Mar. 2, 1934
--

Ragan, Mary E.
July 23, 1933
July 25, 1969

Rambo, Charles A.
Mar. 17, 1877
Feb. 28, 1958

Rambo, Hattie B.
Sept. 22, 1883
Mar. 3, 1969

Rambo, H. Vernon
Nov. 20, 1904
Aug. 26, 1969

Rambo, J. Virgil
Nov. 20, 1904
Nov. 20, 1935

Rivers, Frank M.
1867-1955

Rivers, Mary A.
1879-1966

Rose, George W.
Aug. 16, 1896
Oct. 8, 1918

Sawyers, Mrs. Laura Levey
Died Jan. 26, 1971
78 yrs. 9 mos. 25 days

Sawyers, Walter
1879-1962

Seratt, Donald Wayne
Mar. 27, 1937
Oct. 1, 1938

Seratt, John C.
1876-1961
Seratt, Lula R.
1877-1945

Seratt, Lois Laverne
June 4, 1916
May 9, 1925

Seratt, William S.
May 4, 1917
Sept. 13, 1931

Seratts, Will
Jan. 22, 1901
Nov. 7, 1973
Seratts, Hattie
Nov. 9, 1901
--

Smith, Ezra
June 27, 1891
April 5, 1915

Smith, Dannie
Sept. 12, 1893
May 4, 1917

Smith, Mary Elizabeth
Dau. of Dan &
Neely Smith
Nov. 23, 1916
Oct. 31, 1918

Stafford, Barmo W.
April 11, 1906
--

Stafford, Lautice L.
Oct. 14, 1908
April 12, 1969

Swift, Susan Drewry
Wife of J. B. Swift
Died Feb. 16, 1878

Thorton, John A.
1882-1966

Thorton, Mrs. J. A.
1887-1965

Thorton, John Wesley
Son of J. A. &
Viola Thorton
1913-1924

Todd, Frank
1835-1918

Todd, Sarah
1846-1933

Uselton, L. V. "Bass"
1890-1955
Uselton, Ethel
1895-19

Vaughn, Joseph H.
1891-
Vaughn, Nelma T.
1901-1967

Viar, Florence
Wife of W. M. Viar
Nov. 20, 1867
Jan. 2, 1905

Vincent, Sarah
Wife of H. J. Vincent
1853-1912

Warren, Julia E.
Dau. of P. H. &
F. A. Warren
Feb. 12, 1876
June 10, 1876

Welch, W. C.
Sept. 11, 1837
Nov. 27, 1911
Welch, Mary Frances
July 18, 1844
Jan. 21, 1922

Welch, Willie H.
1898-1974
Welch, Dovie
1902-

White, Cynthia Louise
June 19, 1963
April 23, 1972

Wilson, Jessie L.
1874-1941
Wilson, Minne V.
1880-196_?_

NEGRO CEMETERY

Baxter, Abe
1859-1947
Baxter, Jannie
1868-1945

Branch, Annie H.
1870-1944

Duke, Effie H.
July 14, 1909
June 20, 1972

Fowlkes, Cal
1869-1947

Gauldin, Ezell
1914-1941

Gauldin, Lavetta
Aug. 7, 1892
Jan. 14, 1942

Gilton, John
Tennessee
PVT U. S. Army
World War II
May 11, 1910
Oct. 17, 1971

Harris, Joe
Father
1864-1925
Harris, Ada
Mother
1865-1918

Kelly, Lucy
1864-1944

Martin, Mr. Tom C.
Died Sept. 25, 1975
79 yrs.

Smith, Dewey
Died June 19, 1975
75 yrs.

Smith, Jack
1885-1938
Smith, Della
1874-19

Smith, Mrs. Lela
Died June 1974
88 yrs.

Smith, Rev. Rufus C.
1883-1971
Smith, Avie B.
1891-

Smith, W. B.
1855-1920
Smith, Jennie
1856-1908

Smith, W. B.
Tennessee
PVT
Died Feb. 1, 1928

SHAW CEMETERY

Shaw Cemetery is located in the Tatumville Community. Travel
Highway 104 east from Dyersburg to the by-pass at Tatumville. Turn
left off of the by-pass and go through Tatumville, in front of the
Tatumville Grocery, which is on a curve. Turn to the right on the
first blacktop road and travel east about six hundred yards. The
cemetery is on the south side of the road on a bank.

Akin, Betty H.
1853-1900

Akin, E. L.
1813-1871

Akin, Jasian S.
Feb. 18, 1858
Mar. 25, 1862
4 years

Akin, Jucy J.
Wife of E. L. Akin
1822-1870

Featherston, Wm.
Died Jan. 2, 1870

Shaw, Charles C.
1880-1954

Shaw, Dona Helen
Dau. of G. N. &
P. A. Shaw
Oct. 18, 1874
Jan. 22, 1888

Shaw, Greg Nolen
1844-1914
Shaw, Parthena Akin
1850-1929

Shaw, Samuel
1876-1895

Neal, Sam Cleveland
Oct. 18, 1885
Mar. 23, 1956

I N D E X

Prepared By:
Karen Mac Smith, Nixon, Texas

Cavender, George W. 36
Cavit, Uno W. 142
Cawthon, Abbey Jewell House 94
  Baby 36
  Betty Love 36
  E. J. 36
  James H. Sr. 142
  J. H., Dr. 142
  John L. 36
  M. A. 142
  Roy Emmett 94
  Sarah 142
  Z. H. 142
Chalker, Lexie D. Jr. 36
  Mary Sue 36
Chamberlin, C. C. 15
  Edd Columbus 37
  Marta Anne 15
Chambers, Frelon C. 127
Champion, Emmet A. 37
  Samuel 37
Chandler, Richard T. 127
Chapman, Arebella 1
  J. C. 1, 142
  Lora Vernie 1
  Robert 7
  Sallie Loraine 1
  Viola Bell 1
  Virgie "Bud" 1
  Virginia L. 142
  W. T. 1
  W. W. 1
Cherry, E. O., Dr. 37
  Eunice Fuller 37
Childress, Emma Jane 15
  J. A. 15
  Jerrell 37
Chisman, George W. 142
Chitwood, Alfred Taylor 169
  Alice M. 169
  Allice 169
  Angie K. 169
  Annie E. 169
  Audrain 99
  Audrey 169
  Baby 169
  Bennie Stephenson 170
  Bessie 167
  Bettie 169
  Carrie Hendrix 169
  Charlie C. 169
  Corinne 161
  Creed 169, 170
  E. 170
  Edmund 170
  Effie 170
  Elener 170
  Eliher 170
  Emer A. 170
  Exar 170
  Garry J. 170
  Georgia 170
  Gertrude 169
  Harold L. 99
  Hattie H. 170
  Infant 169, 170
  James W. 170
  John 167
  Lena 170
  Levin H. 170
  Lex 170
  L. H. 170
  L. J. 170
  Lon 170

  Loren Ivy 170
  Lula Mae 170
  Martha Ann 170
  Mary 167
  Mary R. 170
  Matilda Ann 170
  Maude 169
  May 169
  M. B. 170
  Nell 170
  Noel 170
  Oren 170
  Oren Ira 170
  Oaella 170
  Rebecca 179
  R. J. 170
  Roy 169, 170
  S. A. (Bud) 170
  S. H. 170
  S. T. 170(2)
  Steve 167
  William Bostic 170
Churchman, Eliza 142
  Eva Jane 111
  J. R. 4
  M. M. 4
  Robert J. 142
  Ruth 4, 142
  Sarah H. 142
  T. C. 4
  T. G. 142
Churchwell, Brown 37
  J. A. 37
  Katie 37
  Paul 37
  S. E. "Bo" 37
  Verna M. 37
  Winnie Bell 37
Claiborne, E. F. 86
  Eugenia F. 86
  R. F. 86
  Robert E. 86
Caiborne, ____ 86
Clanton, Charlie 1
  Felix 1
  Fred Edward 1
  Hattie Ann 1
  John A. Sr. 1
  Julia M. 37
  Lela Caroline 1
  Leonard 4
  Murrell E. 1
  Rena 1
  Roy 37
  Russell Lee 1
Clark, Amanda C. 27
  Charles P. 27
  Elizabeth Pate 27
  E. M. 142
  Emeline Mitchell 27
  H. 27
  Henderson 27
  Infant 4
  Jake 4
  J. H. 4
  Lula 4
  Ocie F. 120
  Oda 142
  S. B. 142
  Sarah F. 4
  S. F. 4
  Tabmage 142
Clay, Alvie Lee 170
  Ebbie Lee 170

  J. L. 171
  Ollie May 171
Clemen, Mandy S. 113
Clement, Laura A. 142
  Rhodie N. 142
Clift, Celine Johns 37
  H. B., Rev. 37
  James L. 15
  Magtie Snead 37
  Mollie Sue 15
Clifton, Gail Lynn 107
Climer, Jimmie 114
Clopton, Jmaes P. 113
Cobb, A. J. 86
  Allie R. 86
  Charley E. 15
  C. E. 28
  C. R. 15
  Clara 194
  Cleophus F. 15
  Christen 194
  Elvin 194
  Eural R. 37
  Finas 15
  G. E. 15
  Ida F. 37
  Jacob 86
  J. L. 28
  John H. 86
  John Hester 86
  John L. 15
  John Virl 15
  Joseph Covington 86
  Josephene Covington 86
  Josiephene 86
  Lillie B. 15
  Martha 86
  Mary E. 15
  Robert Lee 86
  Sarah E. 15
  Sola Biffle 86
  Tom 194
  William 86
Coburn, G. W. 15
  Mary 15
  Sylvester 15
Cochran, A. 142, 143
  Albert 142
  Albert Hobson 142
  A. O. 140
  Elizabeth L. 143
  Frank Burney 142
  Infant 142
  Ira 142
  James M. 142
  J. M. 142, 143
  John Alison 142
  John C. 142
  Jonnie 142
  Laura 143
  L. E. 142, 143
  L. W. 142, 143
  M. A. 143
  Martha Ann 143
  Masel 143
  Ollie B. 143
  Paul 143
  Robert C. 143
  Robert L. 143
  S. M. 142, 143
  Susan Miley 143
  T. M. 143
  William E. 143
  W. T. 143

www.ingramcontent.com/pod-product-compliance
Lightning Source LLC
Chambersburg PA
CBHW021900020426
42334CB00013B/416